FIREPOWER

A History of
the American Heavy Tank

by
R.P. Hunnicutt

Line Drawings
by
D.P. Dyer

Color Drawing
by
Uwe Feist

PRESIDIO

Published by Presidio Press
31 Pamaron Way, Novato, California 94947

Library of Congress Cataloging in Publication Data

Hunnicutt, R.P., 1926-
  Firepower: a history of the American heavy tank / by R.P.
Hunnicutt; line drawings by D.P. Dyer; color drawing by Uwe
Feist. p.   cm.
  Bibliography: p.
  Includes index.
  ISBN 0-89141-304-9:
  1. Tanks (Military science)—United States—History.   I. Title.
II. Title: Heavy tank.
UG446.5.H846 1988
358'.18—dc19   87-29147

Printed in the United States of America

CONTENTS

ACKNOWLEDGEMENTS

Most of the material on the Mark VIII heavy tank came from the collection of my old friend the late Colonel Robert J. Icks who had personal experience with the vehicle prior to World War II. His collection is now in the Patton Museum at Fort Knox, Kentucky. John Purdy and David Holt of the Patton Museum also provided many items that could not be found elsewhere. Some additional material on the Mark VIII came from the Tank Museum at Bovington Camp, England through the courtesy of George Forty and David Fletcher. James Speraw, Jr of the Fort Meade Museum furnished photographs of the Mark VIII in their collection. These were particularly helpful to Phil Dyer who prepared the four view drawings of all the various tanks.

Leon Burg of the Technical Library at the Tank Automotive Command (TACOM) tracked down many sources of data and similar help was received from the Ballistics Research Laboratory library at Aberdeen Proving Ground. Over the years, many people associated with the heavy tank development program provided valuable information. Among these were Roland Asoklis, Clifford Bradley, Oscar Danielian, Dr. Herbert Dobbs, Clarence Olsen, Dan Smith, and Joe Williams. Most of these have since retired from TACOM.

Dr. Philip W. Lett of the General Dynamics Land Systems Division (formerly Chrysler) shared many experiences from the early development of the T43. Other people who contributed to the research included Major General Andrew Anderson, Michael Armstrong, Joseph Avesian, Major Fred Crismon, Major General Oscar Decker, Paul Denn, Gerry Gardiner, Joseph Hayes, David C. (Doc) Holliday, Briggs Jones, Marvin Kabakoff, Robert Lessels, David Lockhart, Lieutenant Colonel James Loop, Colonel Walter Reynolds, R. Paul Ryan, Roger Smith, General Donn Starry, Anthony Wayne Tommell, Russell P. Vaughan, Clarence Winfree, Steven Zaloga and Major Frank Zink.

Dedicated

to

the memory of

Colonel Robert J. Icks, USAR

1900 – 1985

INTRODUCTION

Except for a short period prior to World War II, the heavy tank was listed as a requirement for the United States Army until the advent of the main battle tank. During this time, the concept of a heavy tank changed drastically. The original vehicle to fit the designation was the Mark VIII developed during World War I. As the final example of the British rhomboidal tanks designed for maximum trench crossing ability, it carried 11 men, weighed over 43 tons, but was only armored against small arms fire. With a maximum speed of about five miles per hour, it was restricted to the World War I role of infantry support over short distances. However, because of limited budgets during the postwar period, the Mark VIII remained in service until the 1930s. By this time, the role of the heavy tank had changed. It now required armor to resist the antitank guns of the period and cannon capable of destroying fortified positions as well as other armored vehicles. Some tanks of this period tried to combine these new requirements with the older role of infantry cooperation. This resulted in complicated designs with large crews, multiple turrets, and weapons of several calibers. In 1940, the original concept for the T1 heavy tank followed this approach with no less than four turrets. Fortunately, the design was simplified to a single turret arrangement prior to development. However, it still retained some features of the earlier concept with both 37mm and 3 inch antitank guns mounted coaxially in the turret. Standardized as the M6 (T1E2), it was a transition vehicle in heavy tank design much as the M3 was to the medium tanks.

By the end of World War II, the heavy tank had evolved into the modern concept with a powerful turret mounted antitank gun protected by heavy armor. Such a design gave priority to firepower and protection, but retained sufficient mobility to permit operations with medium tanks over most terrain. An exception to this was the turretless heavy tank T28, but this vehicle was actually a heavily armored assault gun rather than a tank.

Postwar experiments further refined the same basic design resulting in the development of the heavy tank T43.

At this time, there was a change in nomenclature. Prior to World War II, a tank weighing 30 tons or more was regarded as heavy, but by the early postwar period, medium tanks had reached 45-50 tons and heavy tanks weighing over 70 tons were being considered. A new system was introduced to classify tanks by the caliber of their main armament, but the breakdown between the three basic types remained essentially the same, although they were now referred to as heavy gun, medium gun, and light gun tanks.

After a short development cycle and an extensive rework program on the production vehicles, the 120mm gun tank T43 was standardized as the M103 which became the first U.S. heavy tank in troop service since the Mark VIII. However, the Army only received 74 M103s and equipped a single battalion for service in Europe. Here their heavy firepower was used to support the medium gun tanks in the overwatch role.

The major portion of the new heavy tank production was assigned to the U.S. Marine Corps. The heavy armor of these vehicles was well suited to the infantry support task of the Marine Corps tanks. However, before the Corps accepted the production tanks for troop duty, they were upgraded, first to the M103A1 (T43E2) configuration and at a later date to that of the dieselized M103A2. Thus the Marine Corps, employing their armor in the infantry support role, became the major user of the M103 tank series.

The objective of this volume has been to trace the development of the American heavy tank from World War I until it merged with that of the medium weight vehicles in the new concept of a universal or main battle tank. Such an all purpose tank required armament capable of engaging any target on the battlefield combined with enough armor to insure survival until its mission was completed. Needless to say, such a combination resulted in a heavy vehicle. However, the development of extremely powerful and compact engines improved the mobility of the later main battle tanks until it equaled that of the light tanks a decade earlier. Thus the relatively slow, heavily armored tank disappeared from the inventory of modern armies.

R. P. Hunnicutt
Belmont, California
October 1987

PART I

U. S. ARMY HEAVY TANKS

THROUGH WORLD WAR II

Members of the Anglo-American Tank Commission and other dignataries are shown above with the Mark VIII pilot after its arrival in the United States.

EARLY DEVELOPMENT

The first heavy tank built in production quantities for the U.S. Army resulted from a cooperative Allied effort during World War I. Although often referred to as the Liberty Tank, the International Tank, or the Anglo-American Tank, it was officially designated as the heavy tank Mark VIII and was developed from the earlier British designs first introduced into battle during 1916. Several experimental heavy tanks, such as the Holt gas-electric vehicle and the steam powered tank developed by the Corps of Engineers, were evaluated in the United States, but the Mark VIII design, based on the British experience with the large trench crossing tank, was selected for production. The original plan called for the United States to manufacture the engines and other power train components and Britain would supply the armament, armor plate, and other structural parts. To minimize shipping space requirements, the various components were to be assembled in a new factory constructed in France.

Below are two of the experimental tank designs evaluated in the United States during World War I. The gas-electric vehicle based upon the Holt tractor is at the left and at the right is the steam powered tank built by the U.S. Army Corps of Engineers. The latter was intended to mount a flame thrower.

9

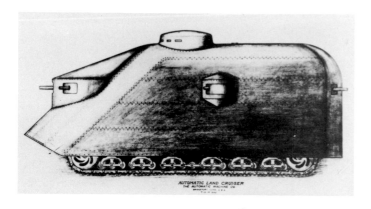

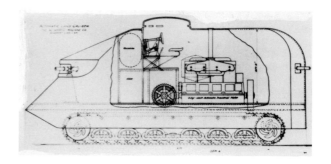

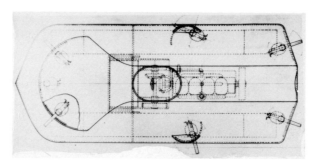

Another early World War I concept appears above and at the right. Proposed by the Automatic Machine Company of Bridgeport, Connecticut, these sketches were dated 14 July 1915. Obviously, its cross-country performance would have been extremely limited in rough terrain.

Above are two views of an experimental chassis with track steering built by General Motors for the United States in late 1916. This resulted from earlier experimental work for the British government which produced the vehicle illustrated at the right and below. Originally built in December 1915, it was reactivated in the photograph at the right for the Armistice Day parade in 1918. Both vehicles were designed by Mr. A.C. Hamilton, chief engineer of the Oakland Motor Car Company, part of General Motors Corporation.

During July 1918, a mild steel hull was fabricated in Britain and shipped to the United States for installation of the engine and power train. The war ended before full production could be achieved, but in early 1919, Colonel Harry B. Jordan, then commanding officer at Rock Island Arsenal, received orders to assemble 100 Mark VIII tanks at that location. These tanks would use 100 sets of component parts purchased from Britain.

On 2 February 1919, the mild steel Mark VIII pilot arrived at Rock Island. After examination and a number of public exhibitions, the tank was shipped to Savanna Proving Ground, Illinois for a road test of 2155 miles. Although generally satisfactory, the road test revealed the need for a number of modifications. For example, the heat from the lower exhaust system made the floor of the engine compartment extremely hot.

Above is the Mark VIII pilot on 1 March 1919 with the original mounts for the British .303 caliber Hotchkiss machine guns, but without the weapons installed.

Above, a Browning tank machine gun has been installed in the turret side mount of the Mark VIII pilot in this photograph dated 29 May 1919. Below, the Mark VIII pilot is fitted with its full complement of British .303 caliber Hotchkiss machine guns.

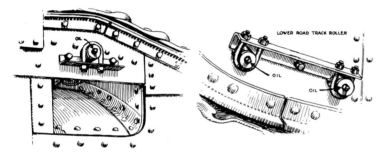

Details of the Mark VIII pilot can be seen in these views. The numbers indicate the following: (top left) 1. towing bracket, 2. commander's cupola, 3. main turret, 4. driver's turret, 5. bullet splash angle, 6. camouflage bracket, 7. track adjusting screw, 8. vision slot, 9. machine gun mount; (above) 1. towing bracket, 2. guide for haulage rope, 3. bullet deflector, 4. unditching gear strut; (below) 1. mud chute, 2. opening for hemispherical machine gun mount, 3. pistol port, 4. vision slot, 5. opening for machine gun mount, 6. side door.

The sketches above show details of the mud chute and mounts for the upper and lower track rollers. The top rear of the tank can be seen below: (at left) 1. roof towing bracket, 2. air inlet, 3. exhaust pipes, 4. water filler pipe; (at right) 1. track, 2. pistol port, 3. vision slot, 4. commander's cupola, 5. cover plate for hemispherical machine gun mount, 6-7. roof hatch, 8. roof towing bracket, 9. camouflage net support socket.

Above are views of the right side 6 pounder sponson on the Mark VIII pilot. Note how it could be retracted to reduce the tank width for transportation.

With a length of 34 feet 2/12 inches, the Mark VIII was a larger version of the earlier rhomboidal British tanks designed for maximum trench crossing ability. In fact, a Mark VIII* version was designed with an overall length of 44 feet, but it was never built. Armament of the Mark VIII pilot consisted of two British 6 pounder (57mm) Hotchkiss cannon and seven Hotchkiss .303 caliber machine guns. One cannon was mounted on each side of the tank in the sponsons. The sponsons were hinged and could be swung inward to reduce the overall width of the tank for rail shipment. The seven machine guns were fitted in ball mounts. Three of these were installed in large hemispherical housings, one of which was located in the rear of the fixed turret and one in each of the two hull side doors. These housings were pivoted at the top and bottom thus increasing the horizontal traverse of the machine guns allowing them to fire upon targets much closer to the tank. The remaining four machine gun ball mounts were fitted in the walls of the fixed turret. Two were in front with one on each side of the driver and one was located in each of the rear side walls. The latter two were eliminated from the Mark VIII tanks produced in the United States and the ports were covered with armor plate. Also, the American built tanks were armed with the .30 caliber M1919 Browning tank machine gun with the barrel enclosed in a heavy protective sleeve.

The .30 caliber Browning tank machine gun is illustrated at the right and below. The shield shown on the sketch was omitted from the guns installed in the Mark VIII.

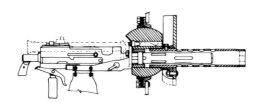

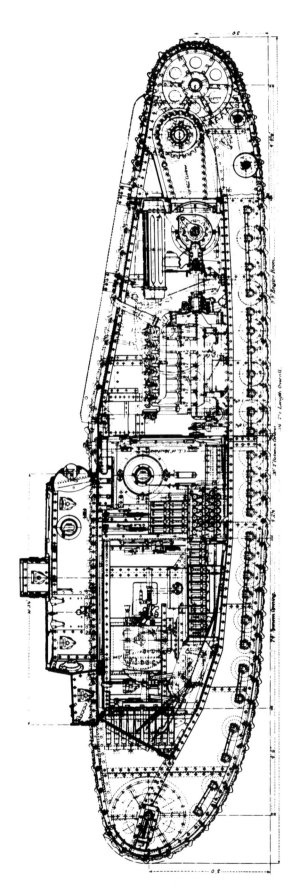 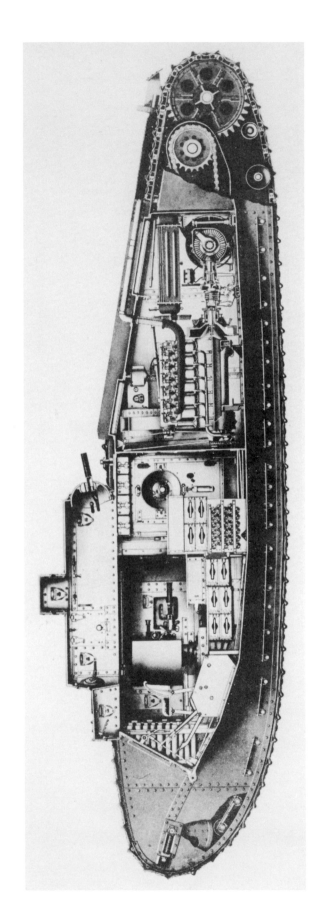

A sectional drawing of the Mark VIII pilot above is compared here with a similar view of the production tank below. Note the changes to the exhaust system and the elimination of the turret side machine gun mounts on the production tank.

14

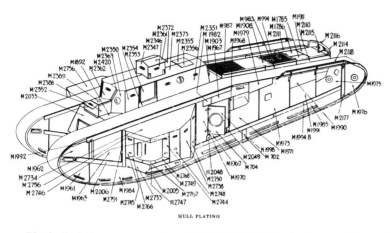

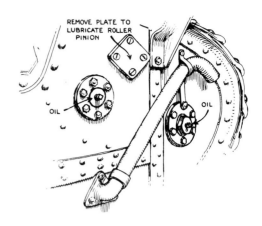

The hull plating arrangement on the Mark VIII pilot is shown at the top left. The numbers for each plate refer to a parts list. At the top right is the external lower exhaust pipe on the pilot tank.

The tank hulls were assembled by riveting the armor plate to a framework of angle iron and steel channels. The face hardened armor plate varied in thickness from 0.236 inches(6mm) on the top to 0.63 inches(16mm) for the fixed turret side plates. Unlike earlier British designs, the hull of the Mark VIII was divided by a bulkhead separating the fighting compartment in the front from the engine compartment in the rear. Two sliding doors, one near each side of the tank, permitted movement between the two compartments. Another opening in the center of the bulkhead was closed by a vertical sliding door. This arrangement provided better ventilation in the fighting compartment and reduced the danger from fire. A 900 cubic feet per minute (cfm) fan installed at the right front of the engine compartment provided air for ventilation.

The ventilation system is sketched at the lower left and the ventilation fan can be seen through the engine compartment bulkhead door below at the right. Note the engine crank in the center of the bulkhead.

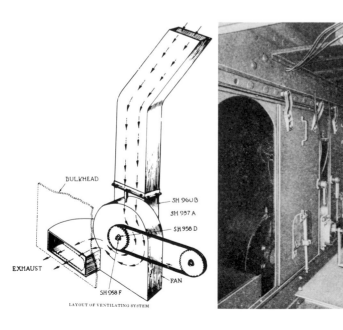

The tank was driven by a 12-cylinder, liquid-cooled, Liberty aircraft engine modified for this application. The power was transmitted through an epicyclic gear box and a chain drive to the track driving wheels(sprockets) at the rear. The Liberty engine was the low compression version developing 338 horsepower (hp) at 1400 revolutions per minute (rpm). On the production tank, the Zenith carburetor used on the aircraft engine was replaced by one manufactured by Ball and Ball and a three inch leather belt was substituted for the V-belt driving the sirocco fan used to cool the engine radiator. Fuel was carried in three gasoline tanks, each with a capacity of 80 gallons, installed in the rear of the hull separated from the engine compartment by another bulkhead. The three tanks were pressurized by an engine driven air pump which forced the gasoline into a gravity feed tank directly above the engine. The Liberty was fitted with an electric starter, however, it was not intended to start a cold engine without help from the hand crank. The latter extended through the bulkhead into the fighting compartment. On the pilot tank, the exhaust could be directed up through two short pipes protruding through the hull roof or down through mufflers installed on each side of the vehicle and then through pipes extending to the rear on each side of the hull. As mentioned previously, the latter arrangement proved to be unsatisfactory during the test program and it was recommended that the mufflers be relocated to the top exhaust pipes. This was done on the tanks manufactured in Britain. However, on the American production Mark VIII, the upper exhaust pipes were extended to the rear of the hull without the installation of any mufflers. The lower exhaust system was eliminated on both the British and American production tanks. The vehicle weight of over 43 tons was carried by 29 unsprung lower rollers on each track. A single top roller was provided where the track angle changed near the center of the hull. The maximum speed was a little over five miles per hour on a level road.

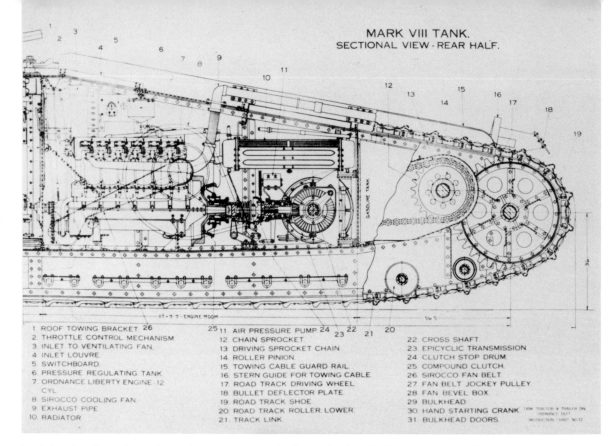

MARK VIII TANK.
SECTIONAL VIEW - REAR HALF.

1 ROOF TOWING BRACKET. 26	11 AIR PRESSURE PUMP 24	22 CROSS SHAFT.
2 THROTTLE CONTROL MECHANISM.	12 CHAIN SPROCKET.	23 EPICYCLIC TRANSMISSION
3 INLET TO VENTILATING FAN.	13 DRIVING SPROCKET CHAIN	24 CLUTCH STOP DRUM.
4 INLET LOUVRE	14 ROLLER PINION.	25 COMPOUND CLUTCH.
5 SWITCHBOARD.	15 TOWING CABLE GUARD RAIL	26 SIROCCO FAN BELT.
6 PRESSURE REGULATING TANK.	16 STERN GUIDE FOR TOWING CABLE	27 FAN BELT JOCKEY PULLEY
7 ORDNANCE LIBERTY ENGINE - 12	17 ROAD TRACK DRIVING WHEEL.	28 FAN BEVEL BOX.
CYL	18 BULLET DEFLECTOR PLATE.	29 BULKHEAD
8 SIROCCO COOLING FAN	19 ROAD TRACK SHOE.	30 HAND STARTING CRANK
9 EXHAUST PIPE	20 ROAD TRACK ROLLER, LOWER	31 BULKHEAD DOORS.
10 RADIATOR	21 TRACK LINK.	

The sectional drawing above shows the engine compartment in the production Mark VIII. Note the fuel tanks in the extreme rear of the hull. Below, a sketch of the fuel system appears at the right and the fuel tanks (1) with the armor covers (2, 3) are at the left. Numbers 4, 5, and 6 refer to the gasoline lines, air pressure lines, and filler caps.

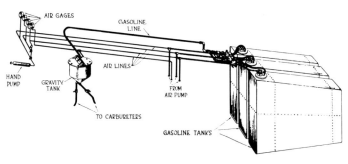

The engine cooling system is sketched at the lower left and the sirocco cooling fan (1) appears below through the engine compartment bulkhead door. Numbers 2, 3, 4, and 5 indicate the fan support and drive components. Number 6 is the auxiliary water tank.

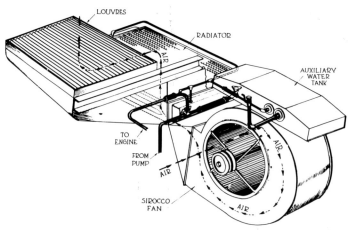

16

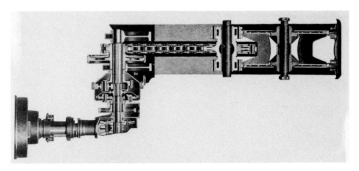

The epicyclic transmission is above at the left and at the top right a sectional view shows the power train components from the clutch through the bevel gears, the epicyclic transmission, the chain drive, the roller sprocket, and the road track driving wheel (track sprocket) to the tracks. Details of the roller sprocket (1, 2, 3) and the road track driving wheel (5) appear below. Numbers 4 and 6 refer to the guide rail and the upper track rail respectively. The drive chain has been removed in the left view.

With the track partially removed in the photograph below, the top rails, upon which the track slides, are exposed. At the right, the inside (upper) and the outside (lower) of the track can be seen. The numbers indicate the following: 1. track link, 2. track link bushing, 3. track shoe. The center of the 8mm thick steel armor plate forming the track shoe was dished to increase the rigidity.

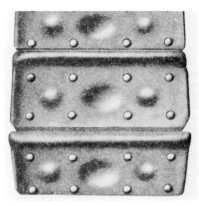

ROCK ISLAND ARSENAL
373-A36-1 April 3, 1920.
Mark VIII Tank; driver's
seat, and front ammuni-
tion storage.

Above, the driver's station on the Mark VIII pilot (left) is compared with that on the production tank (right). Note the changes in the driver's seat. Details of the driver's control levers are sketched at the bottom of the page.

Most documents specified a crew of 11 for the Mark VIII tank. However, one source shows an eight man crew consisting of the tank commander, driver, two 6 pounder gunners, three machine gunners, and a mechanic. The latter rode in the engine compartment. It is probable that another machine gunner and two loaders for the 6 pounders were added to reach the full 11 man crew.

The driver was located at the forward end of the fighting compartment with his head enclosed in the armored housing just in front of the fixed turret. Peep holes were provided for vision and the front plate of the driver's head cover was hinged to permit a direct view when not exposed to enemy fire. The driver's controls consisted of four levers and a brake pedal plus the spark, throttle, and other engine controls. The two inside speed control levers were for shifting between the two gear ratios of the epicyclic transmission. The left outside lever operated the clutch and the right outside lever was used to place the vehicle in reverse. Steering was accomplished by varying the track speed using the speed control levers and braking the track on the inside of the turn if necessary.

The tank commander usually was located in the center of the fixed turret under the small outlook turret or cupola. An officer's kit box on the fighting compartment floor for the commander to stand on, provided sufficient height for him to see out through the peep holes in the cupola. Access to the tank was provided by a hatch in the fixed turret roof and two doors, one in each side of the hull. A mast mounted semaphore signaling device was installed on the left rear of the fixed turret roof. Internal communication was provided by an intratank telephone system frequently referred to as a laryngaphone. The transmitter was a small button shaped device held against the throat by an elastic band and the receiver consisted of earphones. A switch box was located at the stations for the driver, both 6-pounder gunners, and the mechanic and all of these were connected to the commander's switch box. By closing the proper switch, the commander could speak to any of these crew members. As originally installed, he also could speak to a guide outside the tank who wore a headset connected by a long cord to the driver's switch box. However, this feature was discontinued in favor of a flashlight signaling system.

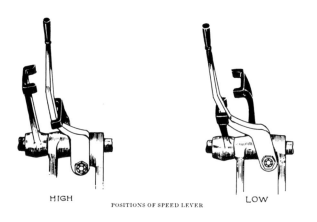

HIGH
POSITIONS OF SPEED LEVER
LOW

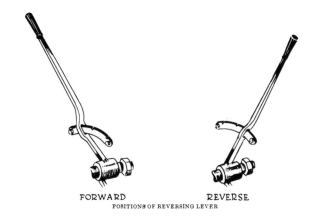

FORWARD
REVERSE
POSITIONS OF REVERSING LEVER

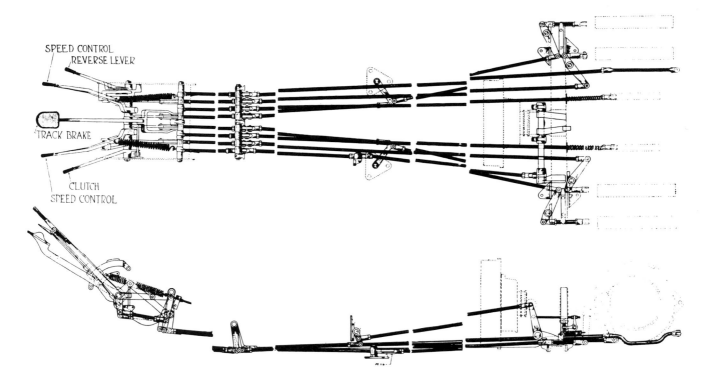

SPEED CONTROL
REVERSE LEVER

TRACK BRAKE

CLUTCH
SPEED CONTROL

The layout of the driver's control system is illustrated above and at the right is a sketch of the spark or throttle lever. They were similar in appearance and were mounted one on each side of the driver.

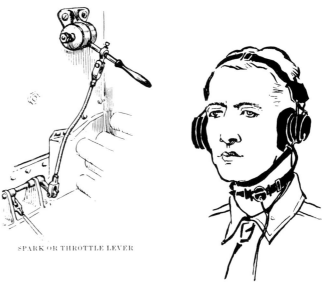

SPARK OR THROTTLE LEVER

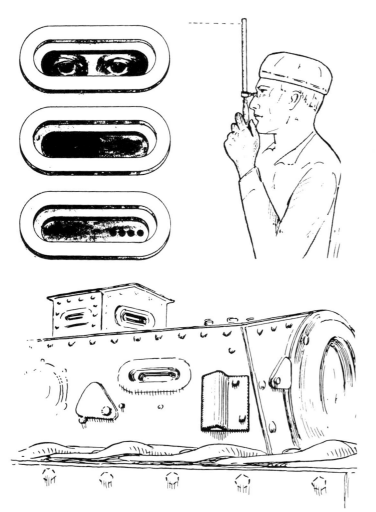

The sketches at the upper left show the three positions of the vision slot covers and the hand held periscope available for use by the driver and the tank commander. The laryngaphone communication system is illustrated above at the right. Below, the opening sequence of the pistol port is shown at the right from the inside of the tank. An external view of the closed pistol port is sketched at the left.

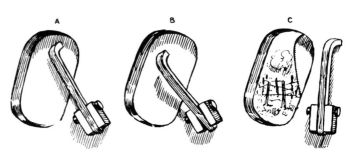

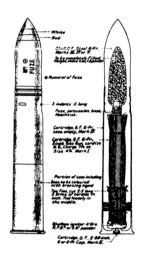

The left side 6 pounder on the Mark VIII pilot can be seen at the top left and a rack for 6 pounder and machine gun ammunition appears at the top right. A 6 pounder high explosive round is sketched above. Below are two views of the 6 pounder installation in the production tank.

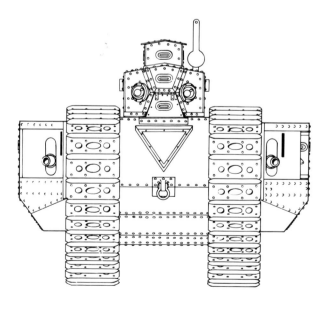
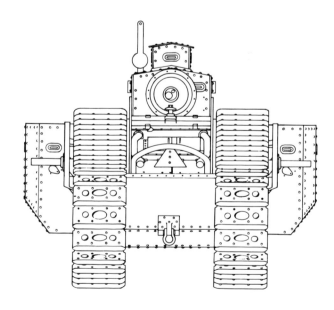

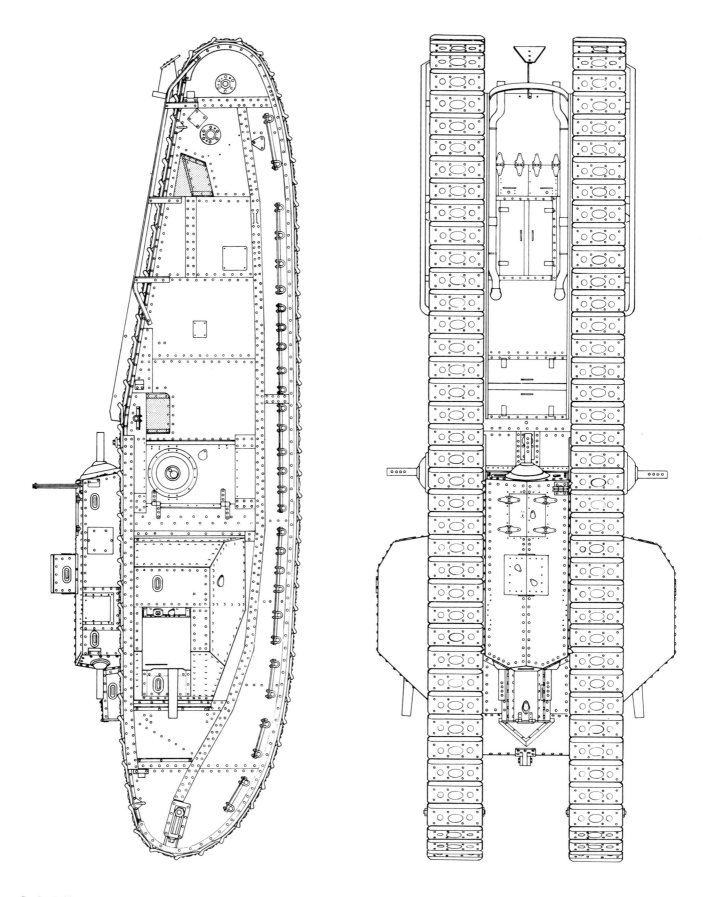

Scale 1:48

Heavy Tank Mark VIII

21

Above is the assembly area at Rock Island Arsenal for the production of the Mark VIII tank. Note the relatively small size of the 6-ton light tank between the first two Mark VIIIs. Details of the machine gun mount and vision slots are visible in the view below. Note that the pistol port in the rear of the main turret on the pilot has been eliminated on the production tanks.

The construction of the first Mark VIII at Rock Island Arsenal started on 1 July 1919 and by 1 September, general assembly of the vehicles was underway with as many as 28 tanks being built at the same time. The first tank was completed on 5 January 1920. The last of the 100 Mark VIIIs was finished and ready for road test on 5 June 1920. The usual number of mishaps occurred during the construction and road tests. During the latter, the most frequent problem was with fires caused by the engine backfiring through the carburetor. Fortunately, these fires were easily handled by the fire extinguishers carried for such emergencies. During the loading for shipment of one tank on 22 March 1920, the sill of the railway flat car gave way and the tank rolled off, landing upside down. Luckily, the driver and mechanic in the tank were only shaken up and not seriously injured. Cables were connected to the vehicle and another tank rolled it back onto its tracks. The tank was then driven back to the shop under its own power. The only damage was a slight dent in the fixed turret roof and a bent semaphore. All damage was repaired without removing the parts from the tank.

Below (left) a train loaded with 34 Mark VIIIs departs from Rock Island on 21 May 1920 for Camp Meade, Maryland. At the right is the Mark VIII which overturned while loading on 22 March 1920.

The inverted Mark VIII also is shown above along with the other tanks during the loading operations.

The photographs at the right and below show the production Mark VIII during the automotive test program. Note that the 6 pounders have been removed in the bottom views.

Above is the Mark VIII fitted with the stroboscopic vision device replacing the commander's cupola. This photograph was taken during a demonstration at Aberdeen Proving Ground.

The 100 Mark VIIIs were used in peacetime training exercises in the infantry support role. By this time, the concept of the slow, lightly armored, heavy tank was obsolete and interest shifted to lighter, faster armored vehicles for future development. However, the Mark VIII was used in several experimental programs. A project extending from 1920 through 1925 studied the application of the stroboscopic vision device to the Mark VIII. Developed in France, this device replaced the commander's cupola on top of the fixed turret. The rotating vertical slots permitted 360 degree vision, although at a reduced light level. Unfortunately, tests showed that the stroboscopic vision cupola was extremely vulnerable to bullet splash from .30 caliber ammunition. Further development attempted to improve the equipment, but on 4 May 1926, the Ordnance Committee concluded that the device was inherently inferior to the periscope and recommended the termination of further development.

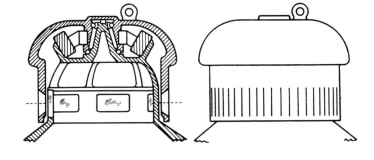

Sectional and exterior sketches are shown above of the stroboscopic vision device.

The Mark VIII below is being used to conduct experiments for transporting the light 6-ton tank.

The Mark VIII at the right has just climbed this vertical wall during test operations.

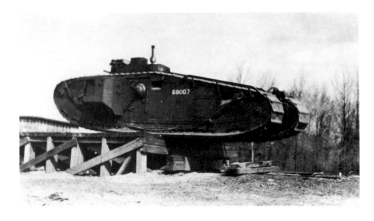

During 1932, an air-cooled Liberty engine was evaluated in the Mark VIII at Aberdeen Proving Ground. Modified by the Heat Controlled Motor Company, it featured an internal and external air cooling system and a higher compression ratio of 6:1. This tank was easily identified by the external ventilator assembly on the left side of the hull. Although the limited testing did not determine the durability of the modified engine, the air-cooled power plant was considered preferable for tank use and its further development was recommended. However, by 1932, the obsolete Mark VIIIs were withdrawn from troop service and placed in storage at Aberdeen Proving Ground. In April 1936, the Ordnance Committee recommended that the requirement for a heavy tank be cancelled and removed from the Ordnance Book of Standards. This action was approved on 7 May. The Mark VIIIs remained in storage at Aberdeen until after the beginning of World War II. At that time, some of them were transferred to Canada for use in the training program.

The photographs at the right and below show the Mark VIII powered by the air-cooled Liberty engine. In the views at the right, the tank is on display by the Ordnance Museum at Aberdeen Proving Ground. At the bottom, the vehicle is manned by R.O.T.C. cadets during training on 11 July 1928.

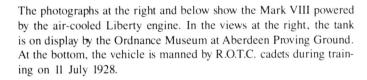

The Mark VIII in service with the troops can be seen in these photographs. Note the large water tank on the rear deck of the vehicles in the top view. There were numerous leakage and overheating problems with the Liberty engine and this arrangement provided a large reserve water supply. Note that it was connected directly to the water inlet of the engine cooling system.

The wooden mock-up of the heavy tank T1 is shown above. This is the final concept from which the pilot tank was built.

With the outbreak of World War II in Europe, interest was revived in the concept of a heavy tank and preliminary studies of such a vehicle began at Aberdeen in September 1939. On 20 May 1940, the Chief of Infantry recommended that a requirement be established for a heavy tank and that a program be undertaken to develop designs for such a vehicle with combat weights of 50 and 80 tons. In response to this request, item 15842 of the Ordnance Committee Minutes (OCM), dated 22 May 1940, recommended that a development project be initiated for a tank weighing about 50 tons.

The initial concept described in OCM 15842 was a multi-turreted vehicle. Two primary turrets, each armed with a low velocity T6 75mm gun, were to be equipped with power traverse to cover approximately 250 degrees. Two secondary turrets, also equipped with power traverse, were intended to cover a full 360 degrees. One secondary turret was to be armed with a 37mm gun and a .30 caliber machine gun in a combination mount while the other was to be fitted with a 20mm gun and a .30 caliber machine gun, also in a combination mount. In addition, the tank was to carry four .30 caliber machine guns in ball mounts. Two of these were to be located in diagonal plates at the rear corners of the hull and the remaining two were to be fitted in the slightly sloping front plate. The latter were to have electric firing mechanisms to permit their use by the driver as fixed sponson guns.

The project was approved on 11 July 1940 and the proposed vehicle was designated as the heavy tank T1. However, the military characteristics soon were revised and a full scale wooden mock-up was constructed incorporating the changes. The multiple turrets were eliminated and the main armament was mounted in a single large turret with a 69 inch diameter ring. The new arrangement was outlined in OCM 16200, dated 24 October 1940, and the changes were approved on 22 November. The new single turret was armed with a modified version of the 3 inch T9 anti-aircraft gun in a combination mount with a 37mm gun M5E1. The turret was traversed 360 degrees either manually or by the electric system developed by Westinghouse. At this time, power elevation also was specified for the combination mount with a gyro-stabilizer. Later, the power elevation feature was dropped, but the elevation stabilizer was retained. The turret crew arrangement differed from that in later medium and heavy tanks with the tank commander located on the left side of the 3 inch gun. A

At the right, Brigadier General Gladeon M. Barnes and key members of industry view the model of the proposed heavy tank T1.

.30 caliber machine gun in a cupola identical to that on the medium tank M3 was provided for the tank commander. The gunner's station in the right front of the turret was equipped with a periscopic sight and a direct sight telescope. A .50 caliber machine gun in a rotor mount was located in the right rear of the turret roof. Operated by the loader, its elevation ranged from -5 to +60 degrees for use against both air and ground targets. A pistol port with a protectoscope was installed in the rear wall of the turret.

At the time that OCM 16200 was published, a crew of six or seven men was proposed for the new heavy tank. Later, this was specified as six, when the tank was standardized. They consisted of the commander, gunner, loader, ammunition passer, driver, and assistant driver. The latter three rode in the hull with the driver in the left front. Two .30 caliber machine guns were mounted in the front armor, one on each side of the hull. Fixed in traverse, these weapons had an elevation range of 15 degrees and were fired electrically by the driver. A door in the front plate could be opened to give the driver a wide field of view and a smaller direct vision port was located just below the door. A protectoscope in the driver's door provided vision when the tank was under fire. Two .50 caliber machine guns in a flexible mount were installed in the right front hull for use by the assistant driver (bow gunner). These guns could be traversed 15 degrees to the left or right of center and elevated from -10 to +60 degrees. In the original design, the two .50 caliber machine guns were installed in the mount, one above the other with the top gun to the left of the lower weapon. Metal sights or rods were attached to the guns to permit aiming through the coupled indirect sighting device. Two escape hatches were provided, one in each top front corner of the hull. An additional escape hatch was located in the hull floor. Two pistol ports with protectoscopes were installed with one in the front side wall of each sponson.

Because of the many problems expected during the development of the new vehicle, the Society of Automotive Engineers (SAE) was requested to form a committee to advise the Ordnance Department on the program. One major problem was the design of a satisfactory power train. The expected weight of 50 tons required an engine of approximately 1000 hp for adequate mobility. The SAE committee considered several engines and the chairman of the engine subcommittee recommended the Wright Cyclone air-cooled radial as the best choice. Other engines considered were the General Motors diesel and the Allison V-1710 aircraft power plant. However, the latter was eliminated because all manufacturing facilities were fully occupied meeting the requirements of the aircraft production program. Also, it was decided not to use the General Motors diesel at that time and

the Wright G-200 was selected as the first choice power plant. Developing 960 gross horsepower at 2300 rpm, it weighed 1350 pounds dry. Unfortunately, no automotive transmission was available for such a high power level and the development of a suitable transmission became a critical part of the project.

Early in the program, the SAE subcommittee on transmissions considered several proposals. These included torque converters designed by the Schneider Hydraulic Corporation, the Twin Disc Clutch Company, and Borg Warner Corporation as well as a new Hydramatic transmission proposed by the Oldsmobile Division of General Motors. Designs for gas-electric drives also were submitted by the Electromotive Division of General Motors and the General Electric Company. However, the gas-electric drive was considered too heavy and it was estimated at that time to weigh about five tons more than the other systems. A conventional synchromesh transmission also was discussed, but it was not considered feasible in such a heavy tank and it would require the development of a clutch since none was available for this power level. After review of the various proposals, the committee voted to select the Hydramatic transmission, but also to study the torque converters as a possible alternate system.

In August 1940, a contract had been signed with the Baldwin Locomotive Works for the design and construction of a pilot heavy tank to be followed by the manufacture of 50 production models. As mentioned earlier, the new vehicle had been designated as the heavy tank T1 by OCM 15946 on 11 July 1940. This was the designation assigned to the vehicle for which the Hydramatic transmission was proposed. However, further studies by the General Electric Company indicated that a gas-electric drive could be developed that would not increase the weight of the tank by more than two tons. Since such a drive would have numerous advantages, it was recommended by OCM 16477 that an electric drive and steering mechanism be developed for installation in the pilot T1. When this equipment was installed, the vehicle was to be redesignated as the heavy tank T1E1.

Work continued on a crash basis at the Baldwin Locomotive Works to complete the design of the new tank and to construct the pilot model. It was expected that the Hydramatic transmission would be available for installation in May 1941. However, numerous problems delayed delivery and in August, the pilot tank was assembled using the Twin Disc torque converter Model T-16001. OCM 16655 on 21 April 1941, had designated the vehicle with this transmission as the heavy tank T1E2. Preliminary testing of the pilot T1E2 began during August at Baldwin parallel with the preparation of plans for production. Modifications were required to minimize vapor lock and to

The pilot heavy tank T1E2 is shown here at the Baldwin Locomotive Works on 19 September 1941. Note that the mounts for the .30 caliber bow machine guns have not yet been installed and the tank is equipped with the early engine exhaust system.

Both sides of the early T1E2 pilot can be seen above and at the left on 19 September 1941 during preliminary tests at the Baldwin Locomotive Works.

improve the transmission and shifting mechanism. A particularly serious problem was the overheating and rapid wear of the steering brakes which subsequently required the development of a completely new brake lining.

Further details of the early exhaust system are visible in this photograph (below) of the T1E2 pilot dated 10 September 1941. At that time, none of the armament had been installed.

Above is the heavy tank T1E2 pilot photographed during the official presentation to the Ordnance Department on 8 December 1941 at the Baldwin Locomotive Works. The tank is fully armed with both cannon and machine guns.

On the day following the attack at Pearl Harbor, the T1E2 pilot heavy tank was officially presented to the Ordnance Department at the Baldwin Locomotive Works with a demonstration alongside a production medium tank M3. Although it made an impressive show, many problems still required solutions, even though the new war situation called for production at the earliest possible date. For example, during the demonstration, the hydraulic system failed cutting off pressure for the power steering and gear shifting mechanisms. Thus for the last three miles of the run, only mechanical steering was available and it was not possible to get the transmission out of gear. Also, the pinion shaft in the traversing mechanism had been twisted off while rotating the turret.

Below at the left, Brigadier General Gladeon M. Barnes (second from the left) stands on the T1E2 pilot during the ceremonies at Baldwin on 8 December 1941. The pilot heavy tank can be compared with a production M3 medium tank in these views.

The photographs on this page, dated 28 February 1942, show the pilot heavy tank T1E2 after its arrival at Aberdeen Proving Ground. The modified rear hull configuration can be seen below.

Following the demonstration, the tank was torn down and numerous changes were made as a result of the initial tests. The four torque converter radiators were combined into two units and the two engine oil cooling radiators were combined into a single unit greatly simplifying the plumbing in the engine compartment. The exhaust manifold was moved from the front to the rear of the Wright G-200 engine and mufflers of a new type were installed. These were located inside the engine compartment and exhausted

into the slip stream of the engine cooling fan. The rear end of the hull was rebuilt to simulate the proposed production configuration.

The T1 was designed parallel with the medium tank M3 and shared many early design features with that vehicle such as the fixed machine guns for use by the driver and the cupola with a .30 caliber machine gun for the tank commander. Troop testing, combined with the British battle experience, resulted in the elimination or modification of many of these

These are additional views of the T1E2 pilot as received at Aberdeen Proving Ground. Note that the tank carries its full armament.

Further details of the T1E2 pilot at Aberdeen can be seen in these photographs. The changes in the rear deck and hull configuration resulting from the modified engine exhaust system are clearly visible.

34

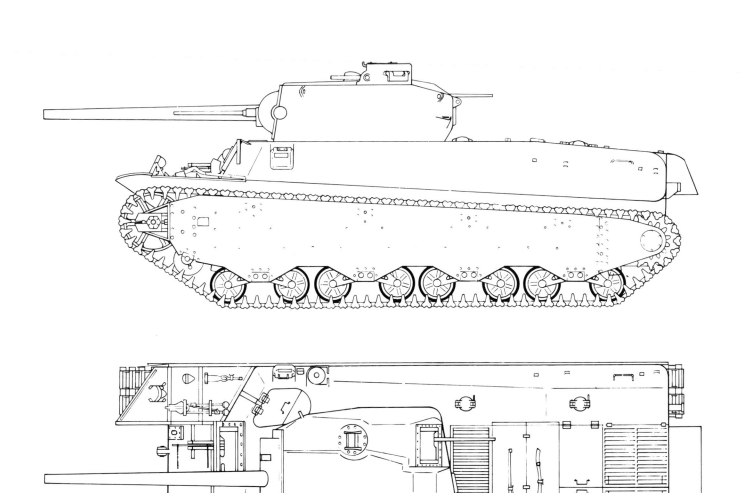

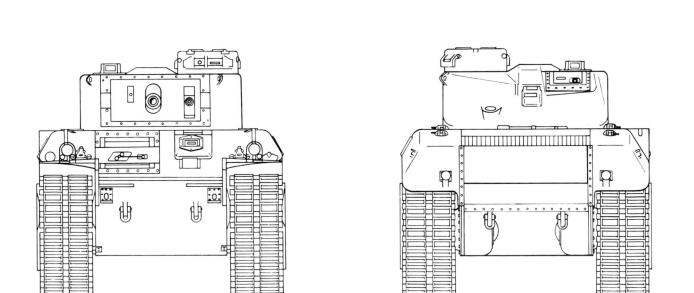

Scale 1:48

Heavy Tank T1E2, Pilot

A production heavy tank M6 is shown here during tests at the General Motors Proving Ground on 4 August 1943.

items and these changes were reflected in the late production M3 and early M4 medium tanks. Similar changes were applied to the production version of the heavy tank. It was recommended that both of the driver's fixed machine guns be deleted. However, the gun on the right side was retained and only the left machine gun was removed and its port covered by a steel plug. Although it was considered desirable to redesign the front hull eliminating the door in front of the driver, such a change was rejected because of delays in production and the modifications were limited to reducing the size of the door and the installation of periscopes for the driver and bow gunner. At first, each had one, but the final design provided two periscopes for the driver and one for the bow gunner. In addition, the driver had a direct vision port installed in the smaller front hull door. At this time, the bow mount for the twin .50 caliber machine guns was redesigned so that the two guns were side by side on the same level.

The production turret replaced the cupola for the tank commander with a flat double door hatch as on the medium tank M4. The rotating ring on this hatch was fitted with either a .30 caliber or .50 caliber antiaircraft machine gun, depending upon the

Armored Force policy at the time. The rotor mounted .50 caliber machine gun in the rear of the pilot tank turret was eliminated. The pistol port in the rear turret wall was retained, but it was shifted toward the right side.

With the United States at war, the pressure increased to get the new heavy tank into production. Following the precedent set with the medium tank M3, it was decided to release the T1E2 for production prior to the completion of the test program. Such an early release was expected to produce tanks

Although none of the machine guns are installed, note that the port for the left bow .30 caliber machine gun has been plated over. This was in accordance with the order to delete that weapon from the production tanks.

The exhaust deflector configuration and the stowage boxes standardized for the production tanks can be seen above.

to meet the critical war situation even if they contained some undesirable features. Any necessary changes resulting from the test program could be introduced later without severely disrupting the production program. Such a policy was already producing M3 medium tanks to meet the critical needs of the British in addition to the American training program. To meet the expected quantity requirements, it was considered necessary to use welded as well as cast hulls and the combination of the General Motors diesel engine and the Hydramatic transmission was proposed as an alternate power train. On 14

February 1942, OCM 17812 sorted out the designations for the different versions of the heavy tank. These were as follow:

Heavy tank T1 - Cast hull, Wright G-200 engine, Hydramatic transmission
Heavy tank T1E1 - Cast hull, Wright G-200 engine, GE electric drive
Heavy tank T1E2 - Cast hull, Wright G-200 engine, Twin Disc torque converter
Heavy tank T1E3 - Welded hull, Wright G-200 engine, Twin Disc torque converter
Heavy tank T1E4 - Welded hull, four GM 6-71 diesel engines, two Hydramatic tank transmissions

At this time, production orders had been placed for the T1E2 and the T1E3 and on 13 April 1942, OCM 18059 recommended standardization of the two vehicles as the heavy tanks M6 and M6A1 respectively. Standardization was approved on 26 May. Although funds had been allocated for 1084 heavy tanks, changing requirements of the Armored Force reduced the number authorized for procurement under OCM 18059 to 115. With the reduced requirements for heavy tanks and the standardization of the

Note the later track design on the production tank at the left compared to the T1E2 pilot.

The photographs above and below show many of the changes in the production tank from the T1E2 pilot. The new turret configuration is obvious with the flat circular hatch replacing the commander's cupola and three periscopes are visible in the front hull roof. The raised rear deck can be seen in the side views.

M6 and M6A1, the development projects for the T1 and T1E4 were cancelled by OCM 18352 on 11 June 1942. Thus the special tank Hydramatic transmission developed by General Motors for the T1 was never installed in a tank, although it was delivered to Aberdeen Proving Ground. Also, the heavy tank T1E4 with the four diesel engines did not progress beyond the design stage. However, the electric drive T1E1 pilot showed exceptionally good performance in tests at the Erie plant of the General Electric Company

At the right is the Hydramatic transmission intended for the heavy tank T1 after delivery to Aberdeen Proving Ground. This photograph was dated 4 September 1942.

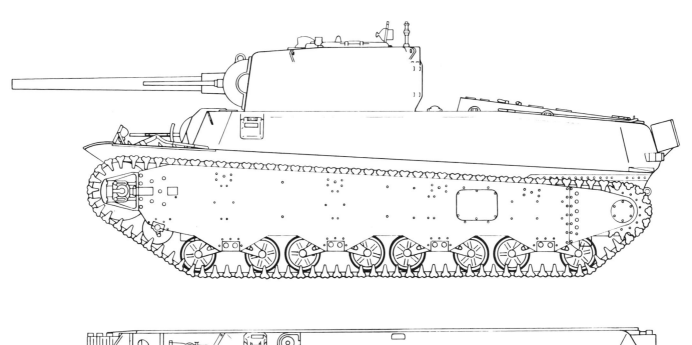

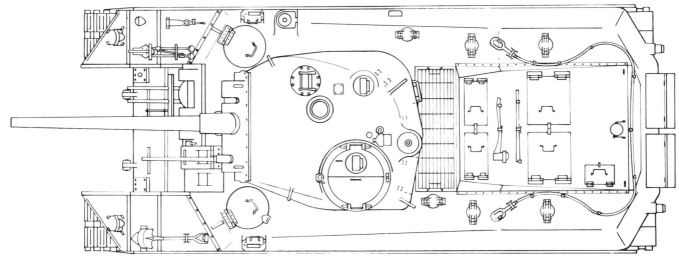

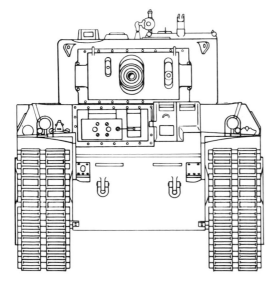

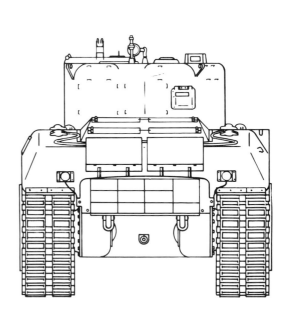

Scale 1:48

Heavy Tank M6

39

The production pilot heavy tank M6A1 is shown here at the General Motors Proving Ground on 22 January 1943. Except for the welded hull, note the similarity to the production M6.

40

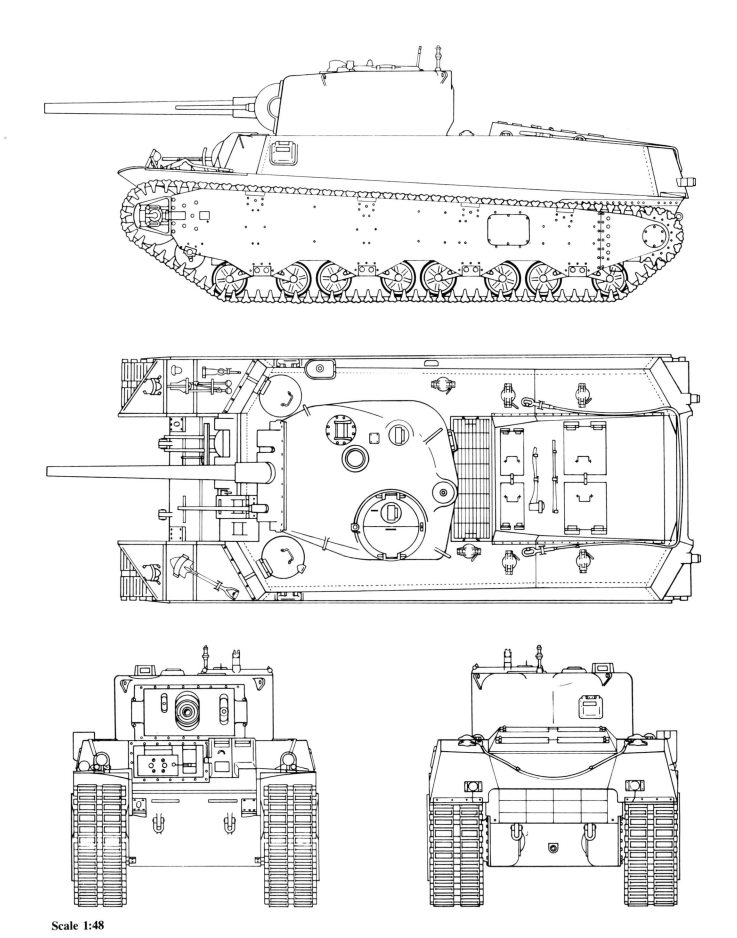

Scale 1:48

Heavy Tank M6A1

41

The production pilot M6A1 can be seen in the four views above and below. Although the production pilot was not fitted with the rear stowage boxes, they were installed on the later M6A1s.

The top view below shows the configuration of the welded hull M6A1. Again, note the similarity to the cast hull M6.

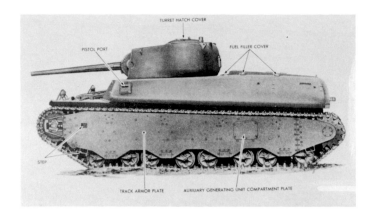

TURRET HATCH COVER

PISTOL PORT · FUEL FILLER COVER

STEP

TRACK ARMOR PLATE · AUXILIARY GENERATING UNIT COMPARTMENT PLATE

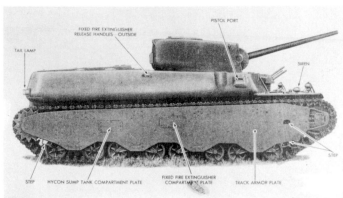

FIXED FIRE EXTINGUISHER RELEASE HANDLES—OUTSIDE · PISTOL PORT

TAIL LAMP

SIREN

STEP · HYCON SUMP TANK COMPARTMENT PLATE · FIXED FIRE EXTINGUISHER COMPARTMENT PLATE · TRACK ARMOR PLATE · STEP

The nomenclature of various components on the M6 can be seen in these illustrations from the technical manual. Note the early .50 caliber machine gun bow mount. This was replaced on the production tanks by the later side by side design. At the left is the Hycon sump tank compartment without its cover.

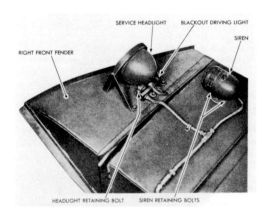

FINAL DRIVE OIL FILTER · HYCON ACCUMULATOR SUMP TANK

3-IN. GUN M7

37-MM GUN M6

CAL. .50 MACHINE GUNS

SIGHT

HEADLIGHT AND HEADLIGHT GUARD

BOW CAL. .30 MACHINE GUN

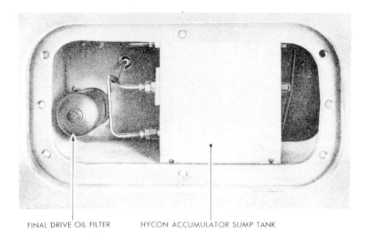

SERVICE HEADLIGHT · BLACKOUT DRIVING LIGHT

SIREN

RIGHT FRONT FENDER

HEADLIGHT RETAINING BOLT · SIREN RETAINING BOLTS

The headlight and siren installation appears at the left and the rear deck of the tank is shown below with the engine compartment hatch covers open and closed.

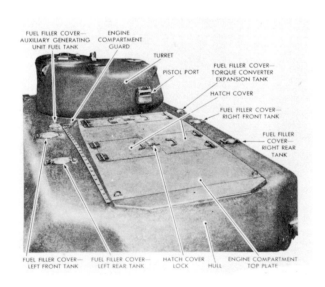

FUEL FILLER COVER—AUXILIARY GENERATING UNIT FUEL TANK · ENGINE COMPARTMENT GUARD · TURRET · PISTOL PORT · FUEL FILLER COVER—TORQUE CONVERTER EXPANSION TANK · HATCH COVER · FUEL FILLER COVER—RIGHT FRONT TANK · FUEL FILLER COVER—RIGHT REAR TANK

FUEL FILLER COVER—LEFT FRONT TANK · FUEL FILLER COVER—LEFT REAR TANK · HATCH COVER LOCK · HULL · ENGINE COMPARTMENT TOP PLATE

SELECTOR GEAR-SHIFT LEVER — POSITION LOCK — BOW CAL. .30 MACHINE GUN ELEVATION LEVER — TRANSMISSION BRAKE PEDAL — PRIMER PUMP — HYCON CONTROLS — FIRE DETECTOR LIGHT — BOW CAL. .30 MACHINE GUN FIRING BUTTON — POSITION LOCKING HANDLE

FOOT REST — HYCON CONTROL BOX — GEARSHIFT LEVER — SIREN BUTTON — STOP LIGHT SWITCHES — MANUAL STEERING LEVERS — DRIVER'S SEAT PEDESTAL — MANUAL STEERING LEVERS — ACCELERATOR PEDAL — HYCON CONTROL PEDESTAL

A—SPEEDOMETER RESET
B—SPEEDOMETER
C—GUN SAFETY SWITCH
D—MAGNETO SWITCH
E—ENERGIZED STARTER SWITCH
F—BOOSTER SWITCH
G—FUEL CUT-OFF SWITCH
H—STARTER SWITCH
J—HEADLIGHT SWITCH
K—CLOCK
L—CONVERTER OIL TEMPERATURE GAGE
M—ENGINE OIL TEMPERATURE GAGE
N—ENGINE OIL PRESSURE GAGE
P—VOLTMETER
Q—AMMETER
R—TACHOMETER
S—OIL DILUTION SWITCH
T—HYCON PRESSURE GAGE
U—WINDSHIELD WIPER SOCKET

V—TROUBLE LIGHT SOCKET
W—CYLINDER TEMPERATURE GAGE
X—FUEL GAGE SELECTOR
Y—FUEL GAGE
Z—DEFROSTER SOCKET
AA—CONVERTER OIL PRESSURE GAGE
BB—TRANSMISSION OIL PRESSURE GAGE
CC—PANEL LIGHT SWITCH
DD—FINAL DRIVE OIL PRESSURE GAGE
EE—FINAL DRIVE OIL TEMPERATURE GAGE
FF—MAIN LIGHT SWITCH
GG—MAIN ENGINE ELECTRICAL SWITCH (COIL)
HH—BOW CAL. .30 MACHINE GUN MAIN FIRING SWITCH
JJ—MAIN BATTERY SWITCH

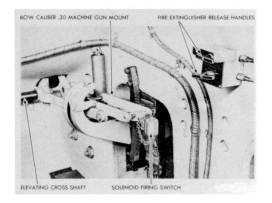

BOW CALIBER .30 MACHINE GUN MOUNT — FIRE EXTINGUISHER RELEASE HANDLES — ELEVATING CROSS SHAFT — SOLENOID FIRING SWITCH

Above are views of the driver's controls (left) and instrument panel (top right). The mount for the .30 caliber bow machine gun can be seen above at the right.

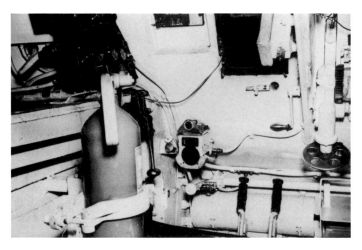

Above, the driver's controls in the M6 (left) are compared with those in the M6A1 (right). Note that the M6A1 is not fitted with the Hycon control system. Below are views of the .50 caliber machine gun bow mount in the M6A1 (left) and the rear of the M6 fighting compartment (right).

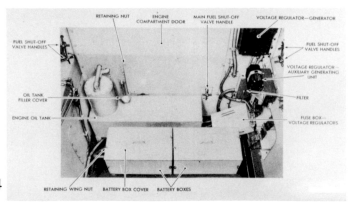

RETAINING NUT — ENGINE COMPARTMENT DOOR — MAIN FUEL SHUT-OFF VALVE HANDLE — VOLTAGE REGULATOR—GENERATOR — FUEL SHUT-OFF VALVE HANDLES — FUEL SHUT-OFF VALVE HANDLES — VOLTAGE REGULATOR—AUXILIARY GENERATING UNIT — FILTER — OIL TANK FILLER COVER — ENGINE OIL TANK — RETAINING WING NUT — BATTERY BOX COVER — BATTERY BOXES — FUSE BOX—VOLTAGE REGULATORS

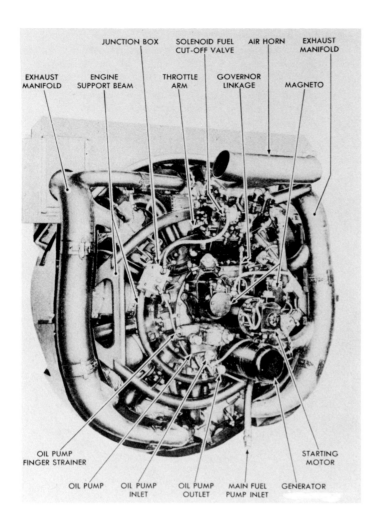

EXHAUST MANIFOLD · ENGINE SUPPORT BEAM · JUNCTION BOX · THROTTLE ARM · SOLENOID FUEL CUT-OFF VALVE · GOVERNOR LINKAGE · AIR HORN · EXHAUST MANIFOLD · MAGNETO

OIL PUMP FINGER STRAINER · OIL PUMP · OIL PUMP INLET · OIL PUMP OUTLET · MAIN FUEL PUMP INLET · GENERATOR · STARTING MOTOR

SHROUD · FAN BLADE · EXHAUST MANIFOLD

TORQUE CONVERTER COMPANION FLANGE · FLYWHEEL

The front (left) and rear (right) of the Wright G-200 engine as installed in the tank can be seen above.

The exhaust tube, muffler, and tail pipe assembly from the Wright G-200 engine is shown at the right.

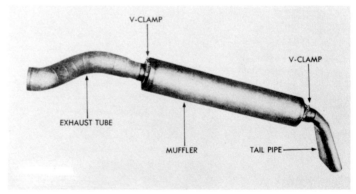

V-CLAMP · V-CLAMP · EXHAUST TUBE · MUFFLER · TAIL PIPE

Below, the torque converter, transmission, and final drive are installed in the M6 without the engine (left) and the complete assembly is shown removed from the vehicle (right).

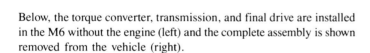

GEARSHIFT · TRANSMISSION · TORQUE CONVERTER · SELECTOR GEARSHIFT · LEFT REAR FUEL TANK PLATE · TRANSMISSION BRAKE DISK · ENGINE MOUNTING BOLTS

REDUCTION GEAR OIL FILTER · CONVERTER FLUID FILTER · TORQUE CONVERTER FLANGE · LEFT FRONT FUEL TANK PLATE

CONVERTER FLUID FILTER · REDUCTION GEAR OIL FILTER · TORQUE CONVERTER · TRANSMISSION · TRANSMISSION BRAKE DISK · FINAL DRIVE · DRIVING SPROCKETS · REDUCTION GEAR CASE BREATHER AND OIL LEVEL GAGE · ARMOR PLATE

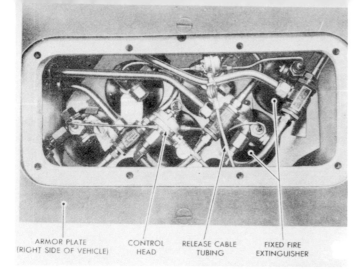

ARMOR PLATE (RIGHT SIDE OF VEHICLE)   CONTROL HEAD   RELEASE CABLE TUBING   FIXED FIRE EXTINGUISHER

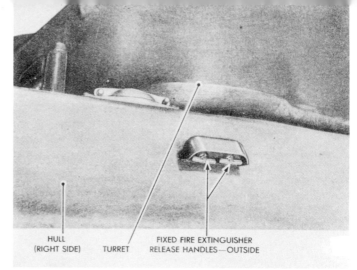

HULL (RIGHT SIDE)   TURRET   FIXED FIRE EXTINGUISHER RELEASE HANDLES—OUTSIDE

Above, the open fire extinguisher compartment can be seen at the left and the exterior fire extinguisher release handles are at the right.

At the right is the auxiliary generator compartment with the cover removed.

AUXILIARY GENERATING UNIT

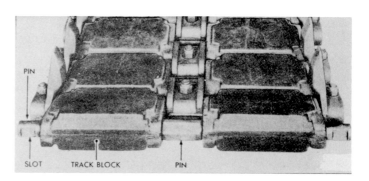

PIN   SLOT   TRACK BLOCK   PIN

The early design track with the detachable rubber pads can be seen above at the left. Above at the right is an assembled section of track. Below, the bogie assembly is shown installed (left) and removed from the tank (right).

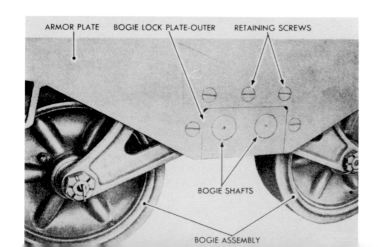

ARMOR PLATE   BOGIE LOCK PLATE-OUTER   RETAINING SCREWS   BOGIE SHAFTS   BOGIE ASSEMBLY

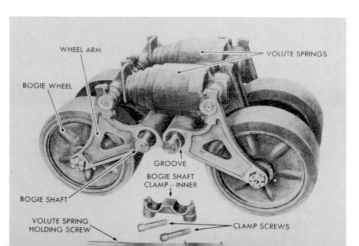

WHEEL ARM   VOLUTE SPRINGS   BOGIE WHEEL   GROOVE   BOGIE SHAFT CLAMP—INNER   BOGIE SHAFT   VOLUTE SPRING HOLDING SCREW   CLAMP SCREWS

The pilot heavy tank T1E1 appears above and below at Aberdeen Proving Ground on 30 May 1942. No armament was installed at that time and steel weights were attached to the vehicle to simulate the weight of a fully loaded tank.

and General Barnes informally ordered 27 additional electric propulsion and control systems to be completed by the end of 1942. Standardization of the T1E1 as the heavy tank M6A2 was proposed, but not approved, although the designation frequently appeared on drawings and in correspondence concerning the vehicle. OCM 18984, dated 10 August 1942, recommended that the T1E1 be classified as a limited procurement type to permit the manufacture of 115

tanks for extended service tests. Since the Services of Supply had directed in June that the procurement of heavy tanks be increased from 115 to 230 with the additional tanks allocated to International Aid, the end result was that all of the T1E1 tanks would be for use by the U.S. Army and the M6 and M6A1 tanks would go to the Lend-Lease program. This was confirmed in a September report which showed that the heavy tank production would consist of 50 M6s and

Above, details on the rear deck of the electric drive T1E1 pilot are clearly visible. The steel slabs brought the total vehicle weight up to 62 tons for the test.

65 M6A1s for Britain and 115 T1E1s for the United States. Production was expected to start in October or November 1942. This schedule was not met and the opinion of the user was shifting against the heavy tank. The Commanding General of the Armored Force, General Jacob Devers, wrote on 7 December 1942 to the Commanding General of the Army Ground Forces stating that "Due to its tremendous

The driver's station in the T1E1 pilot is at the right. Below are two views of the driver's seat and control unit.

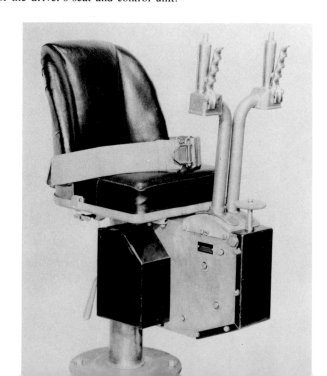

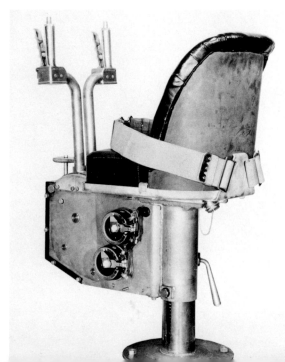

48

The sectional drawings of the heavy tank T1E1 above and below show the general arrangement of the power train and the driver's controls. Note the obvious distortion of the 3 inch gun barrel in this wartime artist's concept.

weight and limited tactical use, there is no requirement in the Armored Force for the heavy tank. The increase in the power of the armament of the heavy tank does not compensate for the heavier armor". Recommending the cancellation of the heavy tank program, General Devers reflected the opinion of the Armored Force that it was preferable to use the available shipping for two 30-ton medium tanks rather than one 60-ton heavy tank. In view of the attitude of the using arm, the Services of Supply approved the termination of heavy tank production. The economical end point was determined to be at 40 vehicles.

Below is a production heavy tank T1E1. This tank is armed with the .50 caliber antiaircraft machine gun.

A production heavy tank T1E1 appears above and below. This vehicle is fitted with the center guide tracks. These tracks were converted from the standard outside guide tracks by the installation of a center guide to replace the center connector. The outside guides were then removed by flame cutting.

The first production M6 was accepted at the Baldwin Locomotive Works in December 1942. A production pilot M6A1 was completed by the Fisher Body Division of General Motors, but the production contract at Fisher was cancelled. All of the 40 production tanks were assembled at Baldwin. They consisted of 8 M6s, 12 M6A1s, and 20 T1E1s with the last tank, a T1E1, being delivered in February 1944.

With the T1E1 and T1E2 pilots and Fisher's production pilot M6A1, the overall total for the series was 43 tanks.

Although the Armored Force had lost interest in the heavy tank, the first production M6 was shipped to Fort Knox for evaluation. Its test program began on 16 January 1943 and it was followed by the production pilot M6A1 which entered the program on 9

Above are two additional views of the production heavy tank T1E1. As in the photographs on the previous page, all of the machine guns have been removed. This is the tank on display today by the Ordnance Museum at Aberdeen Proving Ground.

March. The tests continued until 26 April when both tanks were shipped to the Baldwin Locomotive Works for rebuilding. In addition to the new turret and modified front hull, the production tanks differed from the early pilots on the rear hull. The top plate of the latter was raised several inches to permit better air flow and cooling in the engine compartment.

The test reports on the M6 and M6A1 were highly critical and considered the tanks unsatisfactory without a complete redesign. They noted that the crew positions were awkward making it difficult to operate both the main armament and the various

The production heavy tank M6 is shown above and below during tests by the Armored Force at Fort Knox. The tank is armed with the .50 caliber antiaircraft machine gun which was standard at that time.

The raised rear deck on the production M6 can be clearly seen above. Below, the tank has thrown a track during the tests at Fort Knox.

machine guns. For example, the direct sight telescope was located so close to the 3 inch gun that the gunner could only sight using his left eye. The M6A1 was fitted with new center guide tracks and bogies during the evaluation at Fort Knox and they were later transferred to the M6 test vehicle. Since the original cupola and rotor mounted .50 caliber machine gun had been removed from the production turret, the tank had no means to deliver machine gun fire to the sides and rear without exposing the tank commander. Therefore, as the 37mm gun was considered superfluous, the Armored Force recommended that this problem be solved by replacing the small cannon with a coaxial .30 caliber machine gun.

The later type tracks as well as the final design for the .50 caliber machine gun bow mount are visible on the production M6 below. Also, note the small driver's vision door compared to the pilot M6.

The M6 production tank can be seen here at Fort Knox with the fighting compartment hatches closed (above) and open (below).

At the right, the great size of the M6 is obvious when compared to the M5 light tank during test operations at Fort Knox.

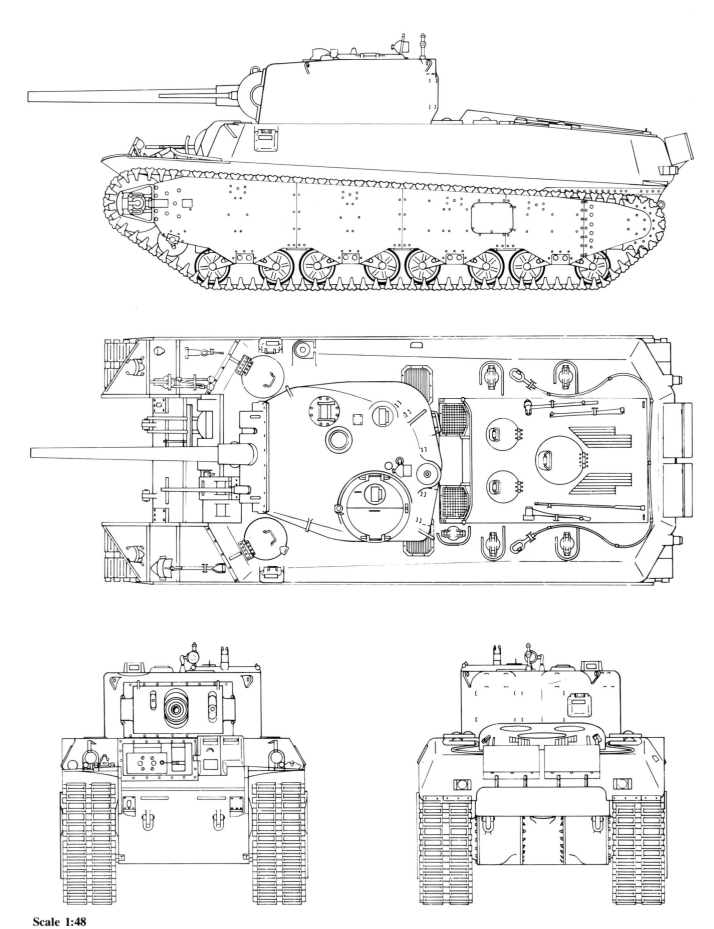

Scale 1:48

Heavy Tank T1E1

Above, the pilot heavy tank T1E1 is at Aberdeen Proving Ground after being rearmed with the 90mm gun T7. The .50 caliber bow machine gun mount and the driver's door have been omitted and replaced by windshields for the test. This photograph was dated 17 March 1943.

The 3 inch gun, now standardized as the M7, was considered inadequate for a heavy tank by the Armored Force. This criticism had been anticipated by the Ordnance Department and a test program had installed the 90mm gun T7 in the pilot T1E1 at Aberdeen. Identical ballistically with the 90mm antiaircraft gun, the T7 was the weapon eventually standardized as the 90mm gun M3 and installed in the Pershing tank. The firing tests were satisfactory with the tank providing a stable gun platform, but as with the 3 inch gun, a redesign of the turret was required to permit efficient operation. By the time the report on the 90mm gun installation was issued, the heavy tank had been rejected for use by the Armored Force and further work on the project was cancelled.

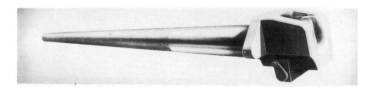

The 3 inch gun M7 above was replaced by the 90mm gun T7 below. The recoil system for the 3 inch gun was used with new throttling groove sleeves to handle the more powerful weapon.

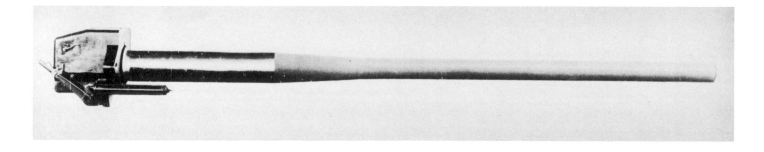

Additional views are shown here of the T1E1 pilot armed with the 90mm gun T7. None of the machine guns were mounted on this test vehicle.

An artist's concept above shows the configuration of the proposed heavy tank M6A2E1 armed with the 105mm gun. Note that the sponson pistol ports have been eliminated.

After the invasion of Europe, the Ordnance Department expected that there would be a requirement for a limited number of tanks with extremely thick armor and powerful armament to break through heavily fortified areas. It was proposed that the T1E1s be modified by removing the bow machine gun mounts and the driver's vision door and then welding additional steel plate on the front to provide protection equivalent to 7 1/2 inches of vertical armor. A new turret was to be installed mounting the high velocity 105mm gun T5E1. This turret, designed for the new heavy tank T29, required an 80 inch diameter turret ring compared to the 69 inch ring on the T1E1. However, it was considered feasible to modify the hulls to accept the larger ring. It was believed that 15 of the T1E1s could be modified in 90 days, if the required high priorities could be obtained. Out of the 20 production T1E1s available, the remaining five were to be used for spare parts. A tentative OCM prepared on 14 August 1944 recommended modification of the 15 tanks and designated them as the heavy tank M6A2E1. The goal for delivery was set as 15 November. The Army Ground Forces had been cool toward the project from the

first and the Army Service Forces had referred the matter to General Eisenhower in a cablegram dated 2 August 1944. His reply on 18 August stated that the 15 modified tanks were not wanted as they were considered impractical for use in the European Theater of Operations. This effectively killed the project and probably it was a very good thing. Tests at Aberdeen on a T1E1 loaded to the expected 77-ton weight of the M6A2E1 showed that it could not climb a 40 per cent slope. Since it was not considered practical to change the final drive gear reduction in the time available, the M6A2E1s would have been limited to operation on favorable terrain.

Another M6A2E1 artist's concept drawing appears at the right. The front armor is a solid rolled plate welded to the front of the tank without a bow machine gun.

57

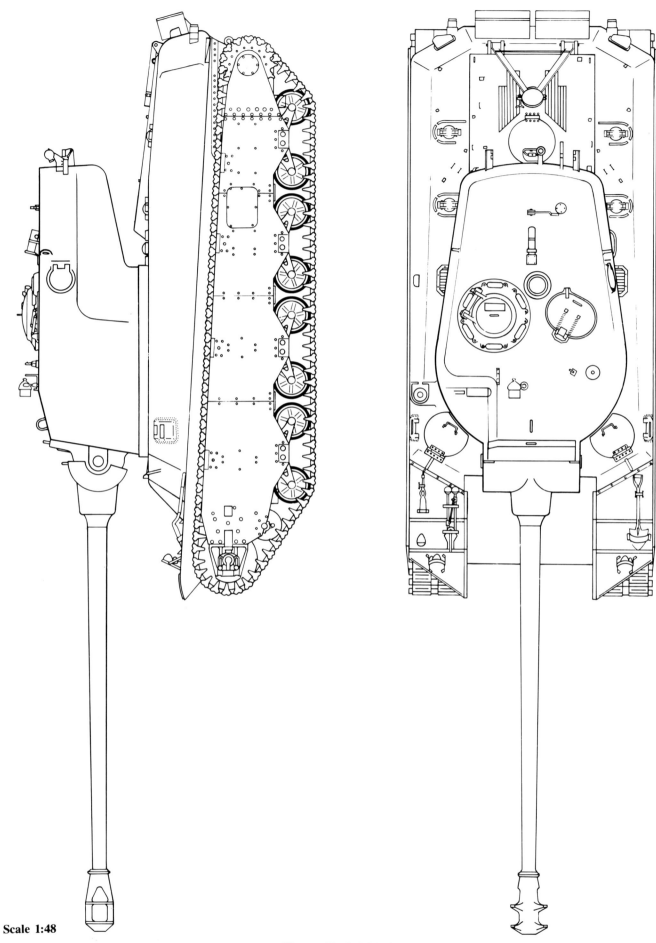

Scale 1:48

Heavy Tank M6A2E1

58

The heavy tank M6A2E1 as finally assembled for the T29 test program is shown here at Aberdeen Proving Ground on 7 June 1945. The original front hull has been retained, but the .50 caliber machine gun bow mount has been removed and a cover installed over the opening.

After cancellation of the project, it was requested that two M6A2E1s be completed to test the turret and armament for the new heavy tank T29. This request was approved and two turrets, gun mounts, and fighting compartments armed with the 105mm gun T5E1 were completed and proof fired at Aberdeen Proving Ground. The two M6A2E1s were not fitted with the additional hull armor specified in the original project since it was not required for this test program. On 14 December 1944, OCM 26039 classified the heavy tanks M6, M6A1, and T1E1 obsolete and subsequently the tanks were scrapped except for a single T1E1 on display today by the Ordnance Museum at Aberdeen.

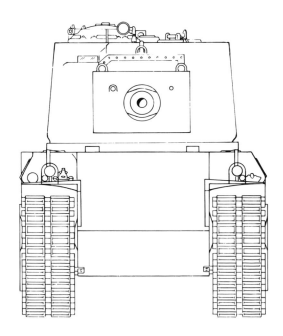

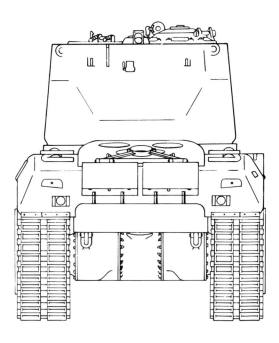

Details of the M6A2E1 turret can be seen above as well as the rear deck configuration of the production T1E1. The hull roof doors have been cut back to clear the larger turret ring and a travel lock has been installed for the 105mm gun. Below, the stowage boxes have been attached to the rear hull and both ports for the .30 caliber bow machine guns have been fitted with cover plates.

The left side of the M6A2E1 is visible in the photographs below. These views, dated 3 July 1945, show the tank operating on the Churchville test course at Aberdeen Proving Ground.

The rejected M6A2E1 project proposed that a limited number of assault vehicles be improvised by modifying the stock of T1E1 heavy tanks. However, a far more extensive program to develop a heavily armed and armored combat vehicle had been initiated in September 1943. Studies by the Ordnance Department indicated that such a vehicle would be required after the invasion of Europe to penetrate heavily fortified areas such as the German West Wall. The original concept proposed mounting the new 105mm gun T5E1 in a tank with the equivalent of 8 inch frontal armor using the electric drive system developed for the heavy tank T1E1 and the medium tank T23. The high velocity T5E1 gun had excellent penetration performance against concrete and when installed in a heavily armored chassis was expected to be extremely effective in reducing heavy fortifications. The Chief of Ordnance proposed that 25 of the new tanks be produced and estimated that they could be completed in eight to twelve months, approximately the same time that would be required to build a single pilot. Such a schedule was expected to make them available in time for operations in Europe. The Army Ground Forces did not agree and recommended that only three pilot models be constructed and that the electric drive be replaced by a mechanical transmission. After a conference with the various parties concerned, the Army Service Forces in March 1944 authorized the procurement of five vehicles,

designating them as the heavy tank T28. The original specification was modified to increase the frontal armor to 12 inches raising the estimated combat weight to 95 tons.

At the top right is an early concept drawing for an assault tank. Note the early volute spring suspension and the short barreled heavy cannon. This may have been based on the original 105mm gun T5. Below, the T28 is shown during a demonstration at Aberdeen on 3 October 1946. At that time, it was designated as a superheavy tank.

The views on this page show the T95 number 1 on 23 January 1946 at Aberdeen Proving Ground after it was redesignated as a gun motor carriage. Its only secondary armament, the .50 caliber antiaircraft machine gun, is installed on the ring above the commander's cupola.

The proposed tank was a low silhouette vehicle without a turret. The 105mm gun T5E1 was to be mounted in the front of the hull with a traverse of 10 degrees to the right and left of center and an elevation range of -5 to +20 degrees. A crew of four was carried with the driver and gunner in the front hull on the left and right of the cannon respectively. The loader was at the left rear of the fighting compartment and the commander at the right rear behind the gunner. The driver and the commander were each provided with a vision cupola. A ring mount for a .50 caliber machine gun was installed around the commander's cupola. It could be used only with the commander standing in the open hatch and was the only secondary armament on the vehicle, except for the individual crew weapons. The gunner was equipped with a telescope alongside the cannon and a periscopic sight in the hull roof.

On 7 February 1945, a memorandum from the Chief of Ordnance requested that the T28 be redesignated as the 105mm gun motor carriage T95 because the cannon was not turret mounted and because of its limited secondary armament. OCM 26898, dated 8 March 1945, approved the name change and recorded the characteristics of the new vehicle. Because of the pressure of the wartime production program as well as the size and weight of the proposed vehicle, there was some difficulty in finding a facility to manufacture the five pilots. However, the Pacific Car and Foundry Company agreed to take on the project

Details of T95 number 1 can be seen in these additional photographs. The extreme width of the vehicle with the outboard tracks installed is obvious in the front and rear views. Note the four inch thick armor skirts on the outboard tracks.

and in May 1945, they were supplied with the basic vehicle design as well as detailed information on the gun mount and the horizontal volute spring suspension. Final design work began immediately. The first front end casting was delivered on 20 June and welding was completed on the first hull in August 1945.

After the end of the war in the Pacific, the number of pilots was reduced from five to two with number 1 being shipped to Aberdeen Proving Ground on 21 December 1945 followed by number 2 on 10 January 1946. The first pilot, registration number 40226809, was used for engineering tests at Aberdeen, but the second, registration number 40226810, was transferred first to Fort Knox and later to the Engineer Board at Yuma, Arizona where it was used for testing floating bridges.

The layout of T95 number 1 and the external stowage arrangement are shown at the top and bottom of this page. However, the radio equipment had not been installed in this vehicle. The view at the left below shows T95 number 2 at Aberdeen on 11 April 1946. The radio equipment had been installed and the antennas are visible on the hull roof.

The power package in the T95 was essentially the same as in the M26 Pershing tank, although the weight of the new vehicle was more than twice that of the latter. To handle the T95, the 500 horsepower Ford GAF engine and the torqmatic transmission required a final drive gear ratio that reduced the maximum vehicle speed to about eight miles per hour. In fact, the maximum recommended sustained speed was seven miles per hour at 2600 rpm. The great weight of the vehicle also required considerable ingenuity in design to reduce the ground pressure to an acceptable level. This objective was achieved by the use of two sets of tracks on each side. The outer set, along with the four inch thick armor side skirts, could be removed and towed behind the vehicle when

The T95 with the outboard tracks removed and arranged for towing can be seen above. Details of the outboard track assembly are shown at the bottom of the page. Below at the right, the vehicle, now redesignated as the superheavy tank T28, is being unloaded from LST 1153 on 3 May 1948.

operating on a hard surface. Removing the outer tracks also reduced the overall width from 179 1/2 inches to 124 inches permitting rail transportation. At Aberdeen, an inexperienced four man crew removed the outer tracks under field conditions in four hours on their first try. An equal amount of time was required to reassemble them onto the vehicle. By the third try, the same team had reduced the time to remove or replace the outer tracks to 2 1/2 hours.

The heavily armed and armored T95 did not quite fit any of the usual categories for U. S. Army fighting vehicles. For example, tanks were expected to carry their armament in fully rotating turrets and self-propelled guns usually were lightly armored to achieve maximum mobility. The T95 did not meet either of these criteria and in June 1946, there was another name change. At that time, OCM 30758 redesignated the vehicle as the superheavy tank T28. It then was considered that the combination of heavy firepower and heavy armor was more appropriate for a tank than a gun motor carriage. Regardless of the

name, the T28 (T95) was under test at Aberdeen Proving Ground until late 1947, primarily to evaluate the durability of components on such a heavy vehicle. A total of 541 miles of operation was completed consisting of 128 miles on roads and 413 miles on

Above, the superheavy tank T28 is loaded on a transporter during the demonstration at Aberdeen Proving Ground on 3 October 1946. At the right, the vehicle is shown during the automotive tests.

gravel. Needless to say, the mileage accumulated slowly because of the low normal operating speed of five to six miles per hour and the low priority assigned to the project. Work was terminated before completion of the program in compliance with a War Department policy to discontinue development on combat vehicles in the 100-ton class. One of the T28 (T95) pilots is on display today in the collection of the Patton Museum at Fort Knox, Kentucky.

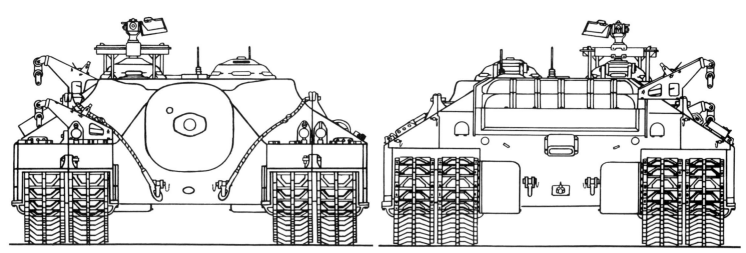

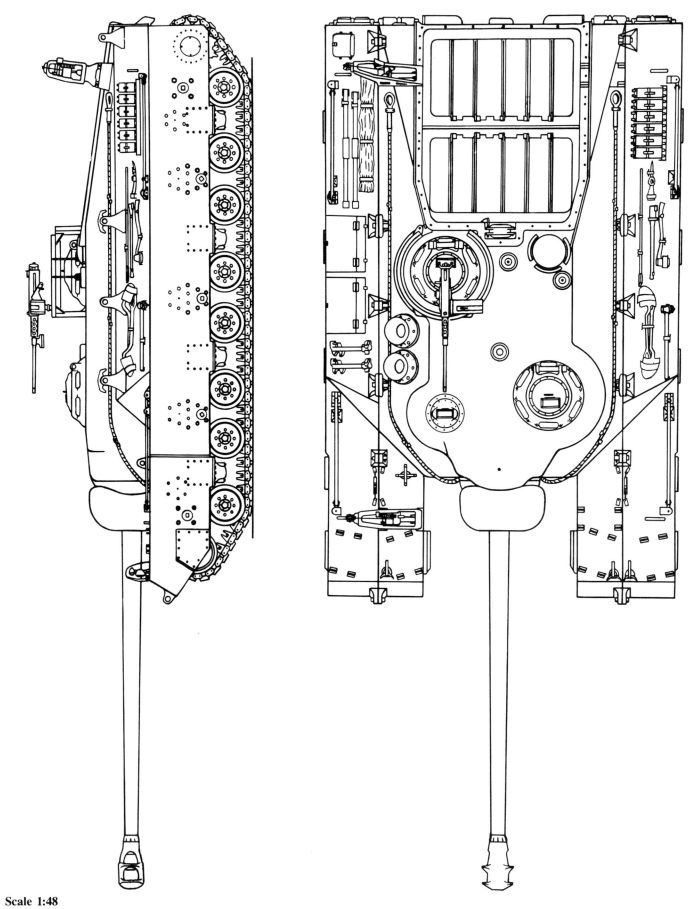

Scale 1:48

Superheavy Tank T28 (105mm Gun Motor Carriage T95)

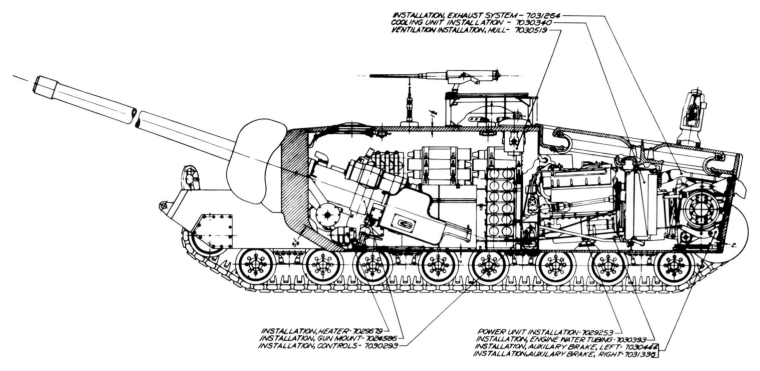

INSTALLATION, EXHAUST SYSTEM - 7031264
COOLING UNIT INSTALLATION - 7030340
VENTILATION INSTALLATION, HULL - 7030519

INSTALLATION, HEATER - 7029519
INSTALLATION, GUN MOUNT - 7024586
INSTALLATION, CONTROLS - 7030293

POWER UNIT INSTALLATION - 7029253
INSTALLATION, ENGINE WATER TUBING - 7030393
INSTALLATION, AUXILARY BRAKE, LEFT - 7030444
INSTALLATION, AUXILIARY BRAKE, RIGHT - 7031336

The interior arrangement of the T95 (T28) can be seen in the sectional drawing above. Note the 12 inch thick front armor.

The interior views above show the left side (left) and right rear (right) of the T95 fighting compartment with the stowage racks for the separated 105mm ammunition. Below, the driver's instrument panel appears at the right and his controls are at the left. The letters indicate the following: A. instrument panel, B. speed range selector, C. driver's seat, D & E. hand throttle and adjusting pin, F & G. steering levers, H. horn, I & J. auxiliary brakes, K. foot throttle.

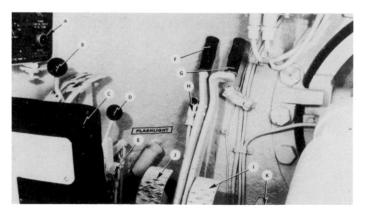

At the left is the original 105mm gun T5. The later 105mm gun T5E1 is shown below. The bore lengths were 48.58 and 65 calibers respectively. However, the T5 was over 200 pounds heavier than the long barreled T5E1.

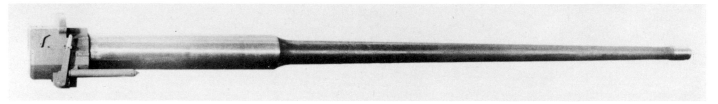

Below, the 105mm gun T5E1 is in its mount at the left and the gunner's station is at the right showing the T139 telescope and the periscope linkage. The nomenclature of the gun and mount at the lower right is as follows: A. recoil mechanism, B. stop, C. trunnion ring, D. gun mount, E. shield, F. elevating mechanism, G. traversing mechanism, H. equilibrator, I. equilibrator roller, J. travel lock, K. firing lever, L-M. breech guard locking lever and cover, N. breech guard, O. breech.

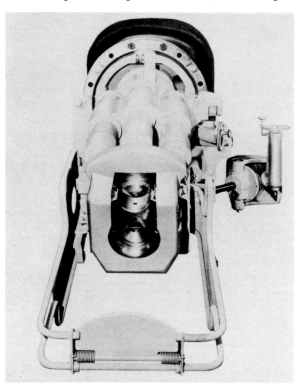

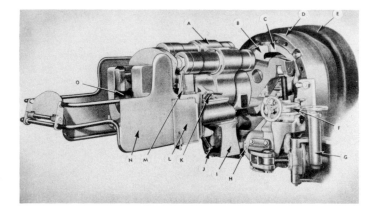

Below, a track link is shown at the left and in the view of the suspension at the right, the letters indicate the following: A. adjustable idler, B. tie bar, C. dual roller, D. intermediate tie bar, E. inner track, F. single roller, G. inner final drive, H. bogie with stop, I. bogie without stop.

Above is the first pilot heavy tank T29 after assembly at Pressed Steel Car Company, Inc. The two coaxial .50 caliber machine guns are clearly visible in the left front view.

By the middle of 1944, combat reports from Europe describing the use of heavy tanks by the Germans stimulated new interest in the development of an equivalent American vehicle. The Pershing medium tank provided an answer to the early model of the German Tiger. However, although the latter was still in first line service, it had first been encountered by U. S. forces during 1943. By 1944, the Germans were introducing even more heavily armed and armored vehicles. Although for morale purposes the Pershing was temporarily redesignated as a heavy tank, it clearly did not provide an answer to the problem. On 14 September 1944, OCM 25117 recommended the development and manufacture of four pilots for a new heavy tank. Two of these were designated as the heavy tank T29 and were to be armed with the 105mm gun T5E1. The remaining two were designated as the heavy tank T30 and were to be armed with the 155mm gun T7.

Procurement of 1200 T29 tanks was recommended by OCM 26825 on 1 March 1945. The new heavy tank was powered by the Ford GAC, V-12, liquid-cooled engine developing 770 horsepower at 2800 rpm. The engine was coupled to the new cross drive transmission developed by General Motors. The latter combined the functions of a transmission, steering gear, and brakes in a single unit. With the original cross drive model EX-120, the driver used an electric control system to operate the transmission under normal conditions. Two mechanical manual steering levers also were provided for emergency use. Lack of sensitivity and feel with the electric control resulted in its replacement by a mechanical system also using a single control lever usually referred to as the wobble stick. The manual steering levers were retained for emergency use. Separate controls were provided for the driver and assistant driver (bow gunner).

The muzzle brake has not yet been installed on the 105mm gun in the first pilot T29 below. Also, the five inch extended end connectors have not been fitted on the double pin tracks.

Above is another view of the first pilot heavy tank T29. At the right are two photographs of the power package, consisting of the Ford GAC engine and the cross drive transmission, removed from the vehicle.

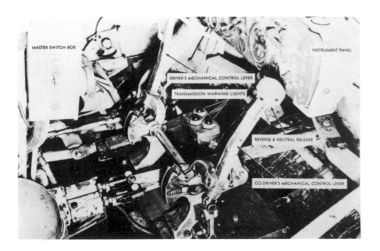

When delivered to the Army, the T29s were fitted with the CD-850-1 version of the cross drive transmission. This unit incorporated two hydraulically selected gear ranges driving through a single phase torque converter. Part of the power was transmitted through a mechanical path bypassing the torque converter. This mechanically transmitted power, as well as that from the torque converter, was

At the left are the mechanical wobble stick transmission controls for both the driver and assistant driver. Below, the early electric transmission controls can be seen for the driver (left) and the assistant driver (right).

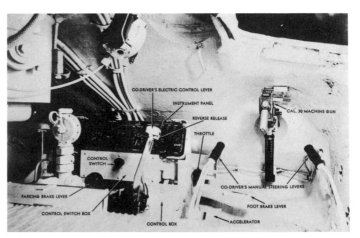

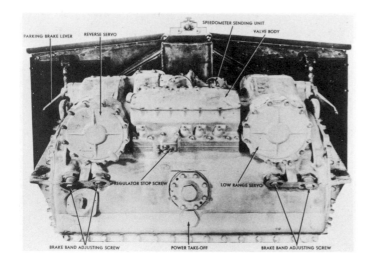

At the left is a view of the cross drive transmission attached to the Ford GAC engine.

applied equally to both output shafts except when steering. At that time, all of the mechanical power was applied to one side to provide the speed difference required for steering. Braking for the vehicle was by means of built in disc brakes actuated mechanically by foot pedals in the drivers' compartment. A later version of the cross drive was installed during the testing program. Designated as the CD-850-2, it replaced the single phase torque converter with a polyphase unit. This later model was more efficient at high speeds and acted as a fluid coupling after the point of 1:1 torque multiplication was reached. The great advantage of the cross drive transmission was its simplicity of operation which greatly eased the task of the driver. Pushing the wobble stick to the left or right steered the tank in that direction when the transmission was in first or second gear. The same action in neutral caused the vehicle to pivot in place with one track going forward and the other in reverse. Such action greatly increased the ability of the tank to extricate itself from difficult terrain where less agile vehicles would be stuck.

Many components in common with the medium tank M26 Pershing were used in the new heavy tanks. The T80E3 tracks were the 23 inch T80E1 tracks of the Pershing fitted with five inch extended end connecters giving a total width of 28 inches. Power was transmitted to the tracks through sprockets at the rear of the vehicle. Eight road wheels per side increased the ground contact length to reduce the ground pressure of the tank which weighed over 70 tons, combat loaded.

The hull was a welded assembly of armor castings and rolled plate similar to the M26. The same maximum thickness of four inches was retained on the upper front, but the angle was increased on the T29 to 54 degrees from the vertical. The driver and assistant driver (bow gunner) were seated on the left and right sides of the front hull respectively. The latter operated the .30 caliber machine gun ball mounted in the front armor. Both the driver and assistant driver were provided with a single periscope in their hatch covers.

The large cast turret was installed on an 80 inch diameter ring well forward on the hull. The turret armor thickness varied from seven inches on the front to four inches on the rear. A crew of four manned the turret with the tank commander seated under a cupola in the center of the turret bustle. The gunner was located in the right front of the turret and was provided with a direct sight telescope in the gun mount and a periscopic sight in the turret roof. The two loaders worked in the rear of the turret ring, one on each side of the cannon. Two hatches, one on each side, were located in the turret roof in addition to the

Below are exterior (left) and interior (right) views of the commander's station in the turret bustle. The two hatches for the loaders also can be seen in the turret roof.

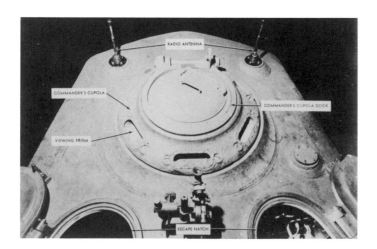

The right side of the commander's station appears at the left and the left side can be seen above.

hatch in the commander's cupola. A circular pistol port was installed in the right side wall of the turret. The 105mm gun T5E1, installed in the combination gun mount T123, was a long barreled weapon with a muzzle velocity of 3000 feet per second using the 39 pound armor piercing shot (AP) T32. During tests, a 24.6 pound hypervelocity armor piercing shot (HVAP) T29E3 achieved a muzzle velocity of 3700 feet per second. A 33.5 pound T30E1 high explosive shell (HE) was provided with a reduced muzzle velocity of 2500 feet per second. A total of 63 rounds of 105mm ammunition was stowed in the turret and hull. Two .50 caliber machine guns were mounted coaxially on the left side of the 105mm gun. Another .50 caliber machine gun was fitted on a pedestal mount in front of the left loader's hatch on the turret roof. Ventilation was provided by two 1500 cfm blowers. One was mounted in the turret roof to the right rear of the commander's station and the other was located in the front hull roof between the driver and the assistant driver.

Below, the 105mm gun breech is visible and one of the .50 caliber coaxial machine guns can be seen at the left. The gunner's station is at the right.

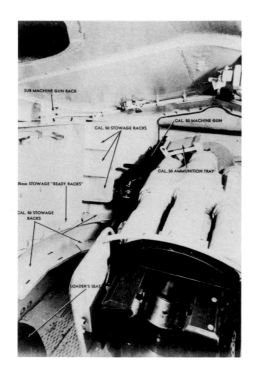

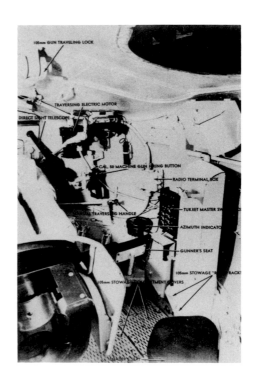

Above, the first production pilot heavy tank T29 is at Aberdeen Proving Ground on 31 October 1947. Note the changes to the gun shield compared to the original pilot.

Procurement of the T29 was approved on 12 April 1945, but the numbers were reduced to 1152. Also in April, four additional pilot T29s were authorized, but later, it was directed that one of these was to be armed with the 120mm gun T53 and redesignated as the heavy tank T34. This was only one of the many changes to the program with the approaching end of hostilities. After the end of the war in the Pacific, the production contract with the Pressed Steel Car Company, Inc. was terminated with one T29 completed and a second partially finished. All material was transferred to Detroit Arsenal for the completion of ten pilots for postwar development studies authorized by OCM 28848 on 23 August 1945. Later, the total of T29 pilots was reduced to eight by OCM 31654, dated 10 July 1947.

The first T29 arrived at Aberdeen Proving Ground in October 1947. By this time, there was no longer any requirement for production of these heavy tanks and the test program was limited to evaluating the various power train components for application to new tank designs. Two additional T29s arrived at Aberdeen in April and May 1948 and they also were used in the endurance and engineering test programs.

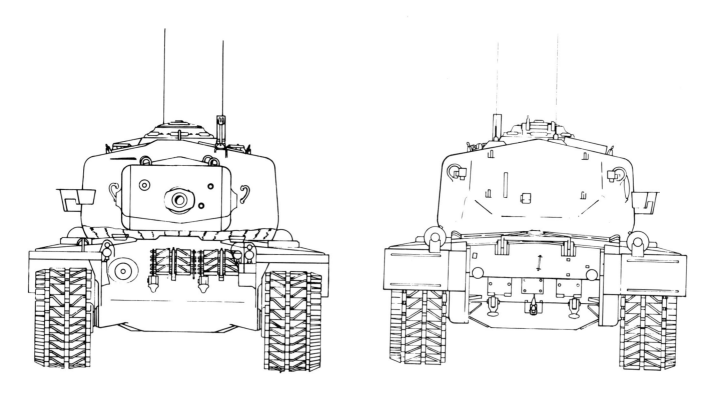

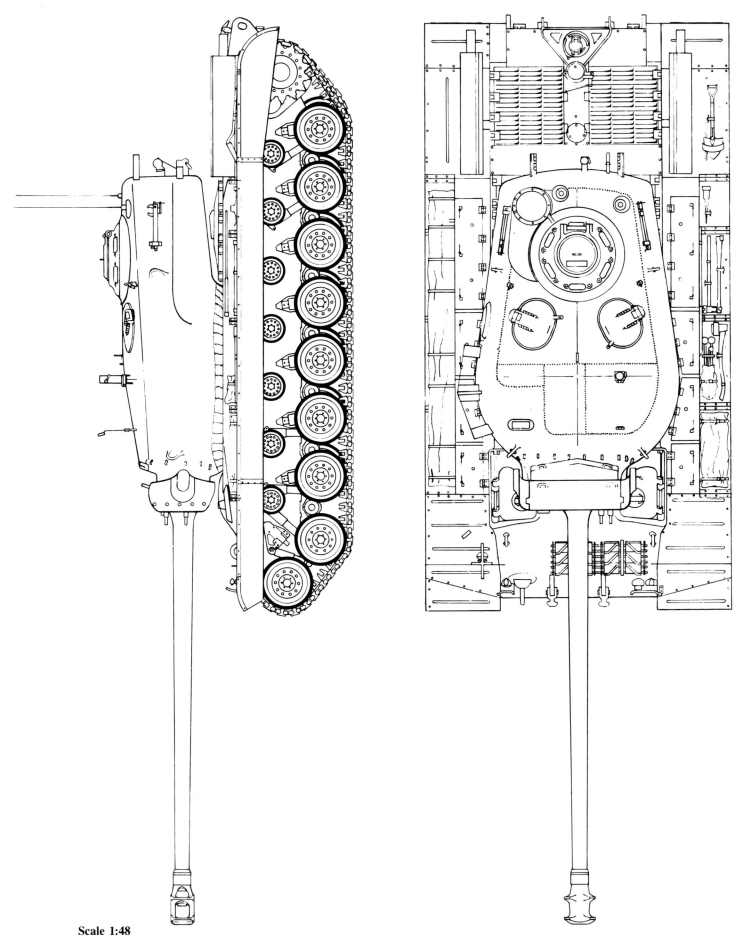

Scale 1:48

Heavy Tank T29

These are additional photographs of the first production pilot heavy tank T29 at Aberdeen on 31 October 1947. The vehicle is fitted with the five inch extended end connectors to increase the track width to 28 inches.

In the front and rear views of the first production pilot T29 above, it is obvious that the machine gun armament has not been installed. Instrumentation for the test program can be seen on the rear deck of the tank. Below, the engine compartment is open at the left and closed in the top rear view at the right. The travel lock for the 105mm gun is visible in both photographs.

The Allison V-1710-E32 engine is shown above with the CD-850-1 transmission. The complete power package is at the right including the cooling system. At the lower right, it is installed in the hull of the heavy tank T29E1.

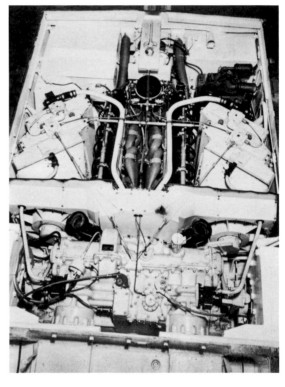

T29 number 1 was diverted to General Motors Corporation for the installation of a modified version of the Allison liquid-cooled V-12 aircraft engine. To accommodate the new power package consisting of the Allison V-1710-E32 engine and the CD-850-1 cross drive transmission, the tank hull was lengthened by 1 31/32 inches. The new engine developed 870 gross horsepower at 2800 rpm and weighed about 1600 pounds dry. This vehicle, armed with the 105mm gun T5E1 in mount T123, was designated as the heavy tank T29E1 in December 1945.

T29 number 2 was fitted with what was designated as the heavy tank turret T5. This turret was equipped with the Massachusetts Institute of Technology combination hydraulic power turret traversing and elevating mechanism and computing sight.

Below are views of the controls for the driver (left) and assistant driver (right) in the T29E1. Note that the manual steering levers have been retained for emergency use as on the T29.

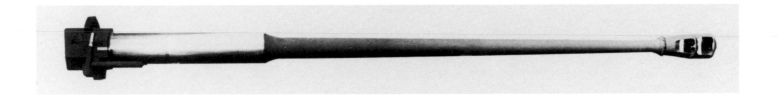

The 105mm gun T5E2 is shown above. In the three photographs below, the breech of this weapon can be seen open and closed.

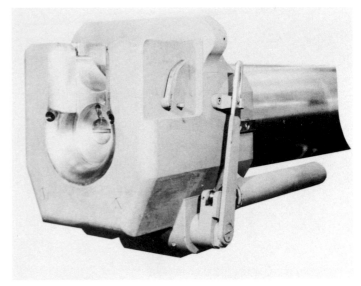

The tank was armed with the 105mm gun T5E2 in mount T123E2. OCM 32107, dated 1 April 1948, designated the T29 with the T5 turret as the heavy tank T29E2.

At this point, a brief description of the guns and mounts is in order. The 105mm gun T5E1 was installed in mount T123 which used three recoil cylinders on top of the gun cradle. This design was modified to have two recoil cylinders on top of the cradle and one on the bottom. This new mount was the T123E1 and the cannon modified to fit it was the 105mm gun T5E2. Installation of the power traversing and elevating system in the T29E2 tank required further modification of the mount and it received the new designation T123E2. Heavy tanks T29 numbers 3, 4, 5, 6, and 7 all were armed with the 105mm gun T5E2 in mount T123E1.

Below are two types of ammunition for the 105mm gun. The hypervelocity armor piercing (HVAP) round appears at the left and the high explosive (HE) round is at the right. With both types of separated ammunition, the projectile and cartridge case were loaded separately.

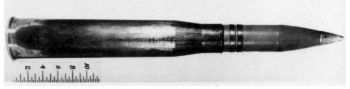

The heavy tank T29E3 appears above and below at Aberdeen Proving Ground on 4 May 1948. The vehicle is easily recognized by the large housings for the range finder extending from each side of the turret.

Heavy tank T29 number 8 was armed with the 105mm gun T5E1 in mount T123. This vehicle was modified to provide for the installation of the range finder T31E1 and telescope T93E2 in mount T136. Provision also was made to install panoramic telescopes T141, T144, and T145 to evaluate their use during indirect fire with the 105mm gun. The T141 and T144 telescopes were used in the gunner's periscopic sight mount and a T156 mount for the T145 telescope was fitted into the turret roof. All this was part of a program to study the effectiveness of integrated fire control systems. The same program also utilized a modified version of the medium tank T25E1. When fitted with the new fire control system,

Except for the .30 caliber bow weapon, the machine gun armament is installed in these photographs of the T29E3 at Aberdeen. Note the muzzles of the .50 caliber coaxial machine guns protruding through the gun shield.

T29 number 8 was redesignated as the heavy tank T29E3. The T31E1 range finder was a stereoscopic instrument with a base length of nine feet. It was not connected to the other fire control system components and was operated by the tank commander who manually relayed the range information using the control box just below the range finder. When the range and the desired lead were set into the control box, it was transmitted by flexible shafting to the telescope mount T136. Thus the gunner could give his undivided attention to tracking the target. Unfortunately, it did not work very well in practice. The tests at Aberdeen showed that backlash as well as windup and binding of the flexible shafting introduced serious errors into the system. However, the test program did show that the stereoscopic range finder was particularly useful for spotting purposes and sensing bursts. It also emphasized the necessity for a range finder if first round hits were to be obtained at ranges over 1000 yards.

The turret configuration with the range finder installation can be seen in the top view of the T29E3 above. Also, two panoramic telescopes are visible, one in the turret roof and one in the gunner's periscope mount.

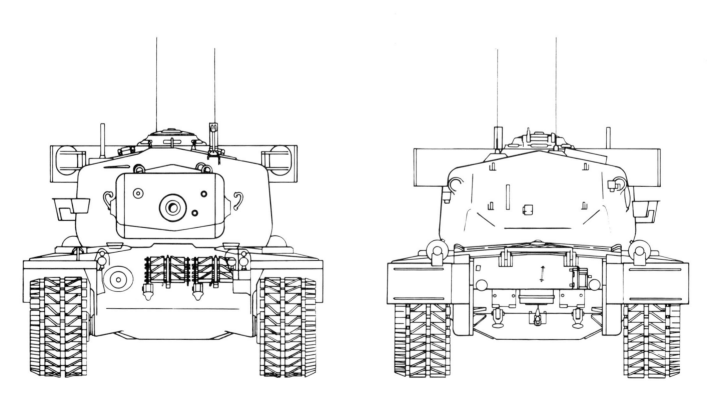

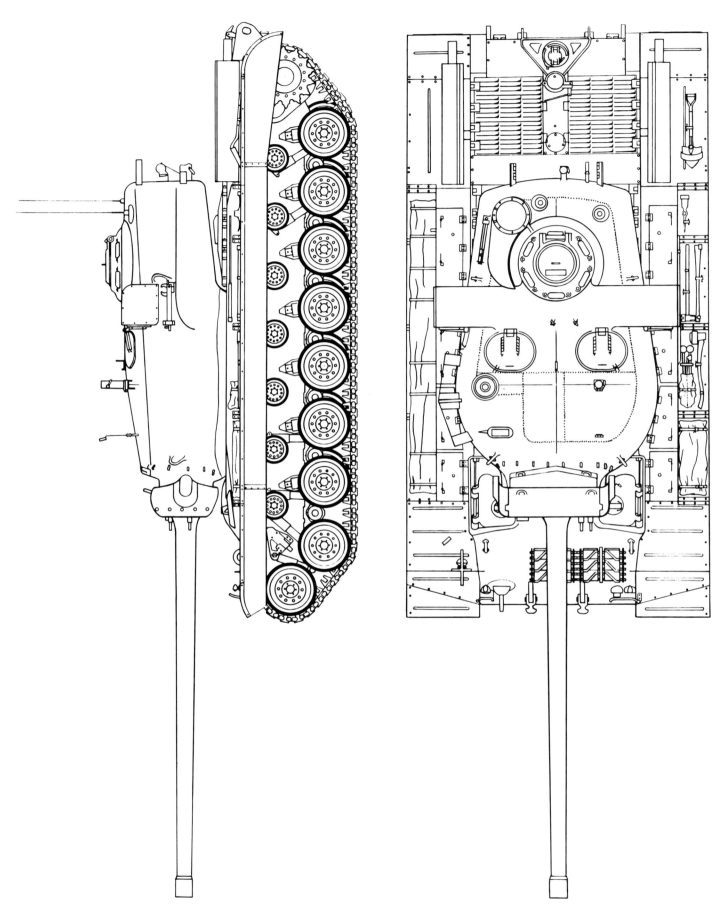

Scale 1:48

Heavy Tank T29E3

83

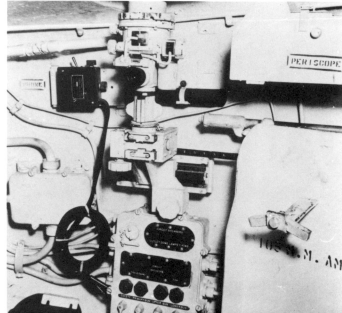

Above are the gunner's controls in the T29E3. At the top right, the panoramic telescope T145 is installed in the mount T156 at the right side of the gunner. At the right, the panoramic telescope T144 is fitted into the gunner's periscopic sight mount. In the background of this view, the T145 panoramic telescope can be seen in the T156 mount.

Below, the controls for the range finder T31E1 are visible at the left through the commander's cupola and at the right, there is an exterior view of the range finder and housing. In the foreground of the latter photograph, the panoramic telescope T141 is installed in the gunner's periscopic sight mount.

Heavy tank T30 number 1 is shown here at Aberdeen Proving Ground on 11 May 1948. The rear of the tank differs from the T29 because of the changes necessary to accommodate the air-cooled AV-1790 engine.

Two T30 heavy tanks entered the test program at Aberdeen shortly after the T29. The first arrived at the Proving Ground in April 1948 followed by the second in July. Originally intended to have the same power train as the T29, the military characteristics of the T30 were changed in late 1945 to substitute the air-cooled Continental V-12 engine for the liquid-cooled Ford GAC. The new engine, designated as the AV-1790-3, developed 810 gross horsepower at 2800

The 155mm gun is secured in the travel lock on the T30 above and test instrumentation is installed on the rear deck. Below, the machine guns have not been mounted on T30 serial number 1. Note that there is an opening for only one coaxial .50 caliber machine gun compared to two on the T29.

rpm and was an early model of what became the standard power plant for American tanks during the next decade. The main objective of the T30 test program at Aberdeen was to evaluate the new engine with the CD-850 cross drive transmission.

The T30 hull was essentially the same as that of the T29 except for the changes to the engine compartment necessary to accommodate the air-cooled engine. The turret also was similar to that on the T29,

but it was armed with the 155mm gun T7. Only one coaxial .50 caliber machine gun was located to the left of the cannon in the T124 combination gun mount. The T7 cannon had a relatively low muzzle velocity of 2300 feet per second, but the 95 pound high explosive shell had a powerful demolition effect. Separated ammunition was used as with the 105mm gun in the T29. The cased propelling charge weighed about 40 pounds bringing the complete 155mm

Above is the air-cooled Continental AV-1790-3 engine and below at the left is a rear view of the CD-850 transmission. At the right below, the complete power package is installed in the T30 with the engine compartment covers open.

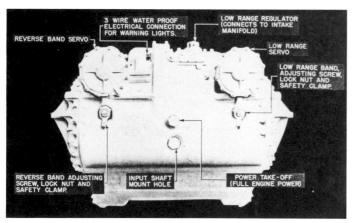

The 155mm gun T7 can be seen below and details of the open breech are visible in the view at the left.

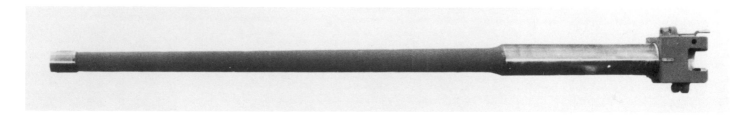

87

Above is another photograph of the heavy tank T30 at Aberdeen. Note the flat fender mounted exhaust mufflers compared to the large cylindrical mufflers on the T29.

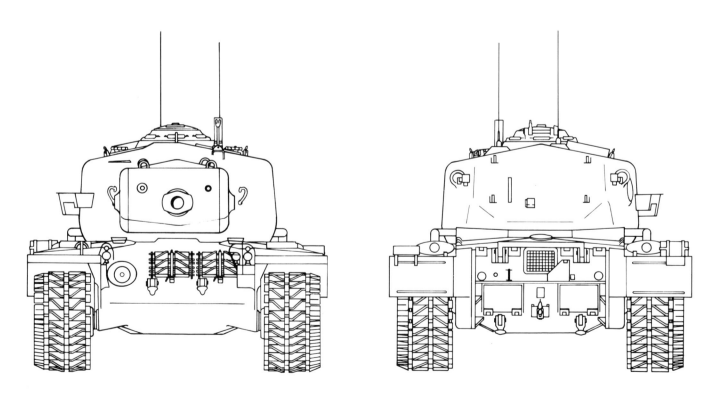

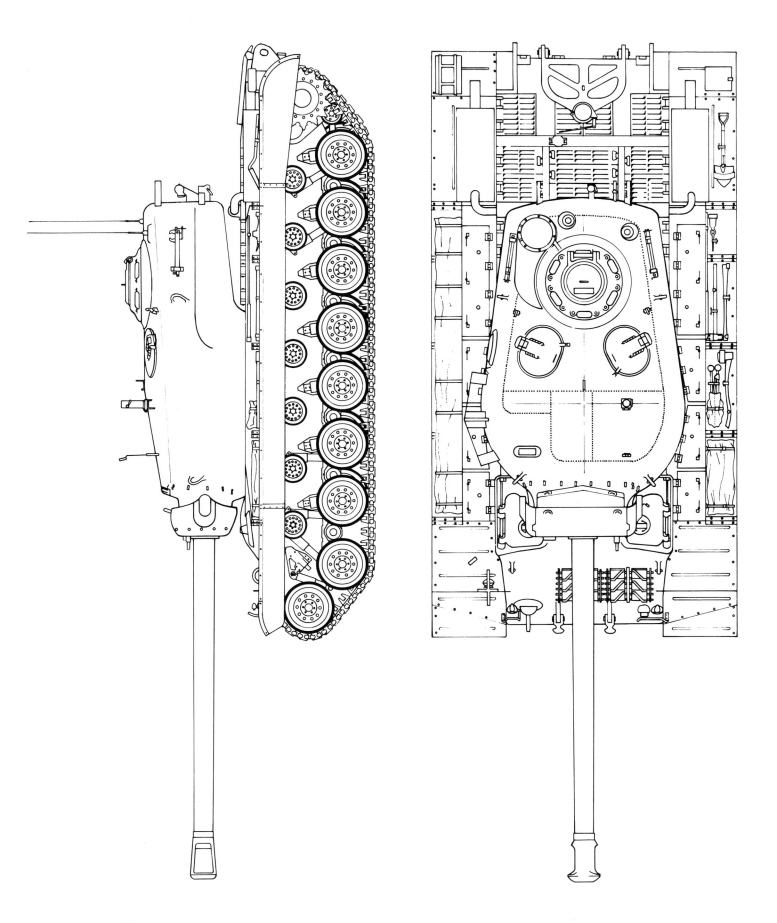

Scale 1:48

Heavy Tank T30

89

Above, the front of the turret interior appears at the left showing the coaxial .50 caliber machine gun at the left of the cannon and the gunner's station at the right. At the top right is a view of the commander's station in the turret bustle. Further details can be seen in the top view of the T30 at the left below.

Although not visible in the photograph at the right, the T30, unlike the T29, was fitted with a single track tension idler between the sprocket and the rear road wheel.

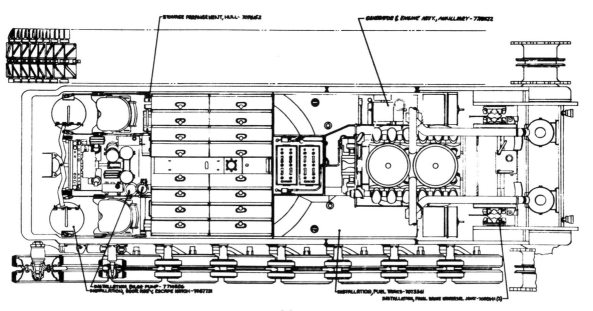

90

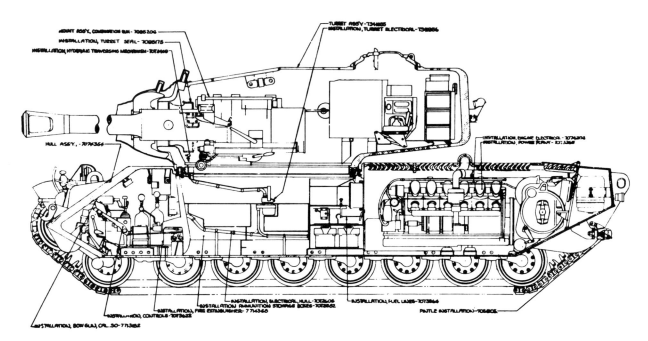

round weight to approximately 135 pounds. Thirty-four complete rounds were carried and a spring rammer was provided for use with the heavy separated ammunition. Even prior to the tests, it had been expected that there would be considerable difficulty in handling the heavy ammunition inside the tank turret. On 24 July 1947, OCM 31668 authorized the diversion of one T30 for the installation of experimental automatic ramming equipment, an automatic cartridge case ejecting mechanism, and a drive mechanism for indexing the mount for loading and returning the weapon to its previous position. The latter was required because the lack of space inside the turret, combined with the size and weight of the ammunition, permitted the loading of the gun only within a very limited range of elevation. The Ordnance Committee action also designated the modified vehicle as the heavy tank T30E1 and the weapon and mount as the 155mm gun T7E1 and the combination gun mount T124E1.

The internal arrangement of the heavy tank T30 can be seen in the sectional drawings above and on the previous page. Note that the track tension idler between the sprocket and the rear road wheel is not included on the drawings. Below, the heavy tank T30E1 is displayed on a railway car as part of a demonstration at Aberdeen Proving Ground.

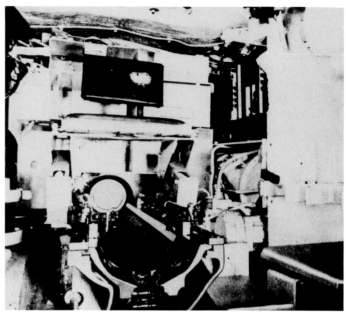

In the exterior view of the T30E1 above, the ejection port for the empty cartridge case is visible at the bottom rear of the turret bustle. Also, note the increased height of the commander's cupola. The was intended to improve his vision over the edge of the large turret. The commander's station in the T30E1 appears above at the right. The cartridge case ejection chute can be seen directly beneath his seat.

The sequence of operations when the cannon fired in the T30E1 was as follows: 1. The gun fired, recoiled, and returned to the battery position. 2. The gun automatically elevated or depressed to line up with the rammer tray. 3. The rammer tray was extended. 4. A port in the rear of the turret bustle opened to allow the ejection of the empty case from the turret. 5. The gun breech opened and ejected the empty case. 6. A new projectile and cartridge case were lifted onto the rammer tray. 7. The projectile and case were rammed and the breech closed. 8. The rammer tray was withdrawn. 9. The gun automatically elevated or depressed to its original firing position parallel with the gunner's sight.

To aid in handling the heavy ammunition, a power lifting device was installed in the T30 and T30E1 during the testing program. From the outside, the only obvious identification point on the T30E1 was the ejection port in the lower rear wall of the turret bustle.

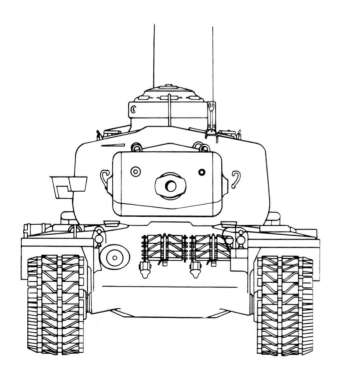
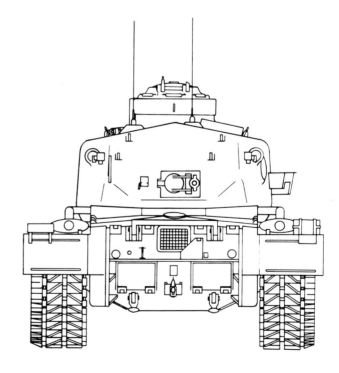

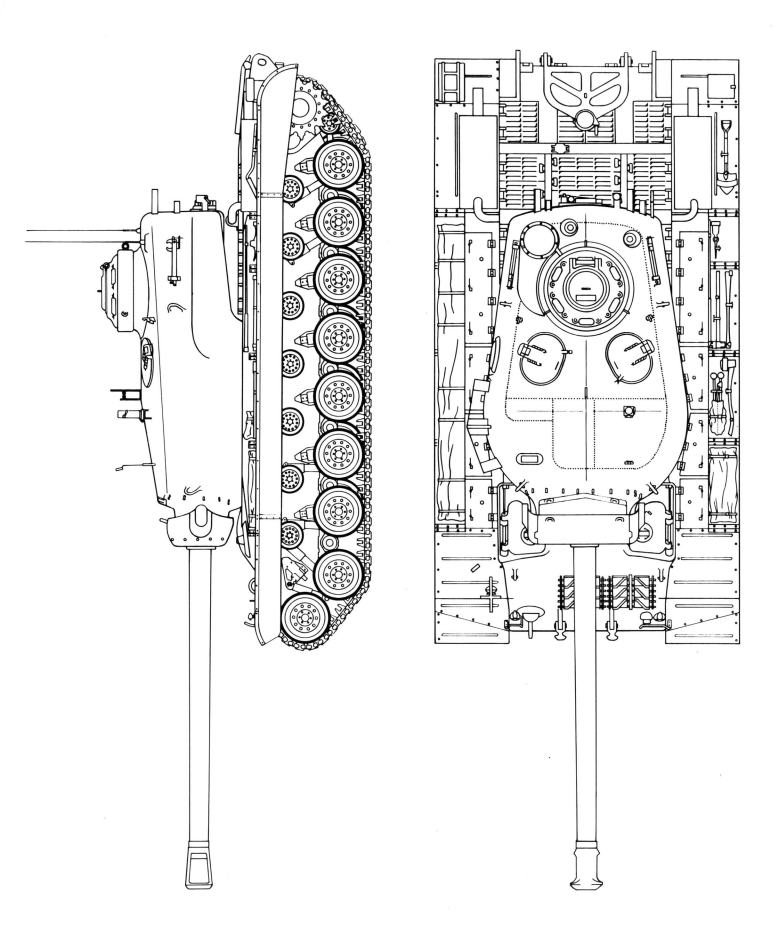

Scale 1:48

Heavy Tank T30E1

93

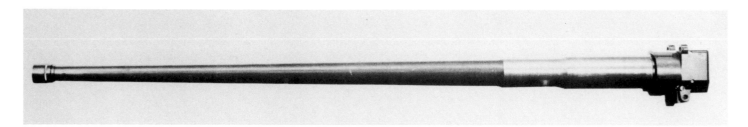

Above is the 120mm gun T53. At the bottom of the page are views of the breech with the breechblock open and closed.

In order to further increase the firepower, the Ordnance Department undertook design studies in early 1945 to modify the 120mm antiaircraft gun for tank use. These studies indicated that such a weapon, designated as the 120mm gun T53, would have armor piercing performance superior to that obtainable with either the 105mm gun T5E1 or the 155mm gun T7. The new 120mm gun had a muzzle velocity of 3150 feet per second with a 50 pound solid shot and development was in progress on a lightweight HVAP round with a muzzle velocity of 4100 feet per second. On 17 May 1945, OCM 27662 recommended that two of the T30 pilot tanks be armed with the 120mm gun and redesignated as the heavy tank T34. This action was approved on 31 May.

Originally, the T29, T30, and T34 heavy tanks all were to be powered by the Ford GAC engine. However, after VJ-day, the program was modified to permit the evaluation of other new power plants and the military characteristics of the T30 were changed to specify the Continental AV-1790 engine, still coupled to the cross drive transmission. On 7 November 1946, OCM 31202 recommended that the two T34 pilots use the T30 chassis and that the characteristics of the T34 also be changed to specify the Continental engine. Prior to this, it had been intended to use the modified Allison V-1710 aircraft engine. However, to minimize costs, OCM 31202 recommended the use of the two chassis diverted from the T30 pilot program.

The T34 pilots were similar in appearance to the T29 and T30 tanks except for the longer barrel of the 120mm gun. As on the T29, the combination gun mount was fitted with two coaxial .50 caliber machine guns on the left side of the cannon. The heavier weight of the 120mm gun required the welding of an additional four inches of armor onto the rear of the turret bustle to balance the long cannon. On the pilot tanks, this provided an obvious identification point. No doubt if the tank had gone into production, the rear of the turret casting would have been thickened up and it would not have been so easily detected.

Like the 120mm antiaircraft gun from which it was developed, the T53 cannon used separated ammunition. Thus the ammunition stowage in the T34 was similar to that in the T29 and T30 tanks which used the same type of round. The 120mm projectile and cartridge case each weighed about 50 pounds so the problem of the two loaders in handling the ammunition was not as severe as with the 155mm gun in the T30. However, another problem arose during test firing both at Aberdeen and Fort Knox. These tests revealed that dangerous concentrations of smoke and carbon monoxide formed inside the turret after firing a few rounds. Also, flarebacks hospitalized at least two men at Fort Knox and singed the hair and eyebrows of several others there and at Aberdeen. These flarebacks were caused by unburned powder gases in the gun tube being sucked back into the turret by the

The heavy tank T34 can be seen in these photographs. The obvious identification points are the long barreled 120mm gun and the additional four inches of armor welded to the turret bustle to balance the heavy weapon.

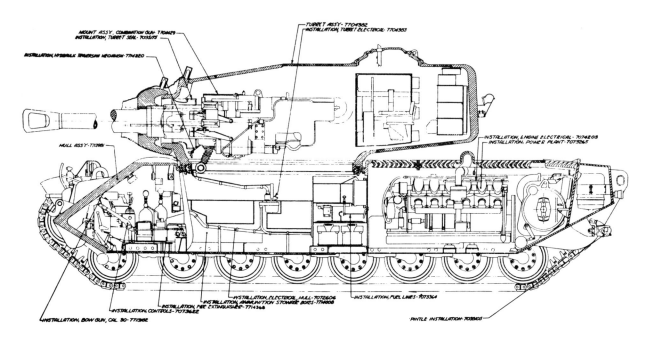

The sectional drawing above shows the internal arrangement of the heavy tank T34. The layout of the T34 suspension can be seen below.

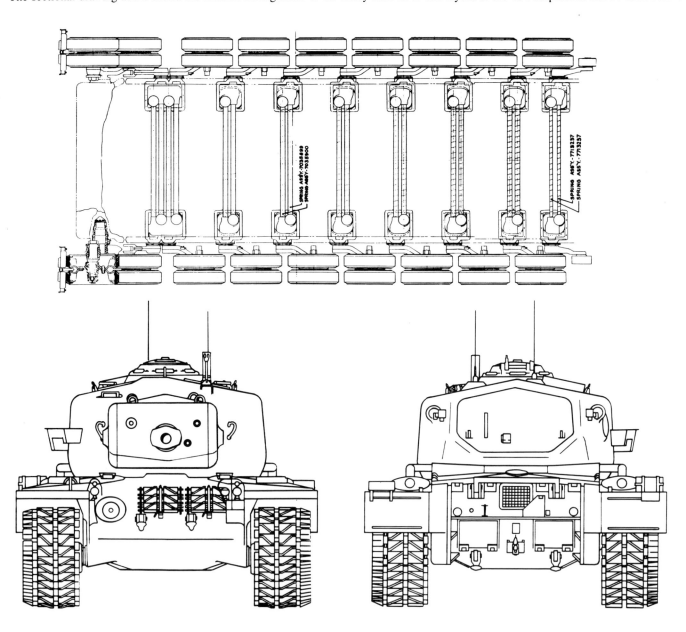

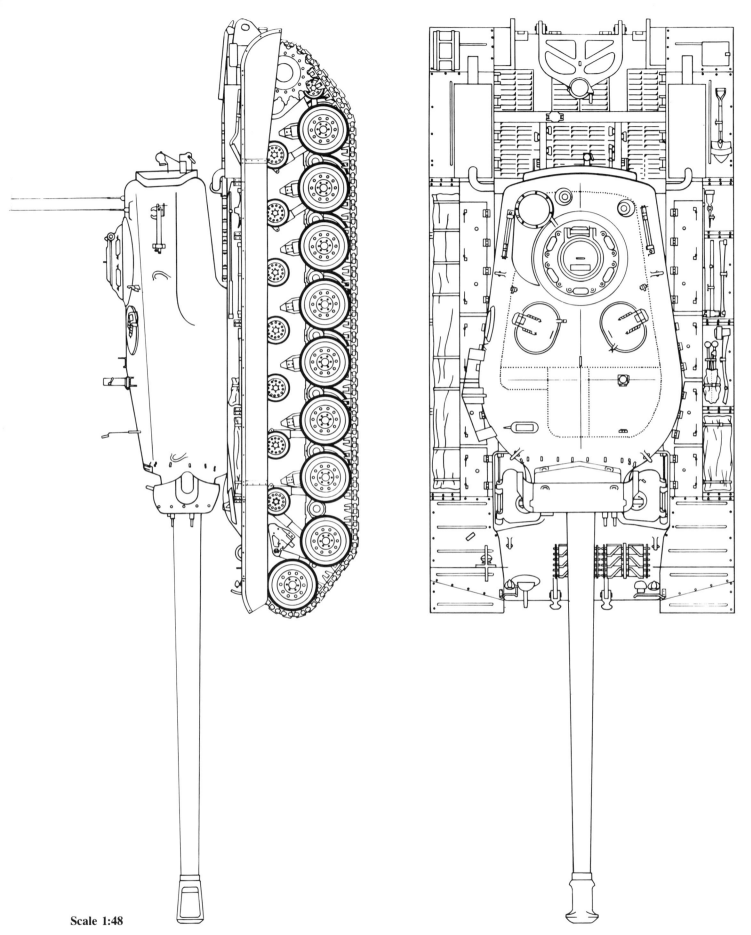

Scale 1:48

Heavy Tank T34

97

Both heavy tanks T34 appear above after the 120mm gun was fitted with the bore evacuator. On T34 number 1 at the left, the muzzle brake has been replaced by a cylindrical blast deflector or counterweight. The registration number for this tank was 30162832. Also, note that, like the T30, the T34 has a single track tension idler between the sprocket and the rear road wheel.

pumping action of the ejected cartridge case. A flash resulted when these hot gases mixed with the oxygen in the turret. To prevent the flarebacks, a bore scavenging system was developed using compressed air to sweep out the gun tube before the breech opened. However, this complex arrangement resulted in leaks at the various valves and required space for an air compressor and reservoir. A simple solution to the problem was the installation of an aspirator type bore evacuator. Previously tested on the 90mm guns T15E4 and M3E4, it consisted of a cylindrical chamber fitted around the gun barrel just back of the muzzle. Holes through the barrel wall, angled toward the muzzle, connected the bore with the evacuator chamber. As the projectile moved down the tube past these evacuator ports, the high gas pressure in the bore also pressurized the evacuator chamber. Once the projectile cleared the muzzle, the pressure in the bore dropped rapidly and the high pressure remaining in the evacuator chamber caused the formation of high

velocity gas jets from the evacuator ports. These jets, angled toward the muzzle, swept the powder gases out of the bore before the breech opened. Tests at Aberdeen and Fort Knox showed that this simple device was extremely effective and it became a standard feature of new tank guns.

At the right is a view of the open 120mm gun breech inside the T34 turret. Below is heavy tank T34 number 2, registration number 30162833, which retains the original single baffle muzzle brake after the installation of the bore evacuator. This tank is on display today by the Patton Museum at Fort Knox.

98

Above is an artist's concept of the heavy tank T32. The track width has been increased to 28 inches by the use of five inch extended end connectors on the double pin tracks.

The successful employment of the heavily armored assault tank M4A3E2 in Europe during the Fall of 1944 emphasized the need for greater armor protection. On 7 December 1944, the Army Ground Forces recommended that the Ordnance Department develop a modification of the new Pershing tank with heavier armor and the Army Services Forces directed that immediate action be taken to comply with this request. Two approaches were followed to solve the problem. The first produced essentially a standard Pershing with thicker armor and a lower final drive gear ratio to maintain a reasonable level of mobility. This vehicle was designated as the heavy (later medium) tank T26E5. A longer range solution was to

develop a new tank utilizing as many Pershing components as possible. OCM 26606, dated 8 February 1945, recommended the construction of four pilots of such a vehicle and designated it as the heavy tank T32. Formal approval of this project was recorded in March.

The design of the new tank proceeded on a high priority basis and by 10 April 1945, a mock-up was almost complete and approximately 80 per cent of the drawings for the first two pilots had been released. A power package consisting of the Ford GAC V-12 engine and the cross drive transmission similar to that planned for the heavy tank T29 was incorporated into the design. As many Pershing components

Below is heavy tank T32 number 1 on 16 January 1946 after completion at Chrysler. The extended end connectors have not been installed on the tracks.

The 90mm gun T15 is illustrated above and below. This weapon used the fixed ammunition shown at the right. To ease the handling problem in the turret, the weapon was redesigned as the 90mm gun T15E2 using the separated ammunition appearing at the lower right. Even so, the separate cartridge case was over three feet long and very difficult to handle inside the turret.

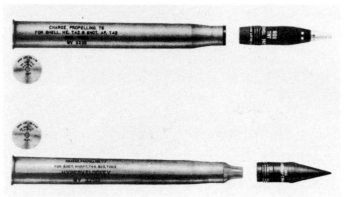

as possible were utilized, but an extra road wheel was added to the torsion bar suspension bringing the total on each side to seven. The Pershing's 23 inch wide T80E1 tracks were fitted with the five inch extended end connectors to further reduce the ground pressure. The high velocity 90mm gun T15E2 with a single coaxial .30 caliber machine gun was specified for all four pilots. This cannon used separated ammunition with a very long cartridge case requiring a rearrangement of the interior stowage as compared to the Pershing. The 90mm gun T15E2 had a muzzle velocity of 3200 feet per second with the 24 pound AP T43 shot and 3750 feet per second with the 16.7 pound HVAP T44 shot. The armor on the front hull was specified as five inches at 54 degrees from the vertical and the turret varied in thickness from 11 3/4 inches in front to 6 inches in the rear. The front hull was cast for the first two pilots and a .30 caliber

The photographs below and on the following page show the heavy tank T32 number 1, registration number 30162828, at Aberdeen Proving Ground on 20 March 1946.

The large cylindrical mufflers mounted on the fenders are similar to those on the heavy tank T29 which used essentially the same power plant. The large housing for the turret mounted ventilation blower can be seen on the rear of the turret bustle.

Heavy tank T32 number 1 is shown here with the 90mm gun forward (above) and locked in the travel position (below). The seven road wheels and the long thin cannon are obvious points of identification for the T32.

The five inch extended end connectors still have not been fitted to the tracks on T32 number 1 and the machine gun armament has not been installed. A closeup view of the gun shield cover can be seen below.

machine gun was installed in a bow mount for the assistant driver. Both the driver and assistant driver had a single periscope fitted in the hatch cover over their seats. Pilots 3 and 4 were assembled using rolled armor plate on the front hull and the bow machine gun was omitted. On the latter two vehicles, the drivers' wide angle periscopes were mounted in the front armor and their hatch covers were pivoted rather than hinged, allowing them to be opened without interference from the traversing turret. OCM 28680, on 9 August 1945, revised the military characteristics and recommended that pilots 3 and 4 be designated as the heavy tank T32E1.

Pilots 1 and 2 were completed on 15 January and 19 April 1946 respectively and both were shipped to Aberdeen Proving Ground. Pilots 3 and 4 (T32E1) were completed on 14 May and 19 June 1946. Number 3 was shipped to Fort Knox and the fourth vehicle was retained at Detroit Arsenal for engineering studies.

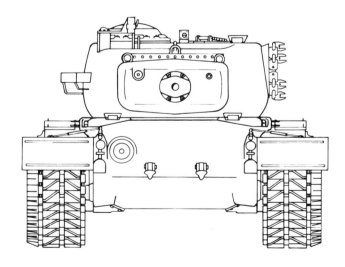

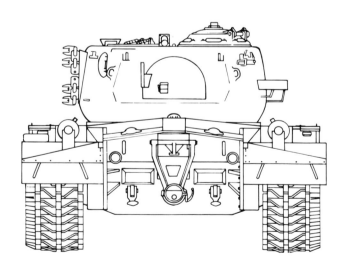

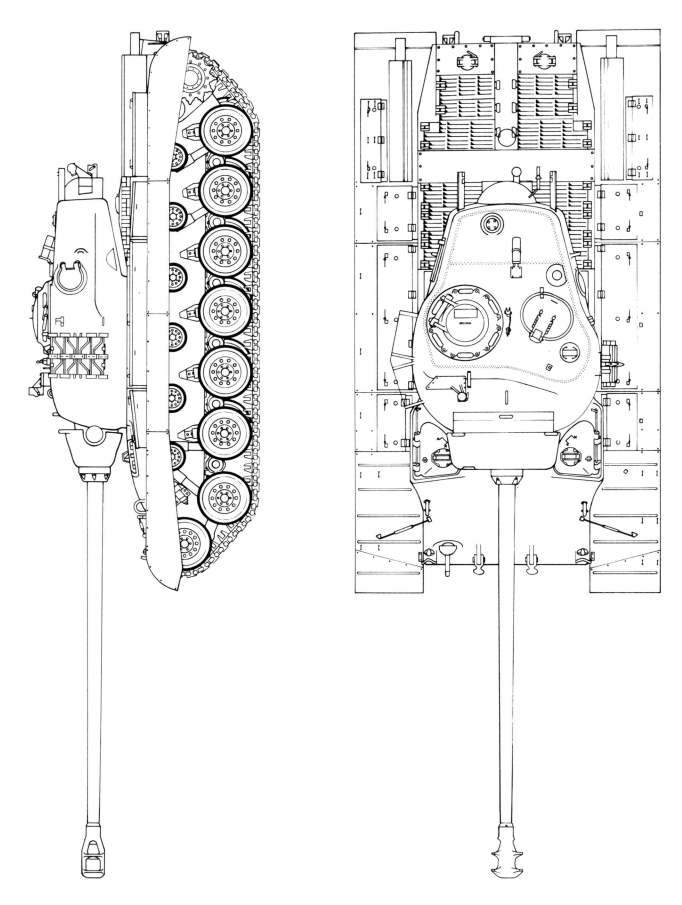

Scale 1:48

Heavy Tank T32

The general arrangement of T32 number 1 is shown in the photograph above. At the right, details of the radio antennas and the pedestal mount for the .50 caliber machine gun are visible on the rear turret roof.

The T32 was the first tank with the cross drive transmission to be tested at Aberdeen and Fort Knox and, as might be expected, a lot of problems were encountered. The early EX-120 version of the cross drive had the usual teething troubles of an experimental design and required excessive maintenance to keep it going. However, it led directly to the development of the CD-850 series of cross drive transmissions which became the standard in American tanks.

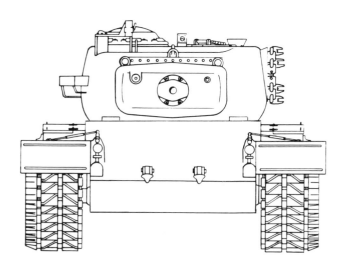

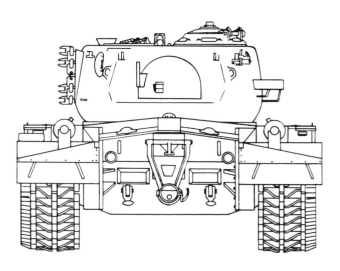

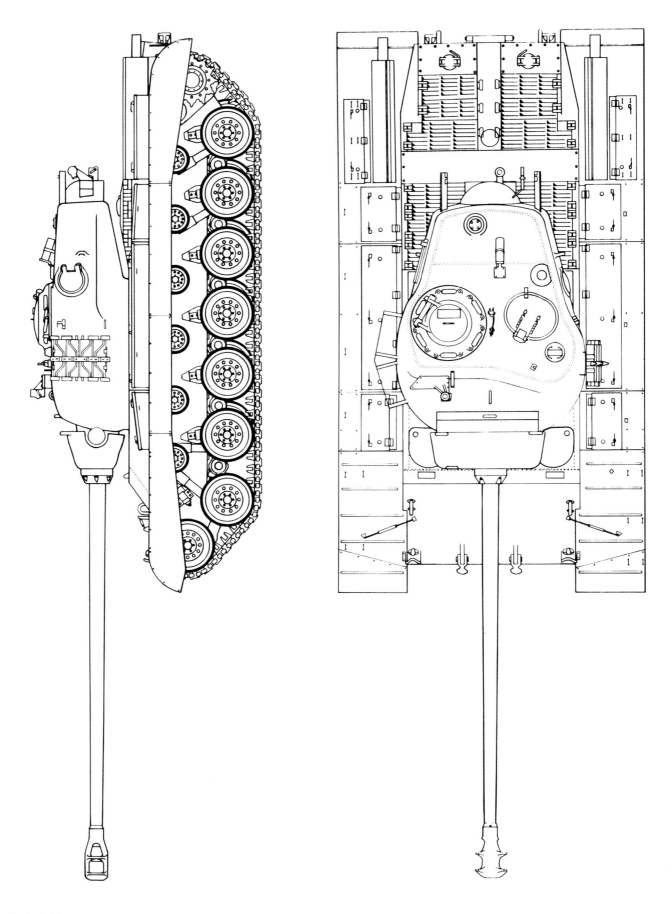

Scale 1:48

Heavy Tank T32E1

Since no photographs of the heavy tank T32E1 could be located, the model shown here was constructed by Gerry Gardiner and Mike Armstrong. Note the differences from the T32 in the front armor and the drivers' hatches as well as the lack of a bow machine gun.

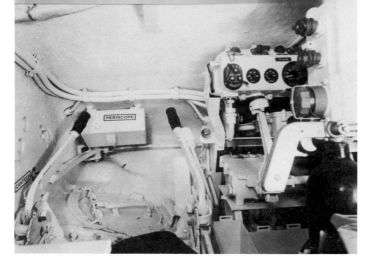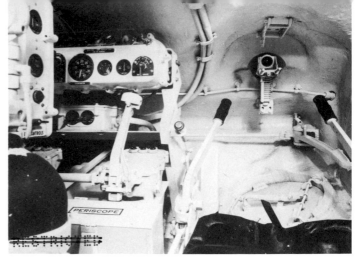

Above, the driver's controls appear at the left and those for the assistant driver at the right. Note that the bow machine gun has not been installed and the manual steering levers have been retained for emergency use. The views below inside the turret show the front from below the gun (left) and the gunner's controls (right).

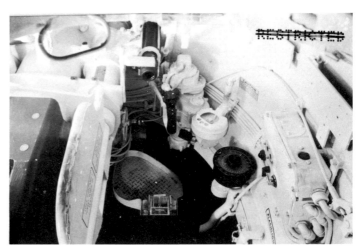

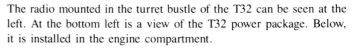

The radio mounted in the turret bustle of the T32 can be seen at the left. At the bottom left is a view of the T32 power package. Below, it is installed in the engine compartment.

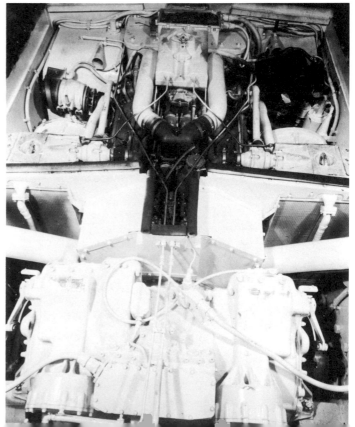

Heavy tank T32 number 2, registration number 30162829, is shown in these photographs at Aberdeen Proving Ground on 27 December 1946. Like the first T32, the tracks have not been fitted with the extended end connectors.

As described earlier, the T29, T30, T32, and T34 series of tanks were used to evaluate numerous experimental components after World War II. Although too late for the war for which they were designed, they provided invaluable service in developing these components for later tanks. Much of the work which made the early AV-1790 engine and the CD-850 transmission a reliable power package utilized these tanks. Later, they were used in the development of other power train components such as the XT-1400 transmission which was tested in the T30.

The heavy tank T32 can be seen below during its evaluation at Fort Knox. At the right is the heavy tank T30 with the installation of the XT-1400 transmission.

PART II

POSTWAR HEAVY TANK DEVELOPMENT

PLAN VIEW

REAR ELEVATION

LEFT ELEVATION

FRONT ELEVATION

Above is the artist's concept of the proposed superheavy semitrailer tank included in the report of the Army Ground Forces Equipment Review Board dated 20 June 1945.

AN ANSWER TO THE STALIN III

With the end of the European war in sight, the Army Ground Forces Equipment Review Board was convened in Washington, D.C. on 2 January 1945. The objective of this board was to outline the equipment requirements for the ground forces in the postwar army. Their report, dated 20 June 1945, included two items under the category of heavy tanks. The first recommended the development of a heavy assault tank weighing about 75 tons with a five man crew. The maximum sustained speed of this vehicle was to be at least 20 miles per hour on a seven per cent slope and it was to have a fording ability at least equal to the height of the tank. Armament was specified not to exceed 90mm in caliber, but it was required to penetrate a minimum of ten inches of armor at 30 degrees from the vertical at a range of 2000 yards, with special ammunition. Fire control equipment was to provide accurate fire at a range of at least 4000 yards with a dispersion limit of .3 mils. Maximum armor on the turret and hull front was requested to be equivalent to 10.5 inches of homogeneous steel at zero degrees from the vertical.

The report also recommended the development of a superheavy tank for research purposes. The characteristics proposed for this vehicle included a

The armor basis for the proposed 75-ton heavy assault tank is shown on the sketch at the right.

minimum weight of 150 tons, a 360 degree traverse power operated turret, and a high velocity gun at least 105mm in caliber. Azimuth and elevation stabilizers were specified for the cannon as well as a dual feed automatic loader to permit the selection of ammunition types. The thickness of the armor was to be the maximum possible, consistent with the weight of the tank. As an example of a vehicle which might meet these requirements, an artists concept was included in the report of a semitrailer tank armed with a 155mm gun. It was considered that such a radical design might be necessary to facilitate the transportation of such a large and heavy vehicle.

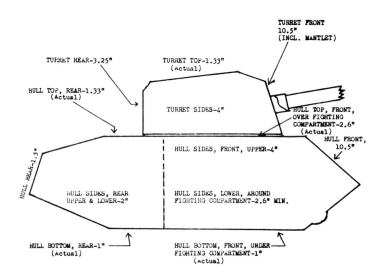

111

A model of the proposed Chrysler K tank can be seen above. The remote control machine guns are located at the four corners of the hull. Note the extremely wide flat track suspension without any track return rollers.

The interest in these heavily armed and armored fighting vehicles was stimulated in part by the discovery of the German experiments such as the Maus and the E100 programs and also by the appearance of the new Soviet Stalin III heavy tank in early 1945. The latter with its 122mm gun and highly sloped armor was to have a profound effect upon United States tank development during the postwar years.

Following the end of the war, another board, headed by General Joseph W. Stilwell, was convened on 1 November 1945. Officially designated as the War Department Equipment Review Board, it was more familiarly known as the Stilwell Board. Its report, submitted on 19 January 1946, generally agreed with the earlier recommendations for light, medium, and heavy tank development, but it dropped the requirement for the experimental super-heavy tank. It also dropped the requirement for tank destroyer development, concurring with the opinion of the Armored School that the best antitank weapon was another tank. Such tank versus tank combat, of course, favored the heavy tank with its powerful armament and thick armor.

Another interesting heavy tank proposal was presented by Chrysler Corporation at the Armored School on 14 May 1946. Dubbed the Chrysler K tank (the first to use that name), it was a large vehicle with an optimistically estimated weight of 60 tons. The arrangement proposed differed from the usual tank layout in that the engine and power train were in front with the turret and fighting compartment at the rear of the hull. Although armed with the long barreled high velocity 105mm gun T5E1, the rear turret arrangement kept the overall length of the tank with the gun forward to only three inches greater than that of the M26 Pershing. Another interesting feature was the location of the entire four man crew in the turret. Consisting of the tank commander, gunner, loader, and driver, they were protected by turret armor ranging from seven inches in front to three inches in the rear. This is believed to be the first application of the driver in turret arrangement to an American tank, although a remote control box allowed the wartime electric drive T23 medium tank to be driven from the turret. The K tank also proposed to use the electric drive with a 1200 horsepower engine mounted transversely in the hull with the final drive and track sprockets located at the front of the vehicle. The hull design consisted of a welded assembly of rolled armor plate varying in thickness from seven inches at 30 degrees from the vertical on the front plate to three inches on the sides. The overall width was 154 inches, but it was intended to remove the sponsons, tracks, and outer road wheels to permit rail transportation. The 30 inch wide tracks were estimated to reduce the ground pressure to only nine psi. This, of

The mock-up of an early version of the heavy tank T43 appears above. It was estimated to weigh about 58 tons with a four man crew. The .30 caliber blister machine guns on the turret of the original design have been eliminated.

course, was based on a combat weight of 60 tons, which was highly unlikely for such a large vehicle. The cast turret mounted the 105mm gun and a coaxial .50 caliber machine gun. One hundred rounds of 105mm ammunition were stowed circumferentially around the rear of the turret. Four hull mounted machine guns also were provided as additional secondary armament. These consisted of two .30 caliber weapons, one at each front corner of the hull and two .50 caliber antiaircraft machine guns, one at each rear corner. These four machine guns were to be operated by remote control from the turret using a simplified version of the gun control system from the B29 bomber. Many of the design innovations proposed for the K tank appeared in later concept studies and the driver in turret arrangement was adopted for the MBT70. However, with the drastic reduction in the available funds after the end of the war, the proposal did not receive any support.

By 1948, a rapidly deteriorating world situation emphasized the need to implement the recommendations of the Stilwell Board for a new tank development program. Postwar studies of these recommendations by the U.S. Army and Marine Corps raised objections to the development of heavy tanks in the 70-ton class of the T34. Further investigation at Detroit Arsenal indicated that the basic T34 design could be modified by shortening the hull, using high obliquity armor, and installing a new lighter weight 120mm gun. It was estimated that such a modified

design would meet the requirements for firepower, protection, and mobility and could be developed with a weight of about 58 tons. OCM 32530, dated 1 December 1948, outlined the characteristics of the proposed vehicle and designated it as the heavy tank T43. The new tank retained the 80 inch diameter turret ring of the T34, but the crew was reduced to four men eliminating the assistant driver and one loader. The shortened vehicle had only seven road wheels per side reducing the ground contact length to 178 inches. However, the 28 inch wide tracks held the estimated ground pressure to 11.6 psi. The 810 horsepower Continental AV-1790 engine was specified with consideration of the possible use of the supercharged version developing 1040 horsepower. The latter engine would have required a new transmission, since the higher power level exceeded the capacity of the CD-850. A lighter weight 120mm gun was to be installed with a single .50 caliber coaxial machine gun in the combination gun mount T140. The original version of this mount utilized three recoil cylinders. Two .30 caliber remote controlled machine guns were to be installed in blisters, one on each side of the turret and the usual .50 caliber antiaircraft machine gun was to be mounted on the turret roof. The main armament was to be powered in both elevation and traverse and a range finder, a direct sight telescope, a lead computer, and a panoramic telescope were to be provided for fire control. The maximum armor was specified as five inches at 58 degrees from the vertical

Here is the early concept of the heavy tank T43 based upon the elliptically shaped cast hull and turret. It retains the seven road wheels of the original design, but the number of track return rollers has been increased to six.

on the front of both the turret and hull. With only one loader, a power system for handling the ammunition was required.

Further development of the design at Detroit Arsenal drastically changed the appearance of the new tank, although it still retained its designation as the T43. The new studies indicated that the use of an elliptically shaped cast hull and turret would result in the least weight for the level of protection required. Mock-ups reflecting the new design concept were constructed and reviewed during conferences at Detroit Arsenal in October and December 1949. As a result, the military characteristics of the T43 were revised and published in OCM 33333 on 24 April 1950. In addition to the new cast hull and turret configuration, the turret ring diameter was increased to 85 inches and the crew was enlarged to five men, consisting of the tank commander, gunner, driver, and two loaders. The extra loader was necessary since any development of automatic loading equipment was deferred to a separate project. The elliptically shaped cast armor was expected to give protection on the turret front and upper front hull equivalent to five inches of homogeneous steel at 60 degrees from the vertical. It was estimated that the combat weight could be reduced to 55 tons with the new armor configuration. The lighter weight 120mm gun was still

specified as the main armament. However, it was installed in a new combination mount with a concentric recoil system which retained the T140 designation originally assigned to the design with three recoil cylinders. The concentric recoil system had already been used with the armament for the light and medium tanks. It replaced the usual separate recoil cylinders with a single hollow cylinder surrounding the gun tube, thus conserving space inside the fighting compartment. Two coaxial machine guns were specified for the new combination mount, one on each side of the cannon. Either .30 caliber or .50 caliber weapons could be installed. Other changes included the elimination of the .30 caliber blister machine guns as well as the gunner's direct sight telescope, the panoramic

The first pilot heavy tank T43 can be seen above and at the bottom of the page. These photographs taken at Aberdeen Proving Ground were dated 7 July 1951.

telescope, and the lead computer. A periscopic sight was provided as backup for the gunner operated range finder which served as the primary sighting device.

On 7 November 1950, OCM 33476 revised the system for designating tanks. The light, medium, and heavy categories were dropped and the vehicles were redesignated according to the caliber of their main armament. Thus the heavy tank T43 became the 120mm gun tank T43.

When the Korean War broke out in June 1950, work on the T43 had not progressed beyond the construction of a full scale mock-up. At that time, it appeared to be a very real possibility that the conflict would escalate into a worldwide war. The limited tank assets available to the U.S. Army consisted mainly of rebuilt World War II vehicles and a few M46 Pattons which were modernized versions of the wartime Pershing. There were no heavy or medium tanks comparable to the Soviet Stalin III. In many

ways, the tank situation was similar to that in 1940-41 when the emergency required production on a crash basis without waiting for a lengthy development and test program. Following this precedent, a production order for 80 T43s was placed with Chrysler Corporation in December 1950. Later, the total production order was increased to 300, providing tanks for both the U.S. Army and the Marine Corps. This was in addition to the six pilot vehicles already ordered.

The first pilot T43 was completed and shipped to Aberdeen Proving Ground in June 1951. Chrysler took over the design responsibility for the T43 pilots after number 3 was finished and manufactured the last three vehicles. These incorporated many features intended for the production tanks and reflected the early results of the test program at Aberdeen. These various changes resulted in a new designation being assigned for the production vehicles by OCM 34359 on 17 July 1952. They now became the 120mm gun

These additional views of T43 number 1 at Aberdeen show the 120mm gun forward (above) and in the travel lock (below). Note the turret with the ladder on the right side and a pistol port in the left side wall.

Above, the 120mm gun T122 (left) is compared with the T123 gun (right). Below, the gun shield on the first pilot T43 can be seen at the left. Note the two coaxial .50 caliber machine guns. At the right below is an interior view showing the right front of the turret with the coaxial machine gun installed.

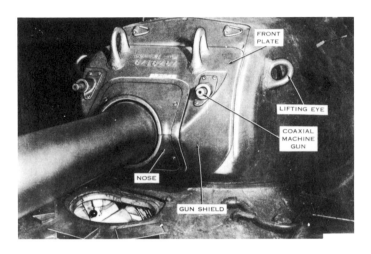
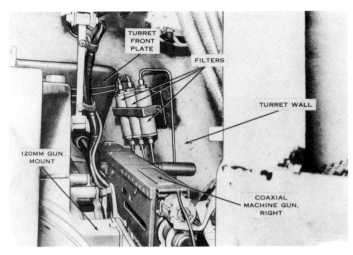

tank T43E1. These T43E1 production tanks differed in a number of respects from the original T43. The first pilot was armed with the 120mm gun T122 which was later replaced by the 120mm gun T123. The T122 was ballistically the same as the earlier 120mm gun T53. However, the maximum powder pressure in the T123 was increased to 48,000 psi compared to 38,000 psi in the T122 and T53. The greater pressure raised the muzzle velocity of the T123 to about 3300 feet per second with a 50 pound shot. The cartridge case for the T123 gun was modified to prevent it being chambered in the lower pressure T122.

The T123 also fitted the same combination gun mount T140 with the concentric recoil system as the T122. However, further studies had resulted in the design of a conventional mount with four recoil cylinders that was approximately equal in weight and space requirements to the concentric type. Past experience had indicated a higher degree of reliability for the conventional design and it was selected to replace the T140 mount in the production tanks. OCM 33834 assigned the designation combination gun mount T154 to the new design on 10 July 1951. The cannon installed in the new mount was the 120mm gun T123E1. It was ballistically identical to the T123 and featured a quick change gun tube. The pilot tanks also differed in being fitted with an early type cupola for the tank commander with five vision blocks and a

The cast hull of the pilot T43 is illustrated at the left and below. The elliptical shape of the front and sides is clearly visible.

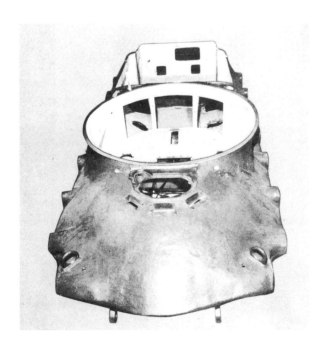
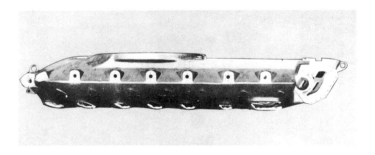

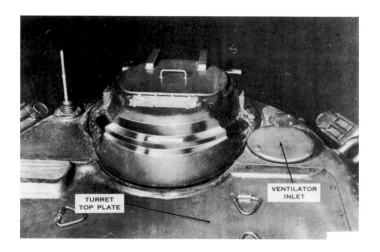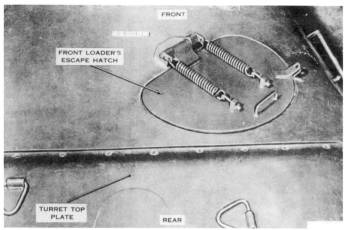

Above, the early type commander's cupola installed on the first pilot T43 can be seen at the left and the loader's hatch is at the right. The gunner's periscope has not been mounted in its holder.

single fixed periscope. This cupola was the same as that installed on the M47 medium tank. Pilot number 1 had a circular pistol port in the left side turret wall. This port was eliminated on the later pilots. The first four pilots were fitted with three T36 periscopes for

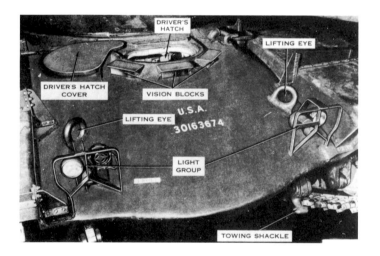

the driver. Later, these were replaced by three T25 (later M26) periscopes on tanks with serial numbers 5 through 59. The driver's hatch also was smaller on these early vehicles. One source indicates that the first 60 tanks had the small driver's hatch similar to that on the 90mm gun tank M48. After number 60, the hatch was redesigned and enlarged in the same manner as on the M48A1 tanks. The driver in these later vehicles was provided with three T36 (later M27) periscopes replacing the earlier T25 model. The driver's hatch cover in all of the large hatch tanks and some of the small hatch vehicles was fitted with a rotating mount for the T41 (later M24) infrared periscope. Other identification points for the early pilot tanks were the flat top brush guards in front of the

The view at the left shows the single piece pivoting hatch cover for the driver and other details of the front hull on the first pilot T43.

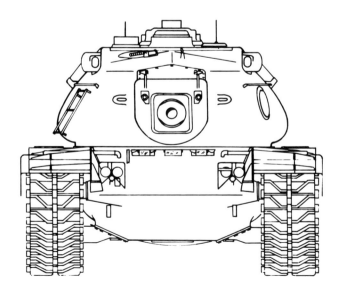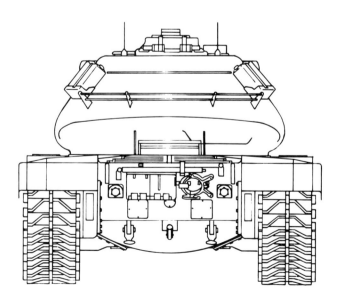

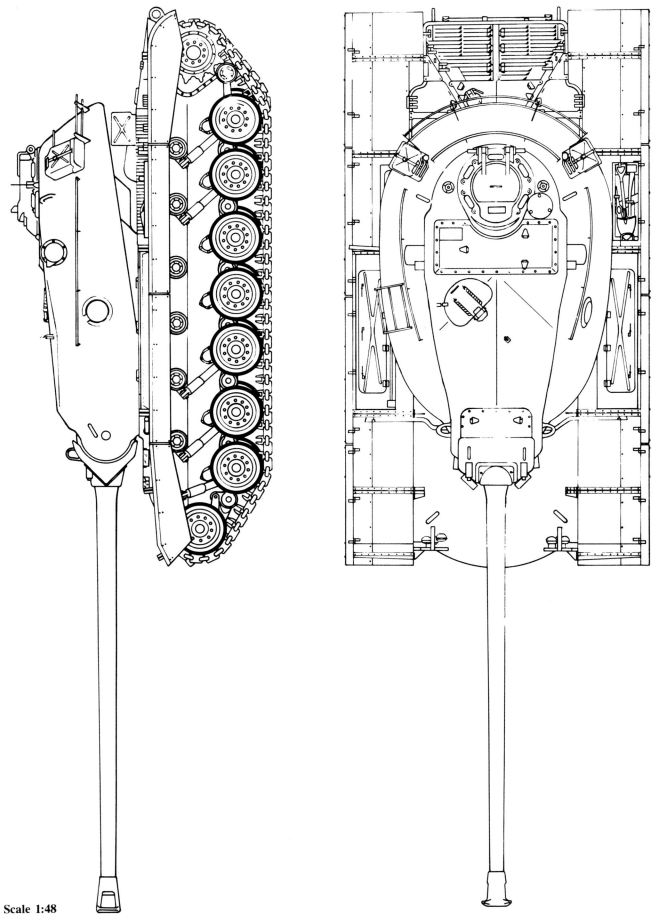

Scale 1:48

Heavy Tank T43, Pilot Number 1

119

Additional details of T43 number 1 are shown here with the headlight assemblies above. Below, the ladder on the right side of the turret appears at the left and the deflectors on each side of the engine exhaust can be seen at the right.

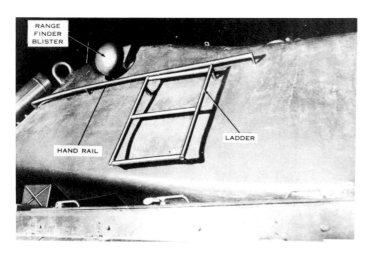 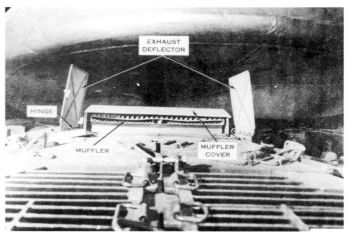

headlight groups and the three rung ladder welded to the right side of the turret. The production tanks were fitted with round top brush guards and the ladder was eliminated. Deflectors mounted at each side of the engine exhaust on the early pilots were found to be unnecessary and were omitted from the production tanks. They had been intended to prevent hot exhaust gases from being sucked into the engine cooling air intakes. A new cupola for the tank commander was introduced with the production tanks. Designed by Chrysler, this was the low silhouette cupola also installed on the early M48s and it was fitted with a .50 caliber machine gun. Although this weapon could be aimed and fired with the turret closed, it could only be reloaded by opening the hatch. The turret was modified on the production tanks with the ventilating blower relocated from alongside the left front of the cupola to a bulge in the left rear of the turret wall. Two receptacles for radio antennas were welded to

The outlets for the bilge pump and personnel heater exhaust are visible in the photograph at the right.

the rear of the turret bustle on the production tanks. On the early pilots, the exhaust pipes from the two personnel heaters were routed through the hull roof, one on each side of the driver's hatch and then extended to opposite sides of the tank. On the production vehicles, both pipes came through the hull roof at the right of the driver's hatch. On some early tanks with this arrangement, no extension pipes were fitted

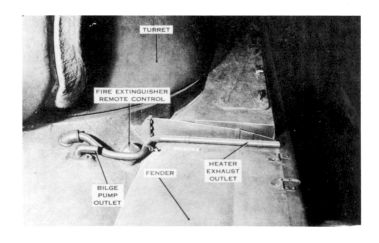

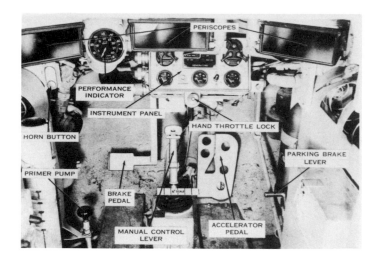

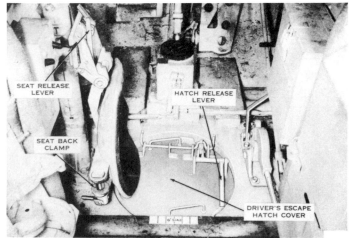

Above are views of the driver's controls (left) and the floor escape hatch (right). The driver's seat has been tilted to the side to permit access to the floor hatch. Below are the stations for the gunner (left) and the tank commander (right).

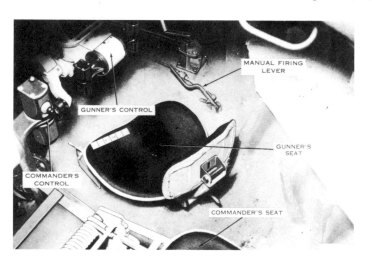

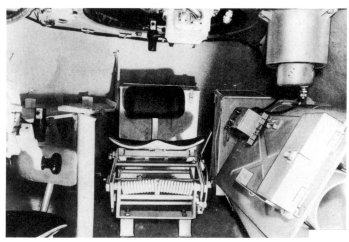

and the exhaust frequently blew into the driver's face. After tests at Aberdeen and Fort Knox, two pipes were attached to the exhaust ports and both extended to the right side of the hull. The travel lock for the 120mm gun on the early tanks consisted of two support arms attached to the rear hull plate. After test, an additional support arm was incorporated in the design and it was attached to the top deck armor.

At the left below, the travel lock for the 120mm gun has been taken apart and stowed on the rear hull plate. The width of the T43 required some disassembly to meet the clearance requirements for some railway travel. Below at the right, the T43 pilot is loaded for shipment. Note the bulge in the bottom of the turret bustle for the gunner's seat.

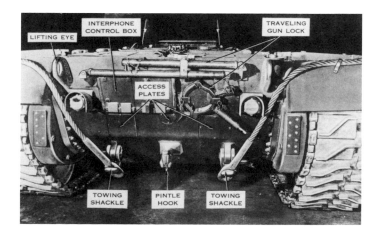

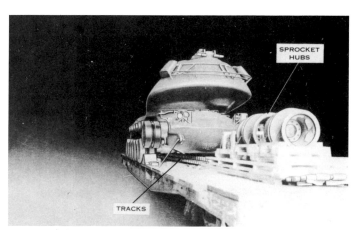

121

On selected railway routes, the T43 could be shipped without disassembly. The third pilot T43, registration number 30163676, is shown above and below after its arrival at Aberdeen Proving Ground on 25 March 1952. The pistol port in the left turret wall has been eliminated, but the ladder is retained on the right side.

This page shows the 120mm gun tank T43E1 during the test program at Fort Knox. On this tank, both the pistol port and the turret ladder have been eliminated as well as the deflectors on each side of the engine exhaust. In the smaller photograph below, the vehicle is climbing a 60 per cent slope.

The production run of 300 T43E1s was completed by Chrysler at the Newark, Delaware plant during 1953 and 1954. Testing began at Fort Knox in May 1953 using pilot number 6 and production tank number 8. The tests of these two vehicles continued until October 1954 during which time they were operated for a combined total of 4367 miles and fired 176 rounds of 120mm ammunition. The test report concluded that the T43E1 was unsatisfactory for army use primarily because the turret and gun controls as well as the sighting system did not meet the Continental Army Command (CONARC) standards for performance and durability. A serious problem also was revealed with the 120mm ammunition. The early rounds were extremely erratic preventing accurate zeroing of the weapon. This difficulty was eventually cured by adding an obturator to the projectile and improving the quality control during manufacture. Other problems included heating of the turret bustle

bottom by the main engine exhaust when the gun was aimed forward and the entry of fumes from the auxiliary engine exhaust into the turret when the cannon was in the travel position.

These additional views of the T43E1 at Fort Knox show many of the changes applied to the production tanks including the new commander's cupola with the remote control .50 caliber machine gun. The two lower photographs show the 120mm gun at maximum and minimum elevation.

After rejection by CONARC, the T43E1 tanks were placed in storage in August 1955 pending completion of a product improvement study intended to correct the various deficiencies. In November of the same year, a Material Requirements Review Board recommended that the tanks in storage be modified to incorporate 98 modifications which would meet all of CONARC's requirements, except for completely new turret control and fire control systems. The durability of the original turret control and fire control systems was to be improved as much as possible. These recommendations were approved in February 1956 and the T43E1 was standardized with these changes as the 120mm gun combat tank M103 by OCM 36177. This action was approved on 26 April 1956.

Above, the 120mm gun tank T43E1 is equipped with the T18 bulldozer in this photograph at Chrysler dated 18 June 1955.

The M103 was armed with two coaxial .30 caliber machine guns, one on each side of the cannon now standardized as 120mm gun M58 (T123E1) in mount M89 (T154). The M4 commander's cupola was the standardized version of the original Chrysler design with minor modifications and it still carried the remote control .50 caliber machine gun. The AV-1790-5B engine and the CD-850-4B transmission which had performed satisfactorily during the tests at Fort Knox were retained in the standard vehicle. However, a heat deflector panel was installed under the turret bustle to minimize the effect of the engine exhaust. Funds were provided to modify 74 of the army T43E1s to the M103 standard. The remaining six tanks of the original 80 had been used in various experimental programs.

The later version of the travel lock for the 120mm gun is shown at the left below. Note the three support arms. At the right below is a front view of the same tank at Aberdeen Proving Ground. Both photographs were dated 11 May 1954.

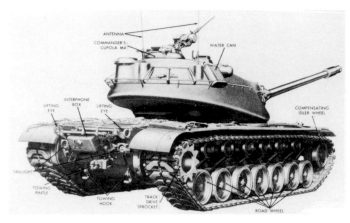

Features of the 120mm gun tank M103 can be seen in these illustrations from the technical manual. The exhaust heat shield or deflector is installed underneath the turret bustle and, unlike the pilot T43, there is no track tension idler between the sprocket and the rear road wheel.

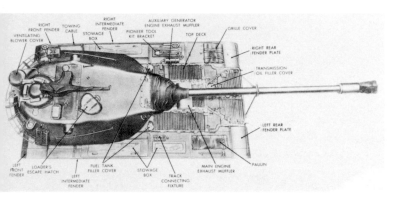

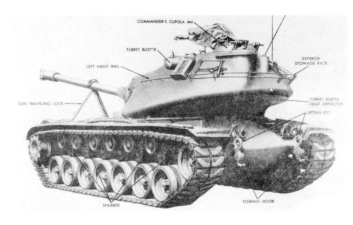

The Marine Corps T43E1 below was photographed at Quantico, Virginia on 9 September 1954. Note the T-shape blast deflector on the 120mm gun. It is still fitted with the early gun travel lock with two support arms.

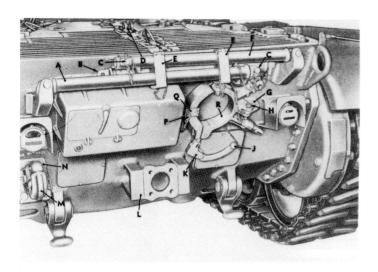

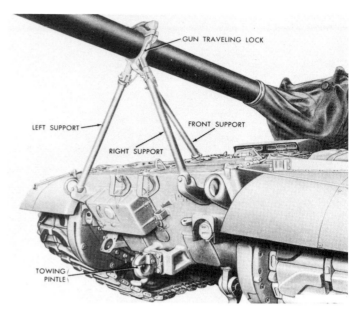

The later version of the gun travel lock with three support arms appears above stowed (left) and assembled (right) with the gun in the travel position on the M103. Below, the M103 driver's controls are shown at the left and his instrument panel is at the right.

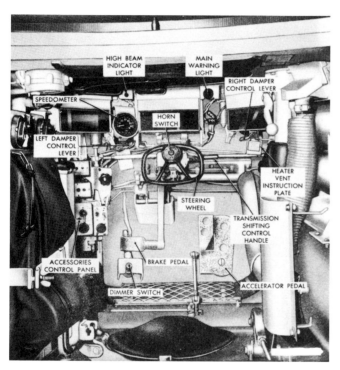

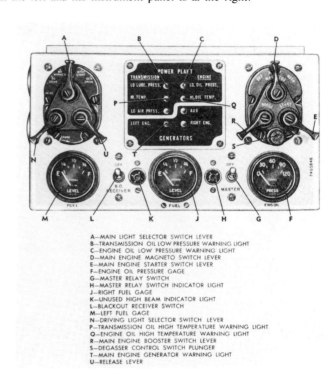

A—MAIN LIGHT SELECTOR SWITCH LEVER
B—TRANSMISSION OIL LOW PRESSURE WARNING LIGHT
C—ENGINE OIL LOW PRESSURE WARNING LIGHT
D—MAIN ENGINE MAGNETO SWITCH LEVER
E—MAIN ENGINE STARTER SWITCH LEVER
F—ENGINE OIL PRESSURE GAGE
G—MASTER RELAY SWITCH
H—MASTER RELAY SWITCH INDICATOR LIGHT
J—RIGHT FUEL GAGE
K—UNUSED HIGH BEAM INDICATOR LIGHT
L—BLACKOUT RECEIVER SWITCH
M—LEFT FUEL GAGE
N—DRIVING LIGHT SELECTOR SWITCH LEVER
P—TRANSMISSION OIL HIGH TEMPERATURE WARNING LIGHT
Q—ENGINE OIL HIGH TEMPERATURE WARNING LIGHT
R—MAIN ENGINE BOOSTER SWITCH LEVER
S—DEGASSER CONTROL SWITCH PLUNGER
T—MAIN ENGINE GENERATOR WARNING LIGHT
U—RELEASE LEVER

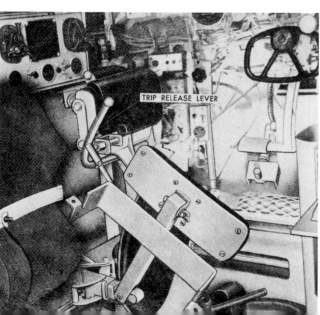

Below, the driver's seat is tilted to one side (left) to expose the floor escape hatch (right).

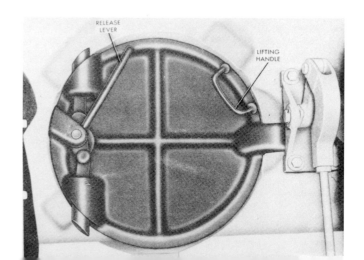

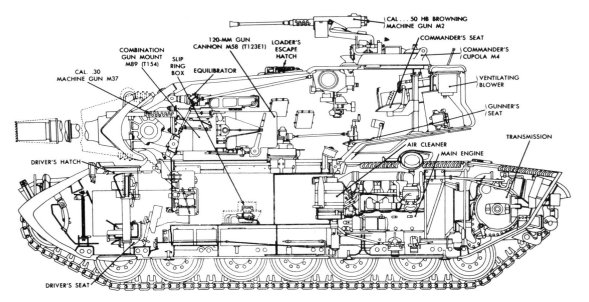

CAL .30
MACHINE GUN M37

COMBINATION
GUN MOUNT
M89 (T154)

SLIP
RING
BOX

EQUILIBRATOR

120-MM GUN
CANNON M58 (T123E1)

LOADER'S
ESCAPE
HATCH

CAL . . . 50 HB BROWNING
MACHINE GUN M2

COMMANDER'S SEAT

COMMANDER'S
CUPOLA M4

VENTILATING
BLOWER

GUNNER'S
SEAT

TRANSMISSION

AIR CLEANER

MAIN ENGINE

DRIVER'S HATCH

DRIVER'S SEAT

The internal arrangement of the 120mm gun tank M103 is shown in these sectional drawings.

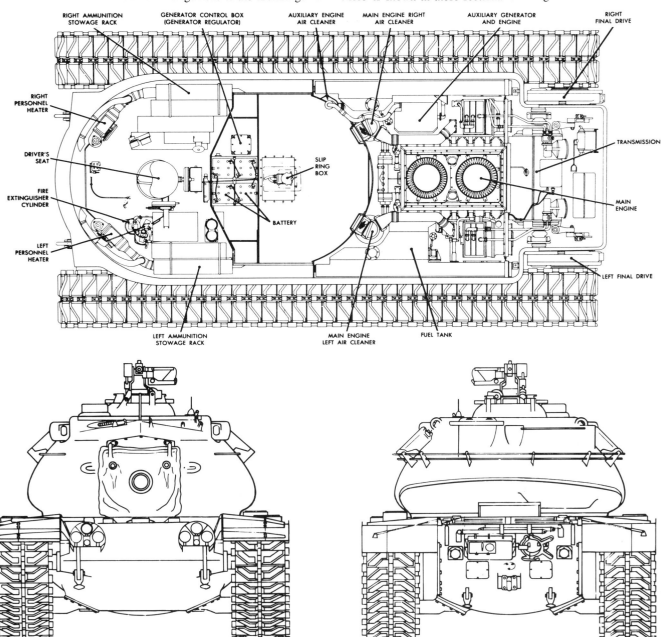

RIGHT AMMUNITION
STOWAGE RACK

GENERATOR CONTROL BOX
(GENERATOR REGULATOR)

AUXILIARY ENGINE
AIR CLEANER

MAIN ENGINE RIGHT
AIR CLEANER

AUXILIARY GENERATOR
AND ENGINE

RIGHT
FINAL DRIVE

RIGHT
PERSONNEL
HEATER

DRIVER'S
SEAT

FIRE
EXTINGUISHER
CYLINDER

LEFT
PERSONNEL
HEATER

SLIP
RING
BOX

BATTERY

TRANSMISSION

MAIN
ENGINE

LEFT FINAL DRIVE

LEFT AMMUNITION
STOWAGE RACK

MAIN ENGINE
LEFT AIR CLEANER

FUEL TANK

128

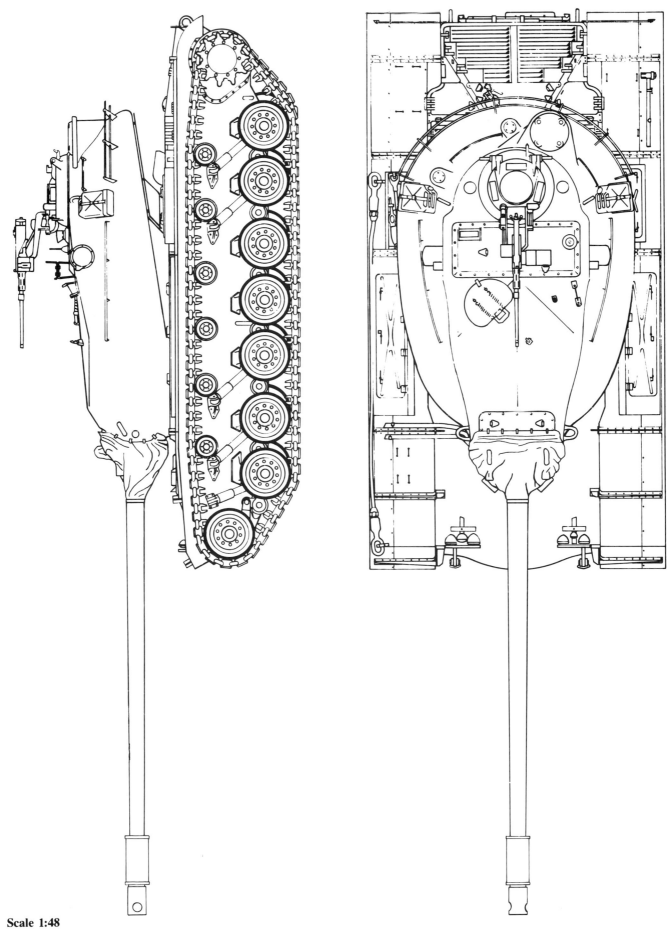

Scale 1:48

120mm Gun Tank M103

129

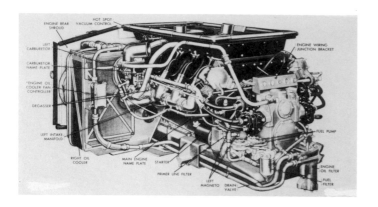

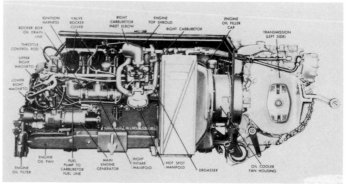

Details of the power package for the M103 are illustrated here. Note the outrigger type of oil coolers on the early model of the AV-1790 engine. A rear view of the CD-850 cross drive transmission appears below at the right.

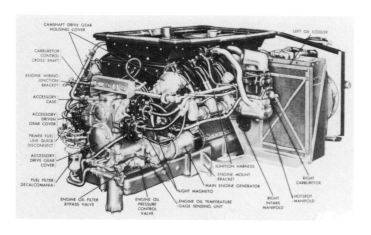

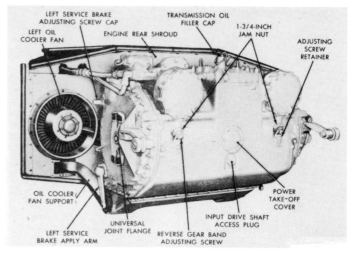

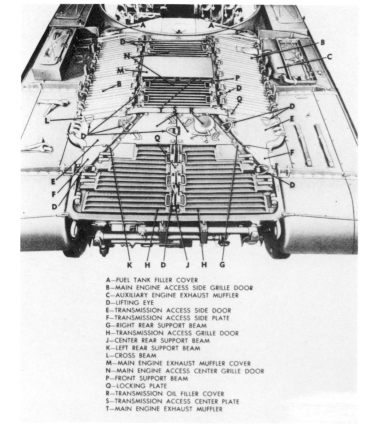

A—FUEL TANK FILLER COVER
B—MAIN ENGINE ACCESS SIDE GRILLE DOOR
C—AUXILIARY ENGINE EXHAUST MUFFLER
D—LIFTING EYE
E—TRANSMISSION ACCESS SIDE DOOR
F—TRANSMISSION ACCESS SIDE PLATE
G—RIGHT REAR SUPPORT BEAM
H—TRANSMISSION ACCESS GRILLE DOOR
J—CENTER REAR SUPPORT BEAM
K—LEFT REAR SUPPORT BEAM
L—CROSS BEAM
M—MAIN ENGINE EXHAUST MUFFLER COVER
N—MAIN ENGINE ACCESS CENTER GRILLE DOOR
P—FRONT SUPPORT BEAM
Q—LOCKING PLATE
R—TRANSMISSION OIL FILLER COVER
S—TRANSMISSION ACCESS CENTER PLATE
T—MAIN ENGINE EXHAUST MUFFLER

The rear deck of the M103 without the turret can be seen at the left. Below is a similar view with some of the access doors open revealing part of the engine compartment.

130

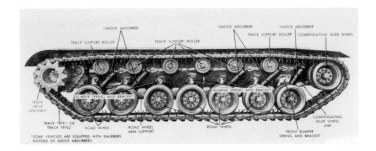

The bottom rear of the M103 appears at the right and above is a right side view of the suspension and tracks. Note the lack of a track tension idler between the sprocket and the rear road wheel. Below is a link from the 28 inch wide double pin track.

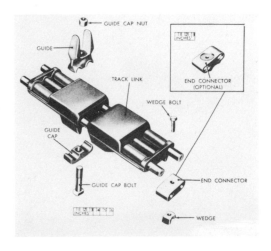

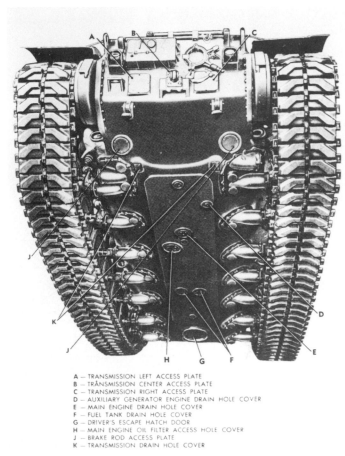

A — TRANSMISSION LEFT ACCESS PLATE
B — TRANSMISSION CENTER ACCESS PLATE
C — TRANSMISSION RIGHT ACCESS PLATE
D — AUXILIARY GENERATOR ENGINE DRAIN HOLE COVER
E — MAIN ENGINE DRAIN HOLE COVER
F — FUEL TANK DRAIN HOLE COVER
G — DRIVER'S ESCAPE HATCH DOOR
H — MAIN ENGINE OIL FILTER ACCESS HOLE COVER
J — BRAKE ROD ACCESS PLATE
K — TRANSMISSION DRAIN HOLE COVER

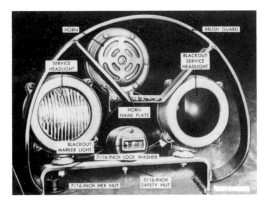

Above, the right headlight group is shown at the left and the left headlight group is at the right. Below, the left taillight is at the left and the right taillight is at the right.

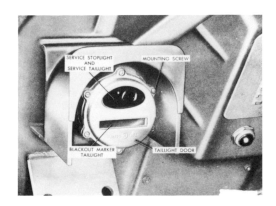

131

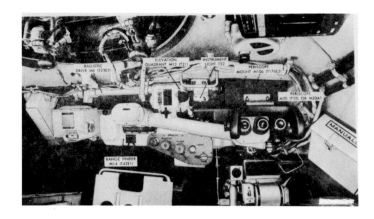

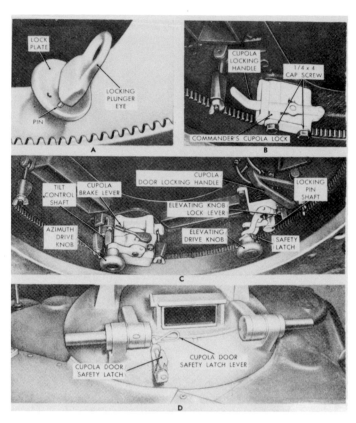

The gunner's instruments and controls are illustrated above. At the right are detailed views of the commander's M4 cupola and controls. The sketch of the fire control instruments below shows the M14 (T42E1) range finder (shaded), the M20 (T35) gunner's periscopic sight, and the M30 (T25) azimuth indicator.

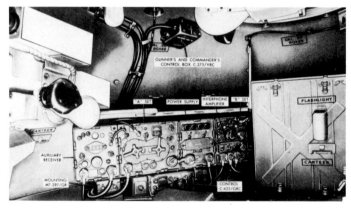

At the right, the radio is installed in the M103 turret bustle. Below are the gunner's seat (left) and the tank commander's seat (right), both in the turret bustle. Note the depression in the bottom of the turret bustle to accommodate the gunner's seat.

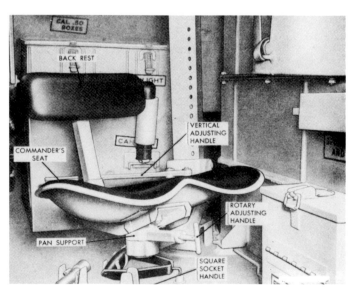

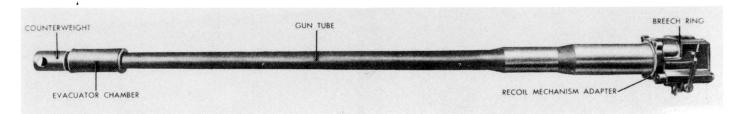

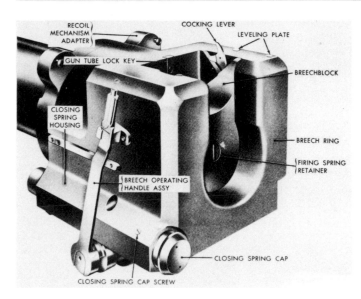

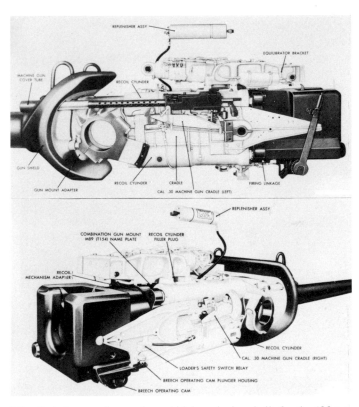

Details of the 120mm gun M58 can be seen above and below. The cylindrical blast deflector also served as a counterweight to balance the gun and as a lock ring to retain the bore evacuator in place. At the right, the gun is installed in the M89 mount. Although only one .30 caliber coaxial machine gun is shown, two were normally fitted in the M89 mount.

Directly below are the smoke and high explosive shells for the 120mm gun with their propelling charge in its cartridge case. At the bottom, the armor piercing and training rounds with the cartridge case containing their propelling charge are at the right and details of the obturator and closing plug appear at the left.

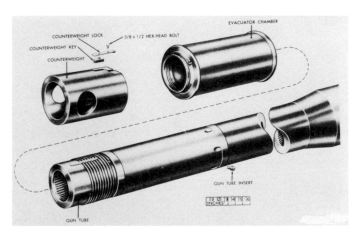

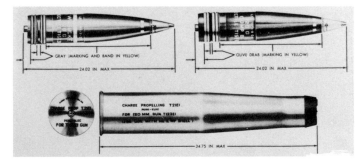

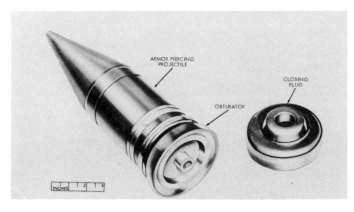

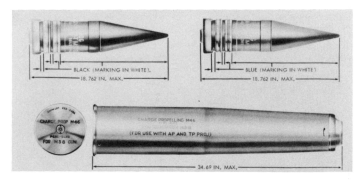

133

Above, two M103 120mm gun tanks from D Company, 33rd Armor are on the firing range in Germany during May 1959. A front view of tank D33 is shown below.

By January 1958, the new M103s were deployed in Europe with the 899th Tank Battalion. In May of the same year, the unit was redesignated as the 2nd Heavy Tank Battalion, 33rd Armor. The organization of this unit differed from that of the standard medium tank battalion. It consisted of four companies, each composed of six platoons. Each platoon was equipped with three tanks and one jeep. This provided a total of 18 tanks per company since the company headquarters tank section was eliminated. During the service in Europe, the heavy gun tanks were well liked by their crews and they proved to be capable of being used in almost any place that the M48 series of medium tanks could be employed. The troops recognized that the powerful 120mm gun was far superior in penetration performance to the 90mm cannon of the medium tanks.

Below is another tank from D Company, 33rd Armor at Grafenwoehr, Germany on 15 September 1959. Note the rack on the rear of the hull for jettisonable fuel tanks to increase the range of the vehicle.

The second pilot 120mm gun tank T43E2 is shown above. Below are two photographs of the same tank during tests at Fort Knox. The new location of the gunner's station is revealed by the periscopic sight in the turret roof.

After the initial tests at Fort Knox indicated that the T43E1 would never completely meet the CON-ARC requirements for the turret and gun control system as well as the fire control system, the Ordnance Committee proposed a re-engineering and product improvement program. Initially, three pilots were authorized for this project, but OCM 35247, dated 22 April 1954, reduced the number to two and designated the improved vehicle as the 120mm gun tank T43E2.

The first T43E2 began engineering tests at Aberdeen Proving Ground in February 1956 and the second was shipped to Fort Knox the following June. As would be expected, changes from the T43E1 were confined primarily to the turret and fire control system. The turret was now fitted with a basket and the gunner was relocated to the right front alongside the cannon. The constant pressure hydraulic turret control on the T43E1 was replaced by the electric amplidyne system. The coaxial machine gun on the right side of the cannon was replaced by an articulated

These photographs of T43E2 pilot number 2 at Fort Knox show many of the changes applied to the tank. The relocation of the gunner's periscopic sight is clearly visible (above). The target obscuration caused by smoke and dust during firing of the 120mm gun is obvious below at the right.

telescope as a secondary sighting device for the gunner. A new T52 stereoscopic range finder was installed for operation by the tank commander. The range finder was coupled electrically to a T33 ballistic computer which, with the gunner's new T44E1 periscopic sight in the turret roof, completed the primary fire control system. The T44E1 sight also provided correction for vehicle cant and projectile drift. The commander's cupola was modified eliminating the geared rotation feature as well as the remote control for the .50 caliber machine gun. This weapon could now only be operated with the hatch open.

During the test firing of the 120mm gun, severe erosion was noted around the holes in the blast deflector (counterweight) on the gun muzzle. It also was observed that the blast deflection produced by these holes had very little effect in reducing target obscuration. Thus the main purpose of this component

The front and rear views below show further details of the T43E2 pilot number 2 at Fort Knox. The new .50 caliber machine gun mount for the tank commander can be seen in both photographs.

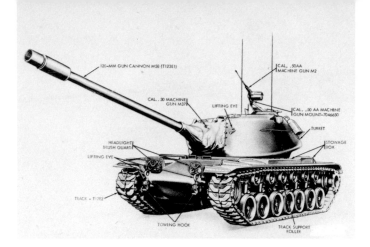

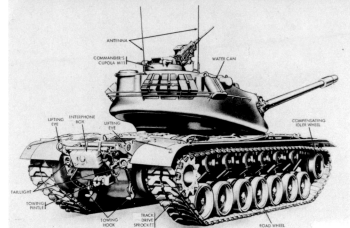

The nomenclature for various components of the T43E2 standardized as the 120mm gun tank M103A1 appears in these views from the technical manual.

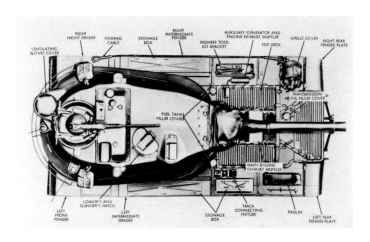

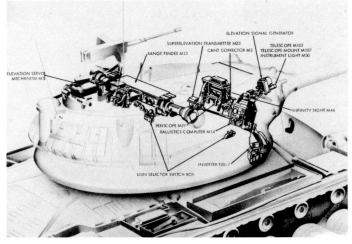

was to lock the bore evacuator in place. To prevent a safety hazard resulting from a possible fracture, the forward part of the cylindrical blast deflector was cut off, converting it into a simple retaining ring for the bore evacuator. At the same time, an experimental T-shape blast deflector was installed on the test tank. However, it did not appear to significantly reduce target obscuration when firing the 120mm gun.

Components of the fire control system on the M103A1 are illustrated at the right. Note that the range finder is now operated by the tank commander. The modified counterweight used to lock the bore evacuator in place can be seen directly below. The driver's controls on the M103A1 appear at the bottom right.

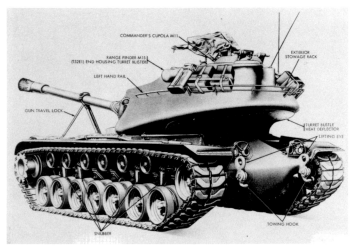

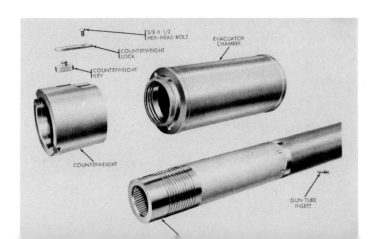

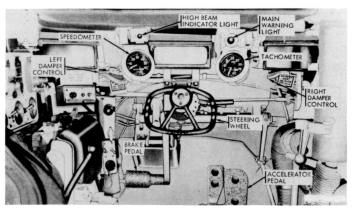

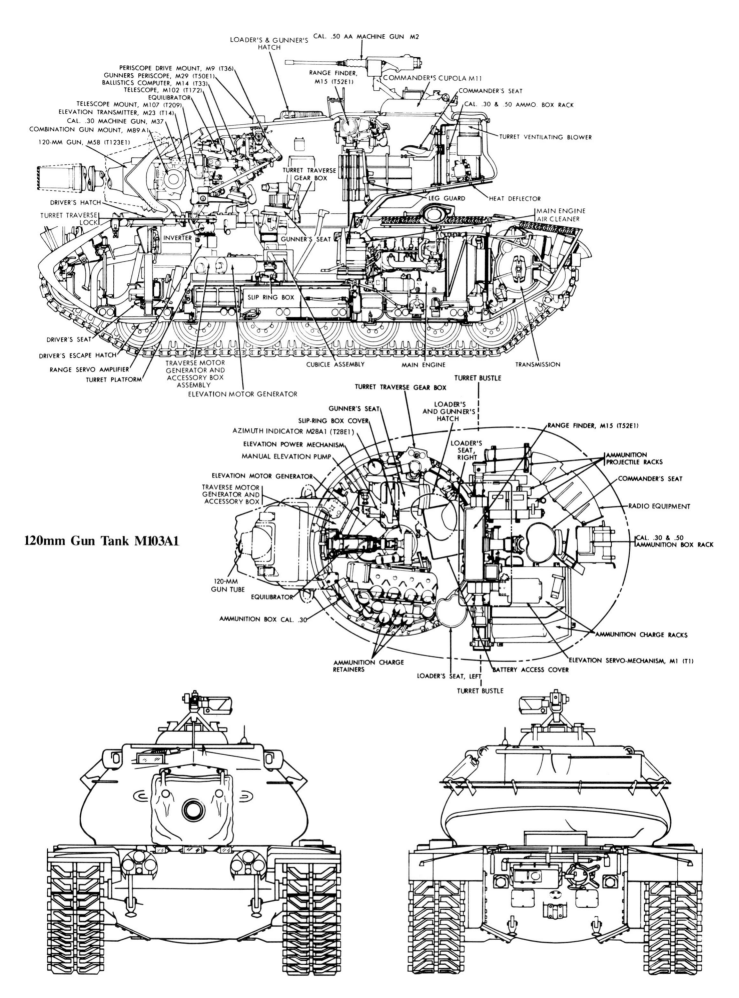

LOADER'S & GUNNER'S HATCH
CAL. .50 AA MACHINE GUN M2
PERISCOPE DRIVE MOUNT, M9 (T36)
GUNNERS PERISCOPE, M29 (T50E1)
BALLISTICS COMPUTER, M14 (T33)
TELESCOPE, M102 (T172)
RANGE FINDER, M15 (T52E1)
COMMANDER'S CUPOLA M11
EQUILIBRATOR
COMMANDER'S SEAT
TELESCOPE MOUNT, M107 (T209)
CAL. .30 & .50 AMMO. BOX RACK
ELEVATION TRANSMITTER, M23 (T14)
CAL. .30 MACHINE GUN, M37
COMBINATION GUN MOUNT, M89A1
120-MM GUN, M58 (T123E1)
TURRET VENTILATING BLOWER
TURRET TRAVERSE GEAR BOX
DRIVER'S HATCH
LEG GUARD
HEAT DEFLECTOR
TURRET TRAVERSE LOCK
MAIN ENGINE AIR CLEANER
INVERTER
GUNNER'S SEAT
SLIP RING BOX
DRIVER'S SEAT
DRIVER'S ESCAPE HATCH
RANGE SERVO AMPLIFIER
TURRET PLATFORM
TRAVERSE MOTOR GENERATOR AND ACCESSORY BOX ASSEMBLY
ELEVATION MOTOR GENERATOR
CUBICLE ASSEMBLY
MAIN ENGINE
TRANSMISSION

TURRET TRAVERSE GEAR BOX
TURRET BUSTLE
GUNNER'S SEAT
SLIP-RING BOX COVER
LOADER'S AND GUNNER'S HATCH
AZIMUTH INDICATOR M28A1 (T28E1)
RANGE FINDER, M15 (T52E1)
ELEVATION POWER MECHANISM
LOADER'S SEAT, RIGHT
MANUAL ELEVATION PUMP
AMMUNITION PROJECTILE RACKS
ELEVATION MOTOR GENERATOR
COMMANDER'S SEAT
TRAVERSE MOTOR GENERATOR AND ACCESSORY BOX
RADIO EQUIPMENT

120mm Gun Tank M103A1

CAL. .30 & .50 AMMUNITION BOX RACK
120-MM GUN TUBE
EQUILIBRATOR
AMMUNITION BOX CAL. .30
AMMUNITION CHARGE RACKS
ELEVATION SERVO-MECHANISM, M1 (T1)
AMMUNITION CHARGE RETAINERS
LOADER'S SEAT, LEFT
BATTERY ACCESS COVER
TURRET BUSTLE

138

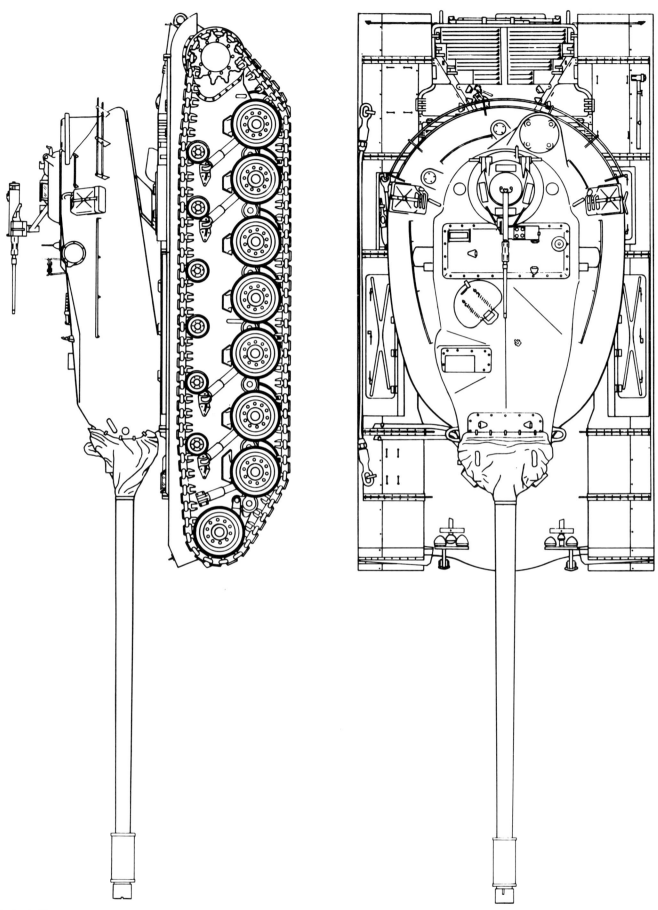

Scale 1:48

120mm Gun Tank M103A1

139

The test report from Fort Knox concluded that the T43E2 met CONARC requirements and that after correction of some minor defects, it was suitable for use by the U.S. Army. At that time, the Army did not plan any additional production and the T43E2 was regarded as a standby design for possible future use. However, the U.S. Marine Corps authorized funds to convert 219 of their T43E1s to the T43E2 standard. On 13 June 1957, OCM 36540 was approved which standardized the T43E2 with the various modifications required by the test program. The same action designated the vehicle as the 120mm gun, full tracked, combat tank M103A1. The modification program for the Marine Corps was completed in July 1959. The heavy tanks were organized into a fourth company assigned to each of the three Marine tank battalions. They also were provided to Marine Corps reserve units. Although the U.S. Army did not modify their tanks, action was initiated in February 1959 to obtain 72 M103A1s on loan from the Marine Corps.

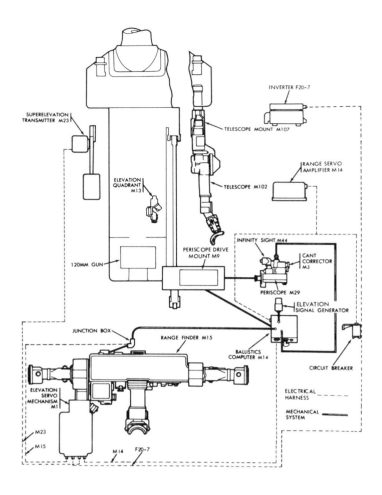

A diagram of the fire control system in the M103A1 can be seen above. Below, a Marine Corps M103A1 from the 2nd Tank Battalion is firing during training exercises near Vieques, Puerto Rico on 25 April 1962.

Above, a 120mm gun tank M103A1E1 is loaded on a tank transporter. Note that this vehicle has only four track return rollers per track.

After the appearance of the diesel powered M60 tank, the Marine Corps provided funds for a modification program to upgrade the M103A1. This product improvement project was initiated on 5 June 1961 with the authorization to build two M103A1E1 pilot tanks incorporating the latest components to improve the operating range, mobility, and fire control. On 4 October, additional funds were assigned to the program for the assembly of a third M103A1E1. The first pilot was completed in March 1962 and shipped to Aberdeen Proving Ground for engineering and endurance tests. In April, the second tank was sent to Fort Knox for service tests by the Armor Board. The third pilot, after completion in May, was retained at Detroit for maintenance evaluation and engineering studies.

Some of the modifications necessary to convert the M103A1 to the diesel engine can be seen in the views of the M103A1E1 below. The use of many rear hull components from the M60 tank is obvious.

141

The M103A1E1 is shown above with the 120mm gun in the travel lock. The new design track drive sprocket and the fender mounted air cleaners used with the diesel engine are visible in all three photographs.

The most important change on the M103A1E1 was the installation of the Continental AVDS-1790-2A diesel engine. Operating with the CD-850-6 cross drive transmission, the new engine increased the cruising range of the tank from about 80 to approximately 300 miles. The engine compartment was modified to incorporate an insulated infrared suppression rear deck as on the M60 tank and the engine exhaust mixed with the cooling air was discharged through the same type of vertical rear door grills. This new rear hull arrangement required the design of a new gun travel lock which was attached at the center rear of the top deck. A new XM24 (later M24) coincidence type range finder was provided for the tank commander. Like the rest of the fire control equipment, it utilized the metric system. The M14E1 (later M14A1) ballistic computer was a modified version of the M14 to improve the night fighting ability and had a cam added for HEAT ammunition. An articulated M102C telescope, which was a metric version of the M102, was provided for the secondary fire control system. A xenon searchlight also was fitted to enhance night fighting capabilities. On the pilot tanks,

an effort was made to reduce the suspension weight by eliminating the second and fifth track support rollers on each side. It also was noted that the light-weight aluminum road wheels and track support rollers from the M60 tank could be installed with only minor modifications.

Meetings in August 1962 reviewed the results of the pilot tank tests and the maintenance evaluation. It was concluded that the tank was suitable for use by the Marine Corps and funds were authorized for the Red River Army Depot to convert 153 M103A1 tanks to the new configuration in addition to the three pilots. On 13 December 1962, the standardization of

The power package for the 120mm gun tank M103A1E1 is illustrated below. This consisted of the Continental AVDS-1790-2A diesel engine and the Allison CD-850-6 cross drive transmission. Note the turbo superchargers on the exhaust system of the engine.

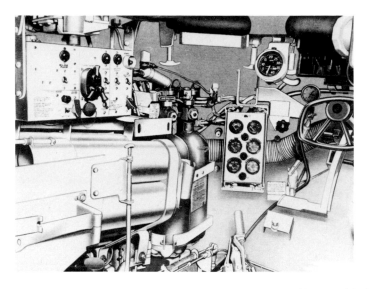

Above are views of the driver's compartment in the M103A1E1 with the control and gage panels visible at the left. Steering with the cross drive transmission is diagrammed at the left below. The 120mm ammunition racks on each side of the driver are visible with the turret removed at the right below.

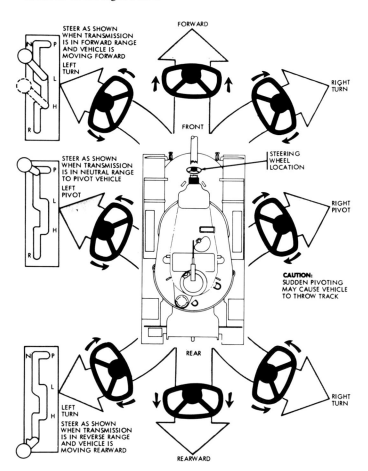

bringing the total to 208. The M103A2 continued in service until 1973 when it was phased out of all operational units.

The bottom of the M103A1E1 hull can be seen below from the rear of the tank.

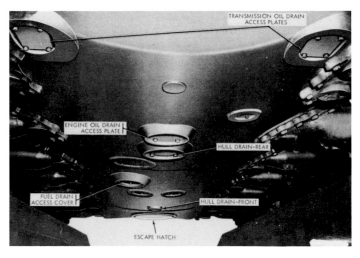

the upgraded vehicle was approved as the 120mm gun, full tracked, combat tank M103A2. Unlike the three pilot tanks, the later conversions retained all six of the track support rollers on each side of the suspension. On 26 August 1963, the M103A2 was designated as the standard operational heavy tank for the U.S. Marine Corps. In fiscal year 1968, an additional 52 M103A1s were converted to the M103A2 standard

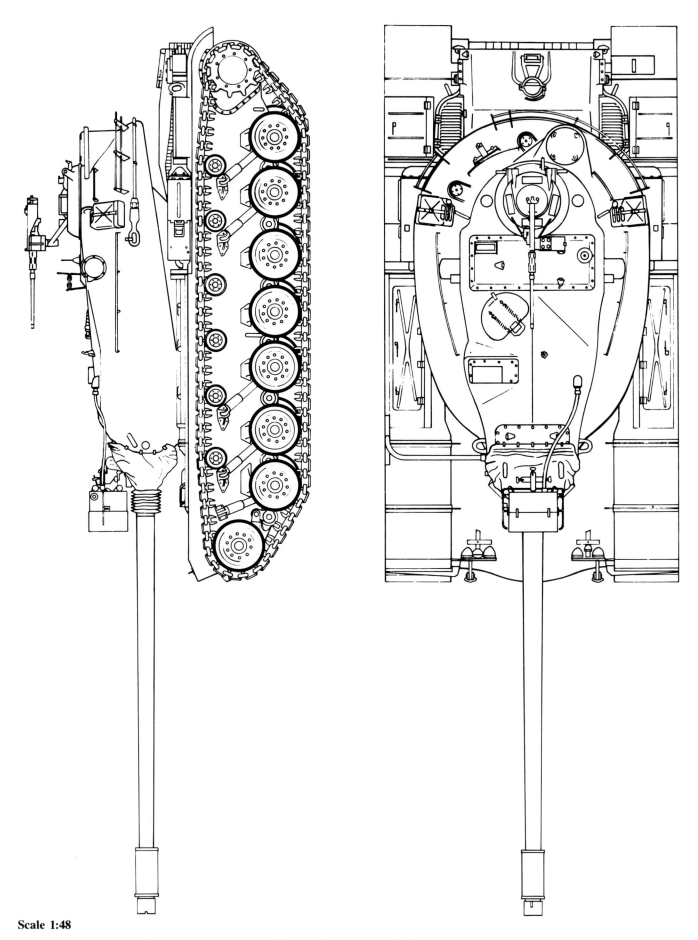

Scale 1:48

120mm Gun Tank M103A2

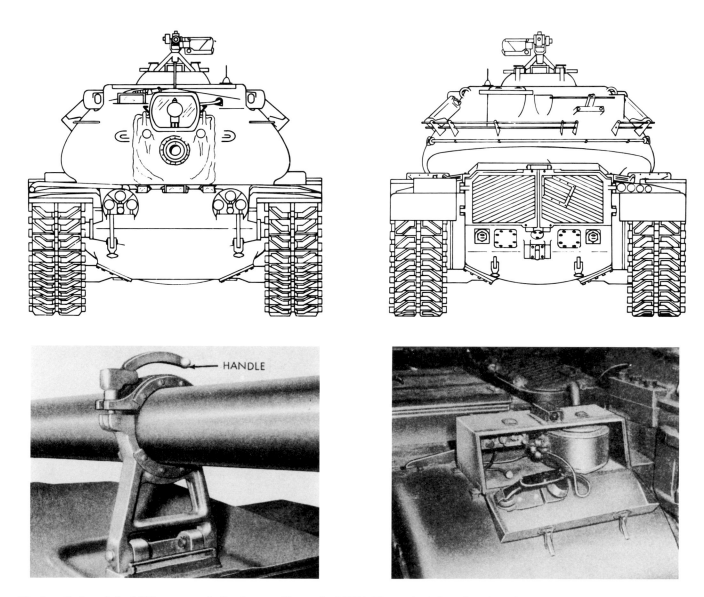

The installation of the M60 type rear hull exhaust grills on the M103A1E1 required the relocation of the travel lock for the 120mm gun (above left) and the external telephone box (above right). Below is the 120mm gun tank M103A2 as standardized. Note that all six of the track return rollers have been retained.

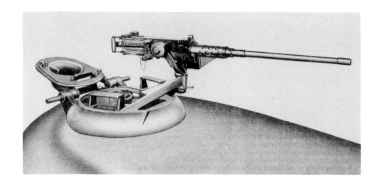

The .50 caliber machine gun and mount on the tank commander's cupola can be seen at the top left and his vane sight is at the top right. Below, the interior of the commander's cupola is shown at the left and his controls are at the right.

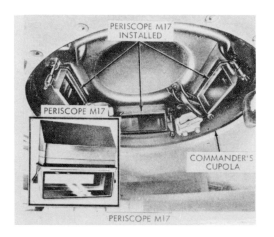

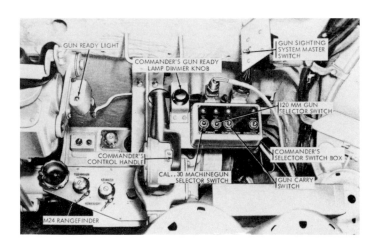

The arrangement of the M103A2 fire control components is sketched below.

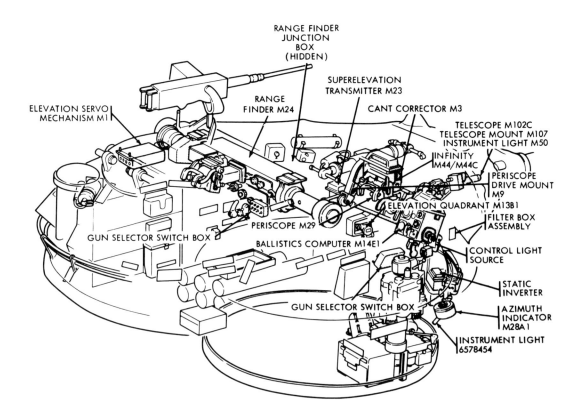

146

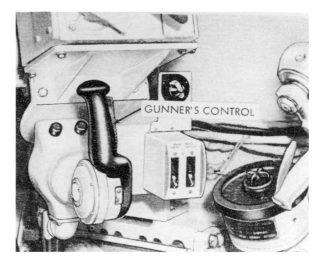

Above, the single .30 caliber coaxial machine gun on the left side of the cannon can be seen at the left and the gunner's controls are at the right. The turret and gun controls of the M103A2 are shown in the schematic drawing below.

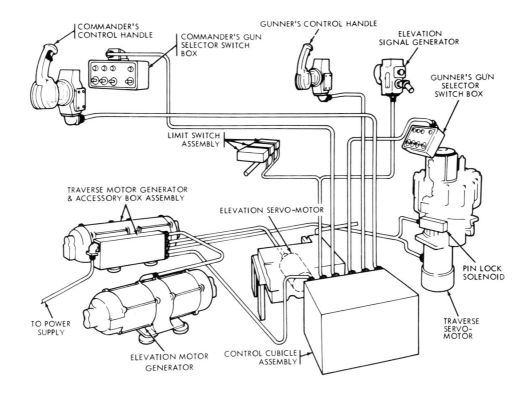

Below, the high explosive antitank (HEAT) projectile T153E14 and the propelling charge T42 are at the left and the sketch at the right shows the 120mm ammunition stowage arrangement in the turret bustle.

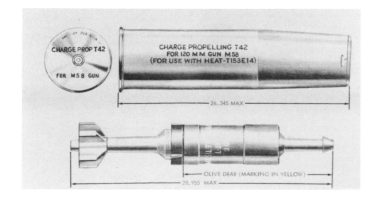

147

Above, four Marine Corps M103A2s during training operations are lined up on the firing range. Below, one of the M103A2s is firing. Note the effect of the muzzle blast and the empty 120mm cartridge cases alongside the tank.

Above, the driver of a Marine Corps M103A2 can be seen operating the tank with the hatch open. Below, another M103A2 is taking part in Operation Silver Lance at Camp Pendleton, California on 10 March 1965. This tank was from the 1st Marine Division.

The M103A2s above and below from the 2nd Platoon, D Company, 5th Marine Tank Battalion are shown operating at Camp Pendleton on 6 June 1967. Note that the tank above is equipped with a xenon searchlight.

Above, two M103A2s from the 5th Marine Tank Battalion pull into the tank park at Camp Pendleton for maintenance on 29 May 1967.

Below, M103A2 tanks are in storage at the Marine Corps Supply Center, Barstow, California. This photograph was dated August 1972. The bore evacuators have been removed and the gun tube muzzles are sealed.

Above and below are two artist's concept drawings of the 120mm gun tank T57 with the oscillating turret on the T43 tank chassis.

EXPERIMENTAL MODIFICATIONS AND VEHICLES BASED ON THE HEAVY TANK

Although the initial investigation showed that it would be extremely difficult to develop automatic loading equipment for the 120mm gun in the T43 turret, further study indicated that such a device might be successful if the weapon were installed in a trunnion mounted turret. In the latter design, also referred to as an oscillating turret, the relative movement between the turret and the cannon was limited to the recoil of the weapon after firing. Such an arrangement greatly simplified the design of an automatic loader. Further studies at Aberdeen indicated that the recoil movement also might be eliminated if the cannon was rigidly mounted in the turret without a recoil system. Experimental rigid mounts for 75mm and 76mm guns had been test fired at the Proving Ground and the results indicated the possibility of designing such a mount for the heavier weapons.

On 12 October 1951, OCM 34048 initiated a development program for a new 120mm gun tank with an oscillating turret and an automatic loader. Two pilots were authorized and the new vehicle was designated as the 120mm gun tank T57. The oscillating turrets with 85 inch diameter rings were to be installed on T43 tank chassis diverted for the purpose. The initial concept envisaged a cylindrical ammunition magazine mounted directly behind the gun in the turret bustle. However, according to preliminary calculations, such a magazine would have diameters of 42 inches, 38 inches, or 30 inches if designed to hold eleven, nine, or six rounds respectively. The Army Field Forces objected to this arrangement, pointing out that such a design would result in a very large turret with a massive bustle to house the magazine. Subsequently, a contract was placed with the Rheem Manufacturing Company for the design and construction of the two pilot tanks.

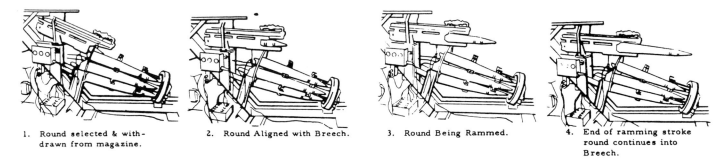

1. Round selected & withdrawn from magazine.
2. Round Aligned with Breech.
3. Round Being Rammed.
4. End of ramming stroke round continues into Breech.

The sequence of operation for the automatic loader in the T57 is illustrated in the sketches above. Note that this mechanism was designed to use fixed 120mm ammunition.

The concept developed by Rheem rigidly mounted the 120mm gun without a recoil system in a low silhouette cast oscillating turret with a long narrow nose. The cannon had a quick change tube and was ballistically identical to the 120mm gun T123E1, but it was modified to use fixed ammunition. The new gun was attached to the turret by a conical shaped tubular adapter surrounding the barrel and screwed onto the forward end of the breech ring. The smaller end of the adapter extended through the turret front and was secured on the outside by an adapter nut. The torque created by the projectile moving down the rifled tube was resisted by keying the adapter to both the breech ring and the turret. Since there was no recoil motion to open the horizontal sliding breechblock, this was accomplished by an hydraulic cylinder actuated by an electric switch after firing. The modified cannon was designated as the 120mm gun T179 and it was fitted with the same bore evacuator and cylindrical blast deflector as the T123E1. The rigid mount was designated as the T169. Initially, two .30 caliber coaxial machine guns were proposed for installation, but later this was reduced to a single .30 caliber weapon on the left side of the cannon. A T173 telescope was located to the right of the mount as a secondary sighting device for the gunner.

The automatic loader consisted of an eight round rotary drum magazine below the gun and a rammer just behind the weapon which pivoted between positions aligned with the gun and magazine. The equipment was intended for fixed ammunition, but an alternate design was prepared for use with separated rounds. In operation, the hydraulically actuated rammer withdrew a round from the magazine and at the same time ejected the cartridge case from the previously fired shot through the port in the top rear of the turret roof. The rammer then moved into alignment with the gun breech and rammed the new round into the weapon tripping the extractors and closing the breech. Firing the gun actuated a toggle switch on the breech ring which operated the hydraulic cylinder that opened the breech. The empty cartridge case was then ejected into the trough back of the round holder assembly. Any one of three types of ammunition could be selected from the magazine by the gunner or the tank commander.

The internal arrangement of the oscillating turret with the rigidly mounted 120mm gun on the T57 can be seen in the sectional drawings below. The ejection port for the empty cartridge cases was in the roof of the turret bustle at the rear.

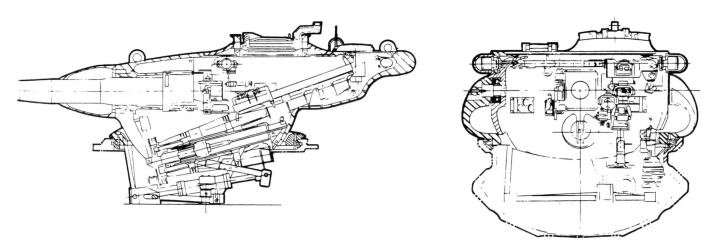

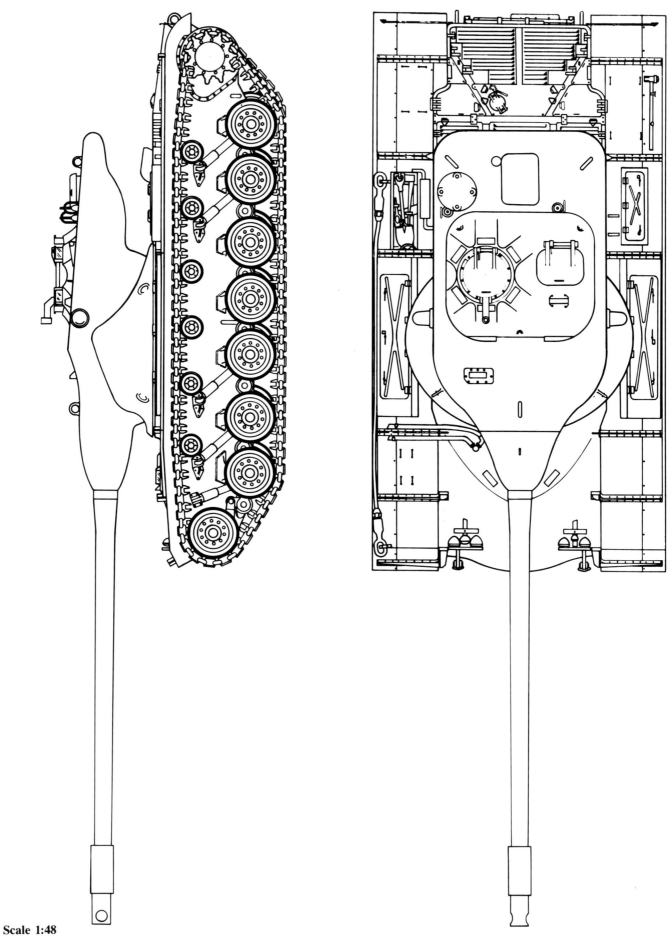

Scale 1:48

120mm Gun Tank T57

154

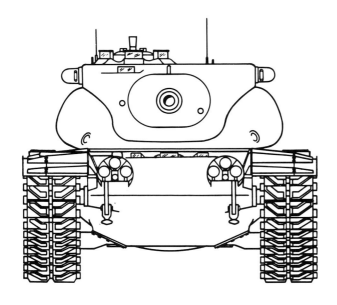
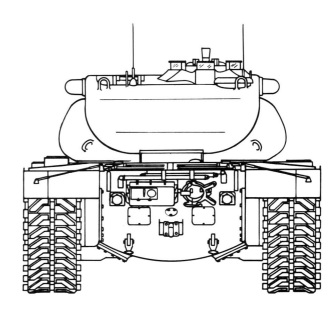

The primary fire control system in the T57 consisted of an M20A1 periscopic sight with the T32E2 range drive for the gunner and a T50 stereoscopic range finder with the T33E2 range drive for the tank commander. The three man turret crew consisted of the gunner and the loader on the right and left sides of the cannon respectively and the tank commander on the right behind the gunner. A cupola over the tank commander's position was fitted with six T36 periscopes and a rotating mount for a .50 caliber antiaircraft machine gun. A separate hatch was installed on the left side of the turret roof for the loader. In addition, a large power operated section of the turret roof, which contained both the cupola and the loader's hatch, could be opened for easy access to the turret. The trunnions on each side of the cast homogenous steel turret were supported in bearings by a cast yoke assembly which was fitted to the standard 85 inch diameter turret ring of the T43E1. An electric amplidyne system powered the turret in both elevation and traverse. The T43E1 hull had stowage modifications to accommodate ten rounds of 120mm ammunition, bringing the total to 18 rounds. The driver occupied his normal position in the T43E1 hull.

Progress was slow on the T57 project because of design problems and delays in obtaining some of the required government furnished equipment. The latter situation reflected changing priorities during this period with interest shifting to newer, lighter tank chassis armed with even more powerful weapons. A T57 turret was installed on a T43E1 chassis with registration number 30170207, but work on the program was ended before the equipment could be tested. Ordnance Committee action cancelled the development on 17 January 1957 and scrapped both T57 turrets. The two T43E1 chassis were returned to supply for future use.

No usable photographs of the 120mm gun tank T57 were available prior to the publication of this volume. The model shown here was constructed by Dave Lockhart to illustrate this vehicle.

Additional views of the 120mm gun tank T57 model built by Dave Lockhart can be seen here.

At the right is an early model of the proposed 155mm gun tank T58 with the oscillating turret mounted on the T43 chassis.

Although the 120mm gun tanks T43 and T57 were expected to meet the requirements outlined in the Army Development Guide of December 1950, the Tripartite Conference on Armor and Bridging in October 1951 recommended the development of a 155mm gun tank. The main weapon for the proposed vehicle was to fire shaped charge (HEAT) and squash head (HEP or HESH) projectiles capable of defeating heavy armor. It was originally intended to mount the 155mm gun T80 in the new tank. However, since the chemical energy rounds did not require a high muzzle velocity to be effective, it was concluded that a modified version of the 155mm gun T7 would be adequate and it would be lighter in weight. The T7 was the weapon previously described as the main armament of the heavy tank T30. The characteristics of the new vehicle were outlined in OCM 34159 on 18 January 1952. The same action recommended the manufacture of two 155m gun oscillating turrets with automatic loaders for installation on T43E1 chassis and designated the resulting vehicle as the 155mm gun tank T58. After approval of these recommendations on 10 April 1952, a contract was negotiated with the United Shoe Machinery Corporation for the design, development, and manufacture of the two pilot turrets and their installation on the T43E1 chassis.

Unlike the rigidly mounted weapon in the T57, the 155mm gun in the T58 was installed with a four cylinder hydrospring recoil system in the mount T170. To conserve space inside the turret, the recoil of the cannon was limited to 12 to 14 inches. Originally, the modified T7 gun was designated as the 155mm gun howitzer T7E2. Later, it became the 155mm gun howitzer T180, but this was only a change in nomenclature. The modified weapon differed from the original T7 in several features. The gun was converted from a horizontal to a vertical sliding breechblock and fitted with a bore evacuator and a new blast deflector. Also, the tube wall was thickened around the chamber and the chamber length was increased by approximately one inch to accommodate the new plastic closing plugs used in the cartridge cases of the separated ammunition.

The automatic loader consisted of a six round magazine and rammer mechanism with controls and interlocks. The magazine extended into the turret bustle directly behind the gun. The projectile and separate cartridge case were rammed at the same time after being placed in the magazine tube by the loader. The loader first manually inserted a cartridge case into the magazine tube. An electrically powered hoist then was used to transfer the 95 pound projectile from the stowage rack to a removable loading tray from which it was slid into the magazine tube. The loader selected the round to fire by rotating the magazine with a crank. After firing, the empty cartridge

Below is the 155mm gun tank T58. At this stage, the range finder had not yet been installed.

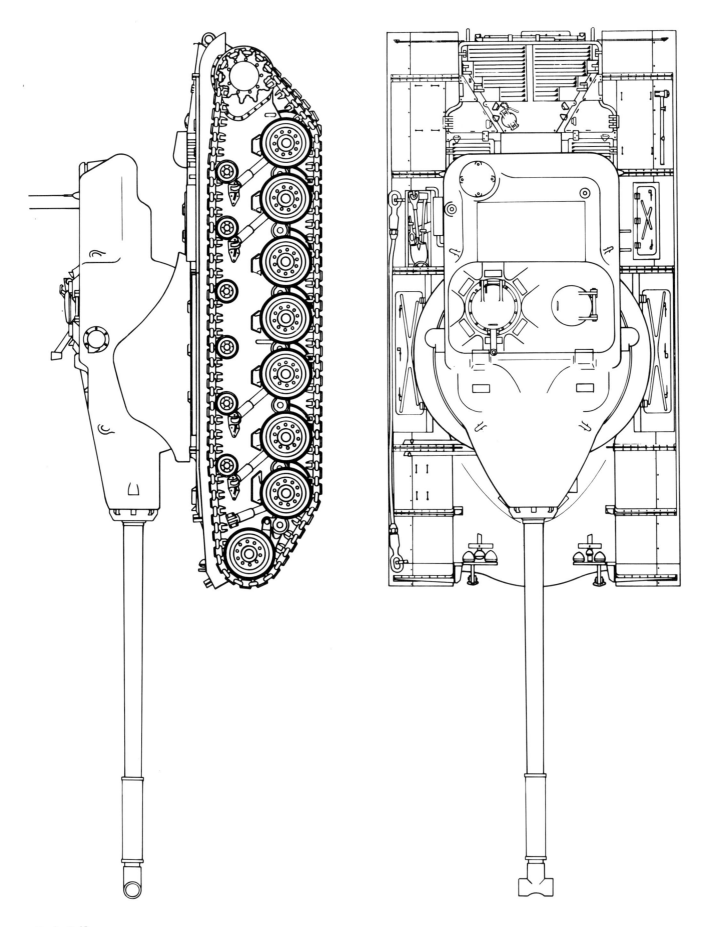

Scale 1:48

155mm Gun Tank T58

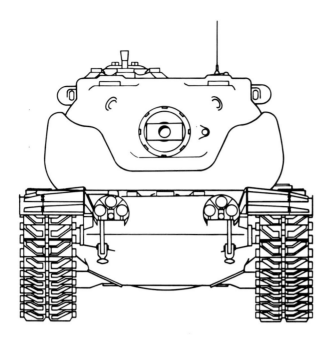

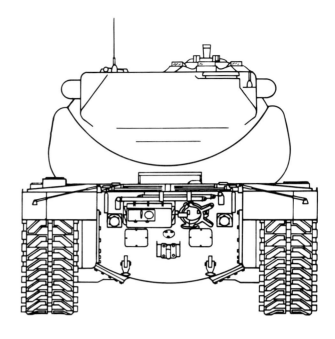

case was ejected back into the magazine from which it was removed by the loader and replaced in the stowage rack. The three man turret crew had the usual arrangement with the gunner at the right of the cannon in front of the tank commander and the loader on the left side of the turret. The cast body of the oscillating turret was assembled with a two section removable roof to permit installation of the automatic loader and other components. The rear part of the roof was bolted in place, but the front section, which carried the commander's cupola and the loader's hatch, was hinged along its forward edge so that it could be raised by an hydraulic cylinder to an angle of 60 degrees. In this position, it provided a shield for the crew during emergency evacuation of the tank. Initially, two coaxial machine guns were specified, but later this was reduced to a single .30

caliber weapon on the left side of the cannon. A .50 caliber antiaircraft machine gun was fitted on the commander's cupola. Six T36 periscopes were installed around the original version of the commander's cupola, but this was increased to seven for the final design. A single M13 periscope, moveable in elevation, but fixed in azimuth, was provided for the loader in the turret roof. The primary fire control equipment consisted of the T184E1 periscopic sight and range drive T33E1 for the gunner and the T50E1 stereoscopic range finder and range drive T32E3 for the tank commander. An improved fire control system including the T30 ballistic computer was intended for any production tanks, but it was not installed in the pilots. A T170 telescope on the right side of the cannon provided a secondary fire control system for the gunner.

The sectional drawing below shows the internal arrangement of the 155mm gun tank T58.

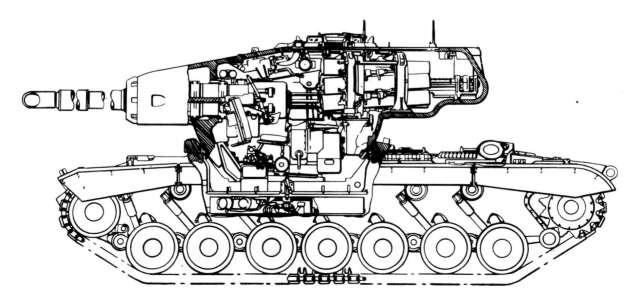

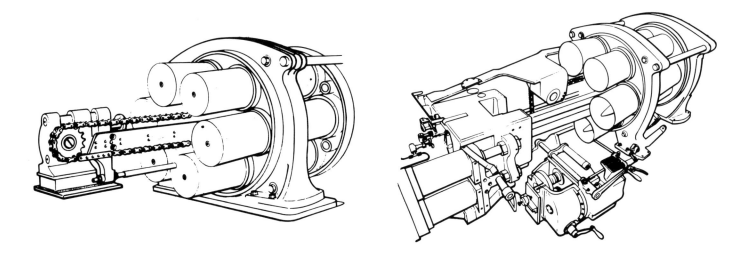

Above is the six round automatic loader installed in the 155mm gun tank T58. A right rear view appears at the left and a left front view can be seen at the right.

As on the T57, the trunnions of the T58 turret body were supported by a cast armor yoke installed on the turret ring of a T43E1. In addition to changes in ammunition stowage, several other modifications were required on the T43E1 hull. At maximum elevation, there was interference between the turret bustle and the mufflers for both the auxiliary generator and the main engine. To correct this problem, the auxiliary generator muffler was shifted to a lower position and the main engine muffler was relocated approximately 20 inches to the rear. A new gun travel lock was provided on the rear deck to accommodate the 155mm gun. The work on the two pilots continued into 1956 at the United Shoe Machinery Corporation despite numerous changes in requirements and delays in obtaining various components required for final assembly. As with the T57, interest had shifted by this time to later designs and there was no longer any requirement for a tank such as the T58. The project was cancelled along with that for the T57 as well as several other programs on 17 January 1957 and subsequently both pilot turrets were scrapped.

Below is a drawing of the 155mm gun T180. In the T58 tank, it was installed with a recoil system.

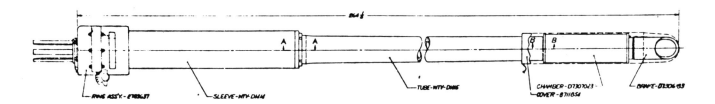

At the right is one of the manned evasive target tanks (METT) built during 1977 using the M103A2 chassis. They were intended for the training of TOW missile crews using missiles with dummy warheads.

160

The pilot heavy recovery vehicle T51 is shown above and at the bottom of the page during its evaluation at Fort Knox in 1951.

With the appearance of the heavier postwar tanks, the recovery vehicles based on the World War II Sherman were obviously inadequate. To meet the new requirements, a design study was started in February 1951. The proposed concept was approved by the Army Field Forces Board Number 2 in April of the same year and construction of a full scale mock-up and two pilot heavy recovery vehicles began that Summer. OCMs 33790 and 33835, dated 5 July 1951 and 2 August 1951 respectively, recommended

and approved this action and assigned the designation heavy recovery vehicle T51. The first pilot arrived at Aberdeen Proving Ground in April 1953 for engineering and endurance tests. Pilot number 2 had already been received at Fort Knox for service tests in February. Following the initial tests, a conference at Fort Monroe, Virginia on 1 September 1953 accepted the new recovery vehicle and it was released for production. The T51 was standardized by OCM 35013 on 22 October 1953 and designated as the heavy

Above is the production pilot heavy recovery vehicle M51, serial number 3, after completion at Chrysler. This photograph was dated 10 February 1954.

recovery vehicle M51. Chrysler started construction of a production pilot at Detroit in October and its tests started at Fort Knox in March 1954. Production by Chrysler at the Detroit Tank Arsenal followed with the release of the first production vehicle in August 1954. A total of 187 M51s were built by Chrysler at this location during 1954 and 1955. Subsequently, it was determined that additional changes were required to make the M51 suitable for troop use. Chrysler constructed a pre-modification pilot incorporating 52 changes and a program was started at the Lima Ordnance Depot in July 1956 to bring the production vehicles up to the new standard. Modification of the last vehicle was complete in July 1958.

The M51 had a combat weight of about 60 tons and was powered by the Continental AVSI-1790-6 engine with the XT-1400-2A cross drive transmission. This engine was the supercharged, fuel injection version of the air-cooled 1790 and it developed approximately 1000 gross horsepower at 2800 rpm. The suspension and tracks utilized the same components as the M103 tank series. The vehicle was equipped with a 30-ton capacity crane, a 45-ton capacity winch, and a 5-ton capacity auxiliary winch for use in recovery operations. The hull was assembled by welding rolled armor plate and it was divided into three compartments. The cab on the front housed the four man crew consisting of the commander, driver, crane operator, and rigger. This compartment also contained the main winch, auxiliary winch, front fuel tank, fixed fire extinguisher cylinders, and auxiliary hydraulic pump. The crane and its associated components were located in the center compartment. The engine compartment was in the rear with the power plant, rear fuel tank, main hydraulic system, power take-off, and auxiliary generator.

The M51 served with both U.S. Army and Marine Corps units which required a heavy recovery vehicle. However, like the M103 tank, its service in the U.S. Army was limited.

A view of the M51 production pilot during test operations is at the left.

162

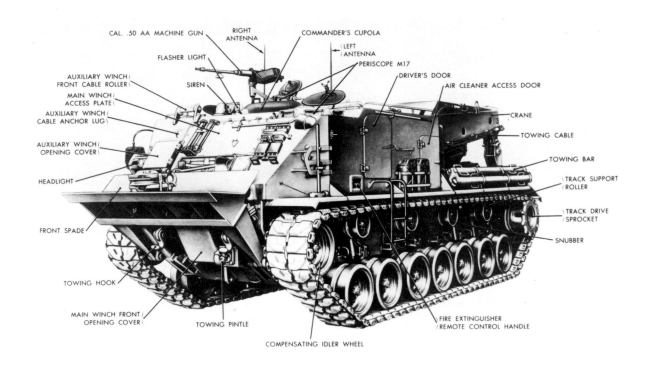

Details of the heavy recovery vehicle M51 after modification can be seen above and below. Note the later type track drive sprocket as on the M103A2 in the side view.

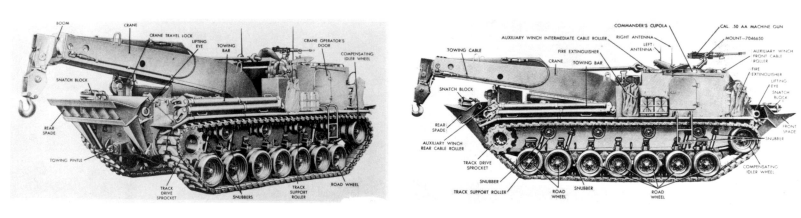

Below, the heavy recovery vehicle M51 is in travel order with the hatches closed and the .50 caliber machine gun covered.

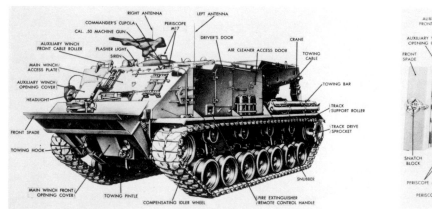
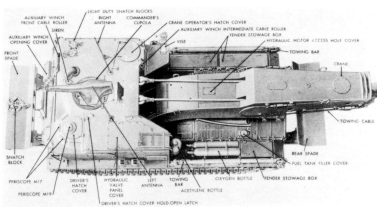

163

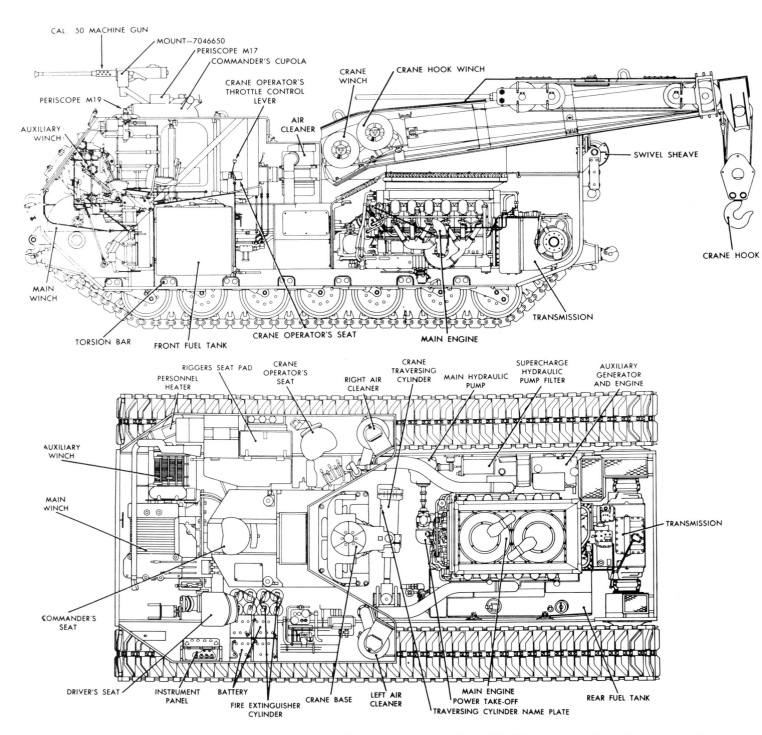

CAL. 50 MACHINE GUN
MOUNT—7046650
PERISCOPE M17
COMMANDER'S CUPOLA
CRANE OPERATOR'S THROTTLE CONTROL LEVER
PERISCOPE M19
AUXILIARY WINCH
CRANE WINCH
CRANE HOOK WINCH
AIR CLEANER
SWIVEL SHEAVE
CRANE HOOK
MAIN WINCH
TRANSMISSION
TORSION BAR
FRONT FUEL TANK
CRANE OPERATOR'S SEAT
MAIN ENGINE

PERSONNEL HEATER
RIGGERS SEAT PAD
CRANE OPERATOR'S SEAT
RIGHT AIR CLEANER
CRANE TRAVERSING CYLINDER
MAIN HYDRAULIC PUMP
SUPERCHARGE HYDRAULIC PUMP FILTER
AUXILIARY GENERATOR AND ENGINE
AUXILIARY WINCH
MAIN WINCH
TRANSMISSION
COMMANDER'S SEAT
DRIVER'S SEAT
INSTRUMENT PANEL
BATTERY
FIRE EXTINGUISHER CYLINDER
CRANE BASE
LEFT AIR CLEANER
MAIN ENGINE POWER TAKE-OFF
TRAVERSING CYLINDER NAME PLATE
REAR FUEL TANK

The sectional drawings above show the internal arrangement of the heavy recovery vehicle M51. Below are two views of the power package removed from the vehicle.

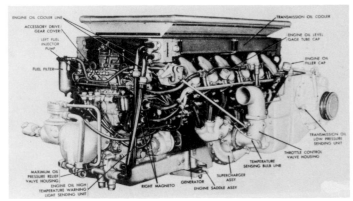

164

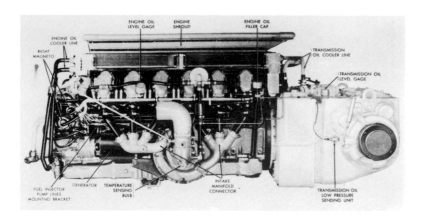

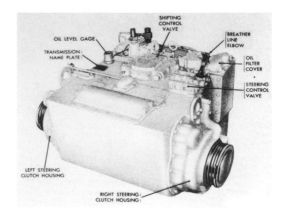

The left side of the power package consisting of the Continental AVSI-1790-6 engine and the XT-1400-2A transmission appears at the top left. Additional views of the transmission are at the top right and below at the left. Details of the suspension on the M51 can be seen below at the right.

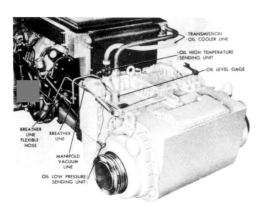

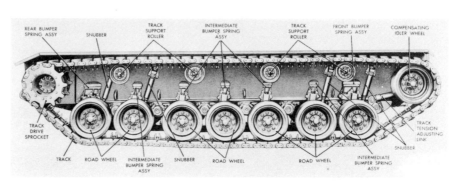

Below is the rear deck of the M51 with the various access doors closed. The heat deflectors (A) are locked in the open position. The exhaust deflector (K) is in place and would have to be opened to permit the cable from the main winch to be extended to the rear of the vehicle. A bottom view of the hull from the front of the vehicle appears at the right.

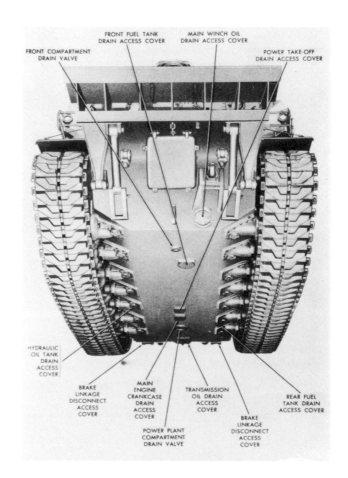

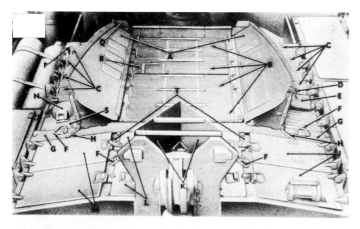

A—HEAT DEFLECTORS
B—ENGINE ACCESS CENTER GRILLE DOOR
C—ENGINE ACCESS SIDE GRILLE DOORS
D—AUXILIARY ENGINE EXHAUST TUBE
E—AUXILIARY ENGINE EXHAUST MUFFLER
F—LIFTING EYE
G—REAR CROSS BEAM
H—HEAT DEFLECTOR RETAINING PIN
J—TRANSMISSION ACCESS RIGHT DOOR

K—EXHAUST DEFLECTOR
L—TRANSMISSION ACCESS CENTER DOOR
M—TRANSMISSION ACCESS LEFT DOOR
N—REAR FUEL TANK FUEL FILLER CAP
   ACCESS COVER
P—FRONT CROSS BEAM
Q—HEAT DEFLECTOR SUPPORT PLATE
R—ACCESS COVER
S—REAR FUEL TANK ACCESS DOOR
T—TRANSMISSION ACCESS DOOR BEAM

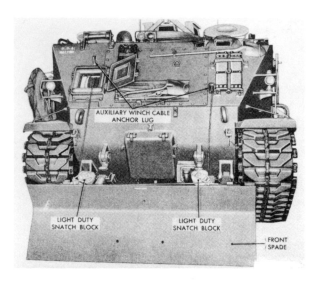

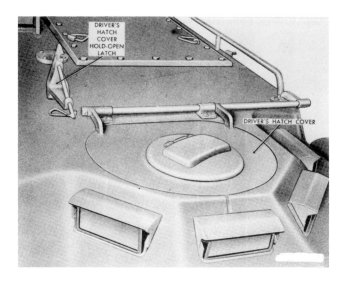

The front spade of the M51 is shown in the lowered position at the top left. At the right are exterior (above) and interior (below) views of the driver's hatch and periscopes. The driver's transmission and winch controls can be seen at the left below.

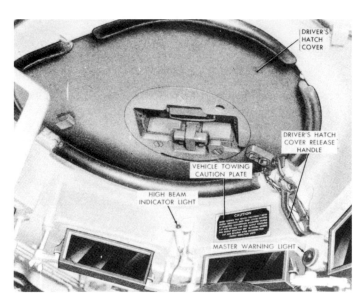

The driver's T-bar steering control appears below in the raised (left) and lowered (right) positions. This permitted operation of the vehicle with the driver standing or sitting in any position of his adjustable seat.

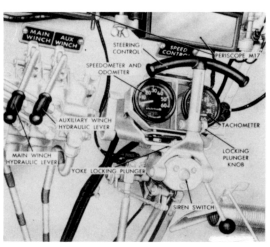

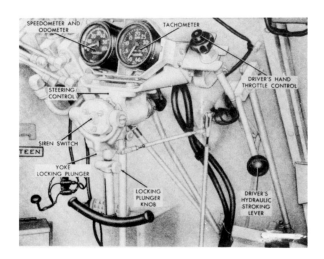

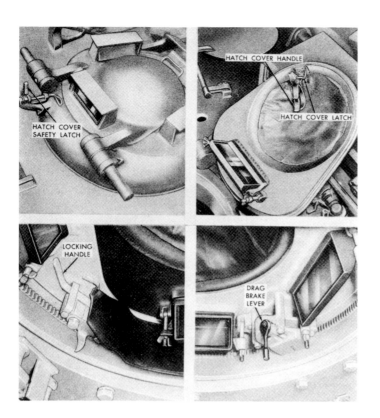

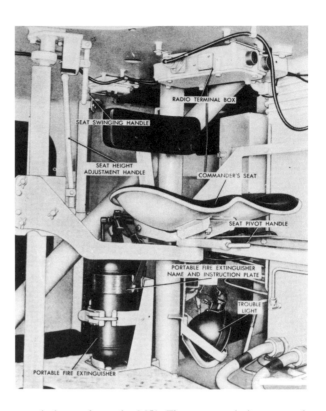

The four views above at the left show exterior and interior details of the commander's cupola on the M51. The commander's seat can be seen above at the right.

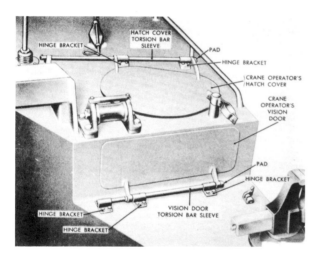

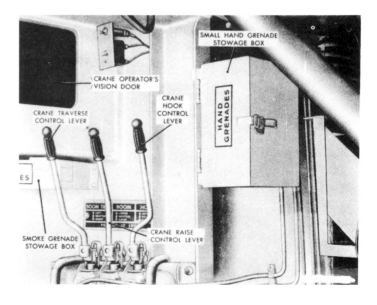

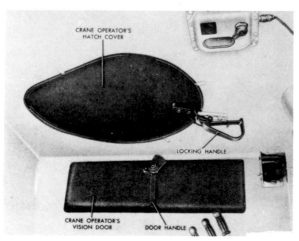

The crane operator's controls are shown directly above. At the left are exterior and interior views of his hatch and vision door.

The heavy recovery vehicle M51 appears above during its test and evaluation program. Below, an M51 of the 3rd Marine Tank Battalion is being unloaded from a landing craft at Dong Ha, Vietnam on 29 June 1967.

A model and sectional drawing of the H1 heavy tank concept presented at the first Question Mark conference appears above. This is the version armed with the 120mm gun. The model and sectional drawing of the H3 concept armed with the 175mm gun from the same conference can be seen at the bottom of the page.

AN IMPROVED HEAVY TANK

Parallel with the development program for the heavy tank T43, other design concepts were being studied as possible candidates to provide a more efficient heavy tank with even greater firepower. In April 1952, the first of what became a series of conferences was held at Detroit Arsenal. Dubbed Operation Question Mark, the objective of this meeting was to bring together the designers and users of armored fighting vehicles and to acquaint each of them with the others problems and requirements. Such a conference enabled the designers to present new vehicle concepts and to receive comments and criticism from those who would have to operate future combat vehicles. It also allowed the users to describe their needs to the people who would design their future equipment. Among the many items presented at the first Question Mark conference were three heavy tank concept proposals. Two of these were identical except for the main armament and both carried the entire four man crew, including the driver, in the turret. One version was armed with the 120mm gun T123E1 and the other with the modified 155mm gun howitzer T7. The armor on the front of both vehicles was five inches at 60 degrees from the vertical and the combat weight was estimated as 50 tons. An interesting feature was the reversed slope on the front hull which, at that time, was expected to offer improved protection against squash head (HEP or HESH) projectiles.

The third heavy tank concept was armed with the 175mm gun T145 in a cleft turret equipped with an automatic loader. The driver rode in the hull and the other four crew members were in the turret. With the same armor basis as the first two proposals, the estimated weight of the 175mm gun tank was about 62 tons. Although none of these proposals were adopted, they provided useful subjects for discussion and many of their features were adapted to other development programs. All three of the proposal concepts utilized a turret ring 108 inches in diameter. Studies indicated that, in addition to the increased space in the turret, such a large ring diameter increased the slope on the turret armor greatly improving its protection. The effect of these large turret rings was evaluated further at Aberdeen starting in 1954 when three turret body castings with 108 inch diameter rings were subjected to ballistic tests. Since no tank hull was available to mount such a large ring, the turret casting was placed on a T43 hull casting to show the relative size. The tests confirmed that the highly sloped turret walls did offer better protection than the standard T43 turret.

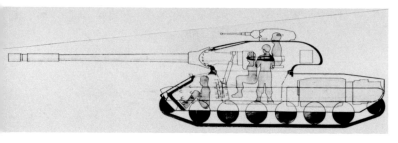

The views above show the sectional drawing and model of the TS-2 heavy gun tank concept armed with the T210 105mm smooth bore cannon in a fully rotating turret. The TS-5 below is armed with the same weapon in a limited traverse mount. A power package consisting of the Continental AOI-1490-1 engine with the XT-500 transmission was proposed for both vehicles, although the sectional drawings appear to be different. Estimated weights for the TS-2 and TS-5 were 45½ tons and 50 tons respectively.

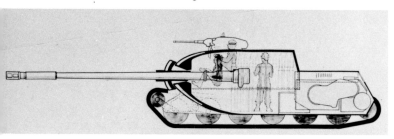

The third Question Mark conference was held at Detroit during June 1954 (Question Mark II in September 1952 had been confined to the consideration of future self-propelled artillery) and several new concepts for improved heavy gun tanks were presented. Six of these were proposed as possible future replacements for the T43E1. Four of the concepts were considered to be fairly short term projects requiring about two years of development time. Two of these, armed with the new 105mm T210 smooth bore cannon, were designated as the TS-2 and the TS-5. The remaining two, mounting the 120mm gun

T123E1, were the TS-6 and the TS-31. The TS designation indicated a tracked vehicle with a short (2 year) development cycle. The TS-2 and the TS-6 concepts carried the main armament in fully rotating turrets with 360 degree traverse. The 105mm gun in the TS-2 was fitted in a rigid mount without a recoil system. The side armor protection on both vehicles was reduced compared to the T43E1 with the combat weights for the TS-2 and the TS-6 estimated as 45 1/2 tons and 54 1/2 tons respectively. The TS-5 and TS-31 proposals utilized a gimbal type mount for the cannon with a limited traverse. They were armed with

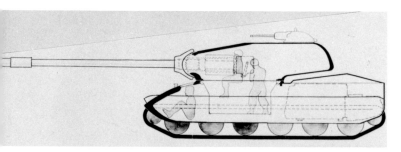

The proposed TS-6 heavy gun tank appears above in the photographs of the sectional drawing and the model. The 120mm gun T123E1 is mounted in a fully rotating turret. Below is the TS-31 concept with the same gun in a limited traverse gimbal mount. The power package proposed for both tanks was the AV-1790-8 engine with the XT-500 transmission. Weights for the TS-6 and TS-31 were estimated to be 54½ tons and 45 tons respectively.

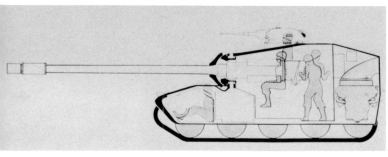

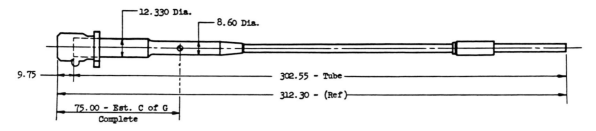

These sketches compare the dimensions of the 105mm smooth bore gun T210 (above) and the 120mm T123E1 rifled gun (below). Note that the two drawings are not to the same scale.

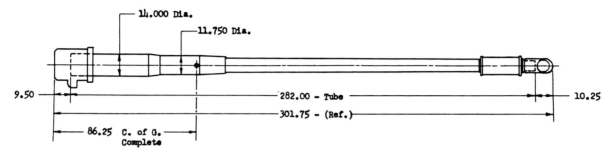

the 105mm gun T210 and the 120mm gun T123E1 respectively. The TS-31 concept was selected for further development as an assault tank and to provide a future replacement for the T43E1, if the T43E2 project and the long term development programs failed.

The two long range concepts presented at the meeting, designated as the TL-4 and the TL-6, were both armed with the smooth bore 105mm gun T210. The first had a fully rotating turret and the latter carried the cannon in a limited traverse gimbal mount. The TL-4 with its rigid gun mount was selected for

development as the future heavy gun tank. A contract was placed with the Ford Motor Company for the design and development of a vehicle based on the TL-4 and it was redesignated as the 105mm gun tank T96. As work on this project progressed, it became obvious that the T96 turret could be mounted on the chassis of the medium gun tank T95 and Ordnance Committee action combined the two programs. The combined vehicle became the 105mm gun tank T95E4 and its further history belongs under that of the T95 program.

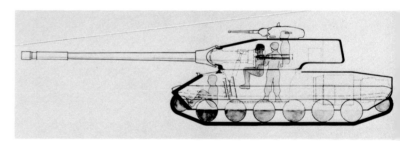

The model and sectional drawing of the TL-4 concept can be seen above. The 105mm smooth bore cannon is rigidly mounted in the fully rotating turret. The TL-6 appears below with the same weapon in a limited traverse gimbal mount. Weights for both concepts were estimated to be about 45 tons.

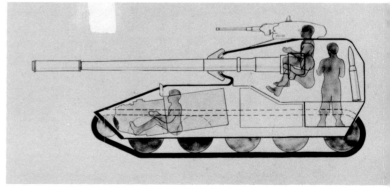

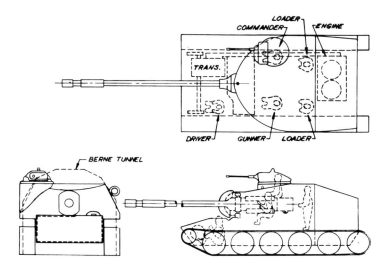

At the left is the original Detroit Arsenal concept drawing for the 120mm gun tank T110. Note the interference of the commander's cupola with the Berne International Tunnel clearance diagram.

The project to develop the TS-31 concept was assigned to Chrysler Corporation and the proposed vehicle was designated as the 120mm gun tank T110. Examination of the initial concept drawings from Detroit Arsenal revealed that the wide cab with the commander's cupola on the right would exceed the dimensions allowed for vehicles to pass through the Berne International Tunnel. This arrangement also limited the field of fire for the cupola machine gun and required additional weight to provide ballistic protection for the tank commander because of the vertical turret walls below the cupola. To correct these problems, Chrysler proposed a modified design with the cab width reduced to 124 inches and the commander relocated to the center rear. This arrangement permitted adequate clearances for the Berne Tunnel and provided a better field of fire for the cupola machine gun. Also, the driver was moved

from the hull to the cab because of control and transmission installation problems as well as large fuel space requirements. However, the Arsenal did not concur with this arrangement and the driver was shifted back into the hull in the second Chrysler proposal. Also, the hull nose was shortened for better obstacle climbing ability. This required some rearrangement of the front idlers and road wheels. The gimbal mount pins for the cannon were changed from the vertical to the horizontal position to reduce weight and to facilitate manufacturing. The fuel tanks were removed from the front hull to provide space for the driver.

Detroit Arsenal now revised their concept of the new vehicle and submitted a second drawing which relocated the transmission from the front hull to the engine compartment. This design required the removal of the cupola to provide adequate clearance for the Berne Tunnel. Fuel was stowed in the front hull with the driver at the left side. At this time, a conventional suspension was specified replacing the flat track design originally required. The flat track suspension supported the top run of track on the road wheels themselves eliminating the track support rollers. Also, a Continental AOI-1490 engine replaced the AV-1790 in the original specification, but the XTG-500 transmission was retained. As its designation indicated, the AOI-1490 was an air-cooled, opposed, fuel injected engine with a displacement of about 1490 cubic inches. It had ten cylinders and developed approximately 700 horsepower at 2800 rpm.

Below are the first (left) and second (right) proposed designs by Chrysler for the 120mm gun tank T110. With the removal of the tracks and the cupola periscope, both concepts meet the Berne Tunnel requirements.

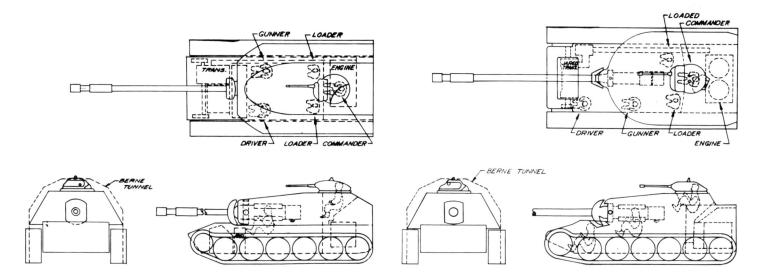

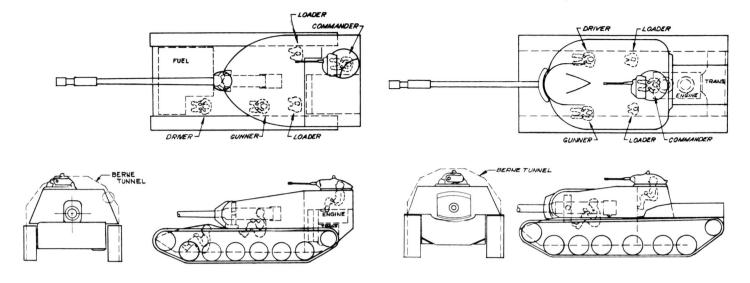

Above, the second Detroit Arsenal concept for the T110 (left) can be compared with the fourth Chrysler proposal (right).

Armament for the T110 was to be the 120mm gun T123E1 modified for installation in a rigid mount. In line with the new requirements, Chrysler began work on a third design, however, numerous problems appeared. To simplify engine and transmission maintenance, it was proposed to mount the power package on rails so that it could slide out of the vehicle through a hinged rear hull plate. Unfortunately, the hinged plate reduced the hull rigidity sufficiently to cause misalignment with the final drive. The engine and transmission also developed severe vibration with this arrangement and several new drive systems were evaluated in an attempt to solve the problem. It also proved to be difficult to provide sufficient grill area to cool the main engine with this configuration.

As a result of the problems with the third design, Chrysler prepared a fourth proposal which placed the AOI-1490 engine and an XTG-510 transmission in the rear of the hull in the conventional manner. Although this arrangement increased the

length of the vehicle, it eliminated many of the problems previously encountered. Infrared shielding was provided on the rear deck with the exhaust gases being ejected, mixed with the engine cooling air, through vertical grill doors at the rear. The 120mm gun was rigidly mounted inside a gimbal ring which permitted a traverse of 15 degrees to each side of center and an elevation range of +20 to -10 degrees. One problem with this design was the requirement for a heavy gun shield. It was nine inches thick and weighed almost two tons. The steeply sloped front of the hull and cab were thickened up to the equivalent of five inches of armor at 60 degrees from the vertical. In addition to the commander's .50 caliber weapon, a .30 caliber coaxial machine gun on the right side of the cannon provided the secondary armament. The gunner's seat was attached to the left side of the mount so that he moved with the weapon when using the T156 telescope which was his primary sighting device. An M16A1 periscopic sight, gimbal mounted in the cab roof and linked to the gun

Below, a model of the 120mm gun tank T110 based on Chrysler's fourth proposal appears at the left with an artist's concept of the same vehicle at the right.

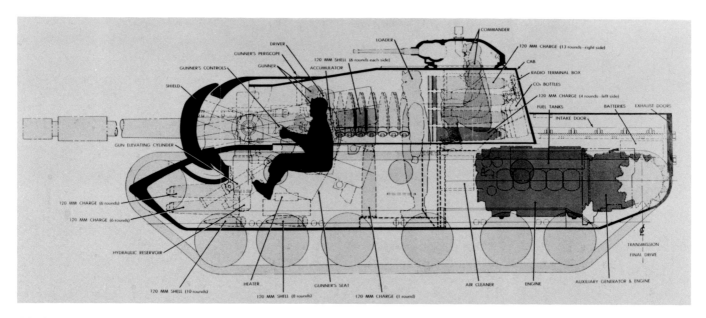

The interior arrangement of the cab type 120mm gun tank T110 with the limited traverse cannon can be seen in these sectional views.

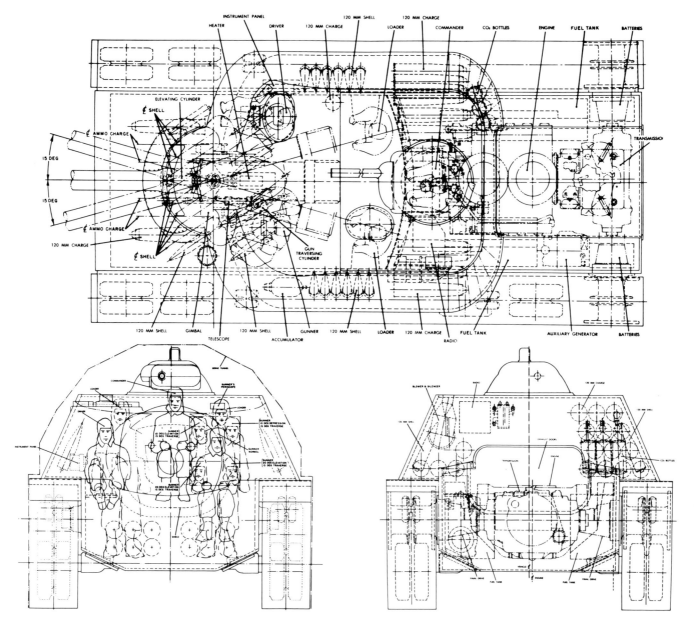

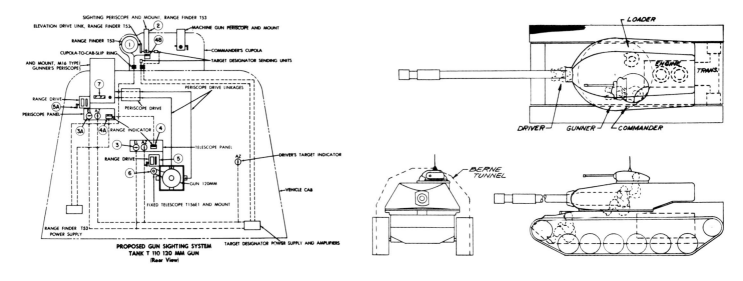

The fire control system for the cab type T110 with the limited traverse main weapon is sketched above at the left. Above at the right is Chrysler's fifth proposal showing the T110 with a full 360 degrees traverse for the turret mounted cannon.

mount, served as a secondary aiming device for the gunner. However, to use it, he had to move to a jump seat attached to the hull side wall. The commander was located in the center rear of the cab and a T53 Optar range finder was planned for installation on his cupola in the final version of this design. The Optar was a pulsed light type range finder which timed the reflection of a light beam from the target to calculate the range. This was, of course, before the time of the laser and it suffered from scattering effects. The installation of the range finder would have required a redesign of the cupola. The driver's position in this proposal was in the right front of the cab alongside the cannon. The location of the driver and gunner required a steeply sloped cab front resulting in very heavy frontal armor to obtain the required ballistic protection. This was a major disadvantage of the cab type arrangement.

Further studies by Chrysler indicated that a heavy assault tank could be designed with a fully rotating turret within the 50 ton weight limit set for the cab type vehicle. The more conventional design also would make use of many standard components thus shortening development time and reducing costs. Such an assault tank was presented in a fifth proposal by Chrysler. The 120mm gun was rigidly mounted in a turret with 360 degree traverse using the standard 85 inch diameter ring from the M103 series. However, the crew arrangement differed from that in the standard tank with the gunner and the tank commander located on the left side of the cannon. The crew was reduced to four with room for only a single loader compared to two in the cab type T110. A power rammer was added to ease his task. The T53 Optar range finder was installed on the left turret wall and could be used by either the gunner or the tank commander. Compared to the cab vehicle, the turreted T110 was expected to have better fire control and to require a shorter time to place the gun on target. It also had a commander's override system which was not possible on the cab type tank. During the final phase of the project, a full size mock-up was

Below is a model and an artist's concept drawing of the 120mm gun tank T110 with the turret mounted cannon having a full 360 degrees traverse. This is the design based on Chrysler's fifth proposal.

175

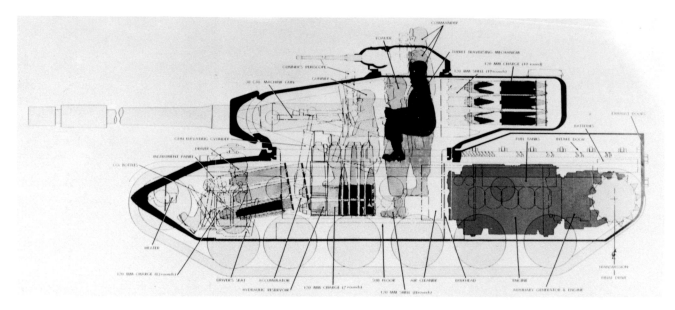

The sectional drawing above shows the internal arrangement of the 120mm gun tank T110 with the cannon mounted in the fully rotating turret.

constructed and presented at Detroit Arsenal. However, by this time, the T43E2 project had been successful and interest had shifted to lighter weight heavy gun tanks for future development. As a result, no further work on the program was authorized.

To obtain additional contributions toward the solution of the heavy tank design problem, proposals were requested from industry. One of these resulted in a contract with the Rheem Manufacturing Company which produced an interesting design concept. Named Project Hunter, the Rheem study investigated a variety of armament, crew arrangements, and other features starting in September 1953. Their final report submitted in June 1955 described a tank of unconventional design armed with a pair of 105mm spin stabilized, rocket boosted guns mounted in an oscillating turret. The Hunter was manned by a crew of four with the driver in the front center of a highly sloped cast armor hull. The gunner was immediately behind the driver and sat between the two 105mm rocket guns in the one man, low silhouette turret. With its automatic loader, each of the rigidly mounted rocket guns had a firing rate of 120 rounds per minute using the seven rounds carried in the

magazine of each loader. With the 80 rounds in the hull, the total 105mm ammunition stowage was 94. Two .30 caliber coaxial machine guns were mounted, one installed outboard of each rocket gun. The tank commander was provided with a cupola in the raised section of the hull just to the rear of the turret. One cupola design was fitted with two .50 caliber antiaircraft machine guns. Alternate arrangements omitted the machine guns or allowed the installation of the standard M1 cupola from the M48A1 tank. The loader was positioned in the hull to the left of the tank commander behind the twin rocket guns. The raised section of the hull at the commander's position limited the turret traverse at an elevation of -10 degrees to 90 degrees to the left or right. A full 360 degrees rotation was possible when the guns were elevated to +20 degrees. An AOI-1490-1 engine in the hull rear powered the vehicle through an hydraulic transmission system. This arrangement eliminated the drive sprockets and used separate hydraulic motors installed in each of the 12 road wheels. This made it possible to use a lightweight rubber band track assembled from six foot sections. With such a drive system, the tank could still move despite the

The dimensions of the Hunter proposed by Rheem can be seen in the front and side views sketched below. The machine gun cupola for the tank commander was omitted in this version of the design.

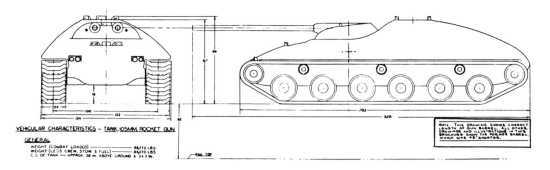

VEHICULAR CHARACTERISTICS - TANK, 105MM ROCKET GUN

GENERAL

WEIGHT (COMBAT LOADED) —————— 88,770 LBS
WEIGHT (LESS CREW, STOW. & FUEL) —— 84,370 LBS
C.G. OF TANK - APPROX 38 IN. ABOVE GROUND & 14.3 IN.

NOTE: THIS DRAWING SHOWS CORRECT LENGTH OF GUN BARREL. ALL OTHER DRAWINGS AND ILLUSTRATIONS IN THIS BROCHURE SHOW THE FORMER BARREL WHICH WAS 42" SHORTER.

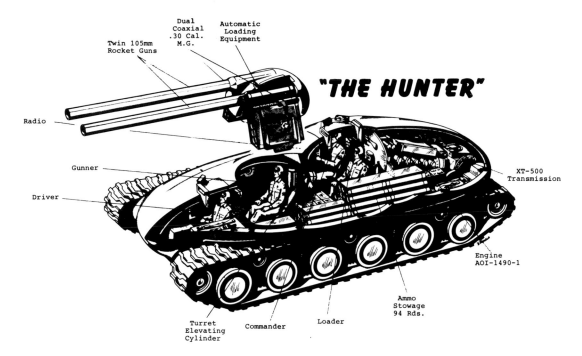

"THE HUNTER"

Twin 105mm Rocket Guns
Dual Coaxial .30 Cal. M.G.
Automatic Loading Equipment
Radio
Gunner
Driver
XT-500 Transmission
Engine AOI-1490-1
Turret Elevating Cylinder
Commander
Loader
Ammo Stowage 94 Rds.

The cutaway drawing of the Hunter above reveals the internal arrangement of the proposed tank. The estimated combat weight of the vehicle was 45 tons.

loss of a track or several road wheels. An alternate design was prepared using the XT-500 transmission with conventional drive sprockets and tracks.

The Hunter, with its highly sloped configuration and low silhouette, provided exceptionally good protection and siliceous cored armor was utilized in the front of both the hull and the turret. This type of armor was cast around a fused silica core and it was particularly effective against shaped charge rounds. The top rear deck was hinged just in front of the commander's cupola and it could be raised by an hydraulic cylinder. This allowed easy access to the vehicle for maintenance and stowage and also provided a quick emergency exit for the crew.

A model of the Hunter is shown directly below. In the sketches at the right, the frontal area of the Hunter is compared with that of the 120mm gun tank T43 (top) and the use of the hinged rear deck to allow the crew to escape from the vehicle is illustrated (bottom).

Although the Hunter concept had many innovative features, long range development interest at that time was concentrated on armored vehicles which could be transported by air, such as the Rex tank and other vehicles studied under the ASTRON project. As a result no further work was authorized on the Hunter.

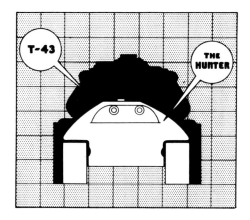

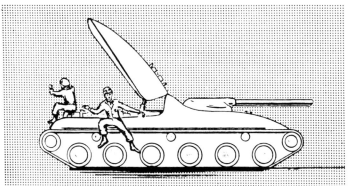

177

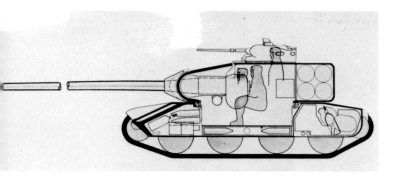

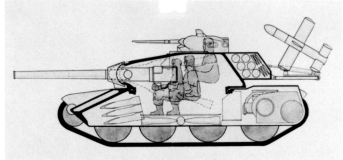

The three concepts proposed for the heavy gun tank role at the Question Mark IV conference are shown here. Above, the R33 is at the left and the R8 is at the right. The R29 is below at the left.

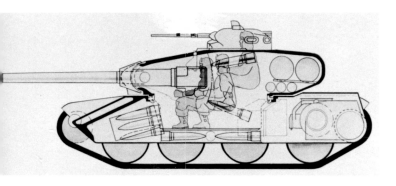

The Question Mark IV conference in August 1955 included three concepts proposed as possible replacements for the T43E1. All of these utilized new lighter weight main armament and siliceous cored armor. The first proposal, designated as R33, was armed with a 120mm gas gun using a mixture of hydrogen, helium, and oxygen as the propellant. It was expected to defeat six inches of armor at 60 degrees from the vertical at a 2000 yard range using a 30mm penetrator and it also could fire 120mm chemical energy rounds at lower velocities. The propellant was separated from the crew in the turret bustle. A gas turbine was proposed as the power plant for this vehicle and it had an estimated weight of 31 tons.

The other two concepts reflected the increasing interest in guided missiles as main armament for tanks. They were armed with a low velocity 120mm gun firing chemical energy ammunition for use at ranges below 1000 yards. For longer ranges, the R8 concept carried eight Dart missiles and the R29 had ten modified D40 missiles. With estimated weights of 30-31 tons, these vehicles were to be powered by the AOI-628 or the AOSI-628 engines. All three proposed tanks located the driver in the turret.

In the sketch at the right, a mobile nuclear power plant provides power for an entire convoy of electrically driven vehicles.

During this period, all three branches of the military service were investigating the possible use of nuclear power in their operations. For the Army, an obvious possible application was as a power plant for armored vehicles. Some studies considered the development of armored carriers for a small nuclear plant to generate electricity to power an entire convoy of vehicles. Such an arrangement would have saved each vehicle's fuel supply until it reached the area of operations. Other projects investigated the development of nuclear power plants for individual vehicles. The Question Mark III and IV conferences both included concepts for a nuclear powered tank. The first of these, armed with a modified 105mm gun T140, was designated as the TV-1 and was estimated to weigh about 70 tons with 14 inches of armor on the front of the hull and turret. Its nuclear powered, open air cycle, gas turbine could operate at full load for 500 hours without refueling. The TV-1 designation indicated a tracked vehicle with a very long development cycle under the terminology of Question Mark III. By the time of Question Mark IV in August 1955, advances in nuclear technology had indicated the possible development of a lighter weight atomic powered tank. The R32 concept presented at that

A model of the 105mm gun nuclear powered tank TV-1 proposed at the Question Mark III conference is shown above and below at the left. The internal arrangement of the vehicle can be seen in the sectional view below at the right.

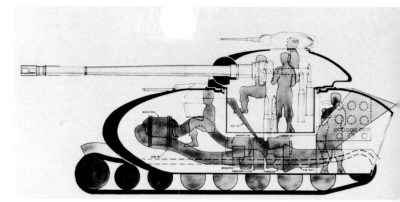

meeting showed a 50-ton vehicle armed with a modified 90mm T208 smooth bore cannon. Such a tank was expected to have a 4000 mile cruising range, but the front armor protection was limited to 4.8 inches at 60 degrees from the vertical. Needless to say, any

atomic powered vehicle would have been extremely expensive and the radiation level would have required frequent crew changes to avoid excessive exposure. Despite these obvious drawbacks, studies as late as 1959 considered the feasibility of mounting a nuclear propulsion system on the M103 chassis. This, of course, would have been only a propulsion test bed and the tank's turret would have been removed to make room for the reactor.

A side view drawing of the gun armed nuclear powered tank proposed at the Question Mark IV conference is at the left.

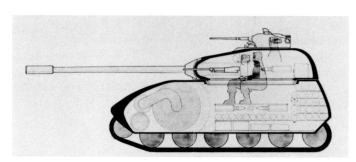

The existance of the Soviet Stalin III (top left) and T-10 (top right) heavy tanks provided the major incentive for the development of the U.S. heavy tanks after World War II.

CONCLUSION

If the World War I Mark VIII is excepted, the interest of the U.S. Army in heavy tanks spanned about two decades and during that time only a single battalion saw troop service in Europe. The reasons for such limited application of a weapon which took so long to develop may be found in the Armored Force doctrine that evolved at the beginning of World War II. This operational concept envisioned fast moving armored units penetrating deeply into enemy areas and, if necessary, bypassing strongly fortified localities. Such a role was suitable for a light tank and the early armored divisions were organized with two light tank regiments and only one with medium tanks. Prior to his death in 1941, General Chaffee was not fully convinced of the value of the medium tank and preferred to wait for operational experience with the new M3 before increasing their numbers in the armored division. At that time, it was expected that a few heavy tanks might be useful for reducing strong points, but much of the impetus for their early development came from the rumored use of such tanks by the Germans in Poland and France. Later, after full acceptance of the medium tank, the heavy M6 was rejected on the grounds that its thicker armor and greater firepower did not compensate for the heavier weight. Faced with the logistics of a worldwide war, the Army considered it preferable to ship two 30-ton tanks instead of one which weighed 60 tons. Also, loading and unloading was much easier for the lighter vehicles in the limited port facilities found in some foreign operational areas. In addition, from a tactical standpoint, it often was better to have a large number of lighter tanks than a few heavy

ones. Thus it would be possible to send columns down several roads rather than being confined to a single line of advance.

After the rejection of the heavy tank M6, wartime development was concentrated on the medium tank T20 series. However, after the appearance of the German Tiger I, the armor and firepower were increased and it eventually appeared as the M26 Pershing. For a short period, it was reclassified as a heavy tank, primarily for morale purposes. However, the encounters with German Panthers and Tigers in Europe during the final months of the war allowed the Ordnance Department to initiate several development programs for a true heavy tank. Although none of these were available prior to the end of hostilities, they provided valuable information for later development. The experience of the tank versus tank battles with the heavy German armor also resulted in a heavy tank being included in the requirements specified for the postwar army by the various review boards. This requirement, together with the existence of the Soviet Stalin III, resulted in the T43 heavy tank program. With the start of the Cold War, the presence of the Stalin III and its successor the T-10 served as a constant reminder that a powerfully armed heavy tank might be required in the future. Even so, there was little enthusiasm for such a vehicle and production for the Army was limited to 80 tanks. These eventually armed the single battalion in Europe.

The Marine Corps view of armor differed from that of the U.S. Army. The primary task of Marine Corps tanks was infantry support. In this role, the heavy armor and firepower were important advantages and the limitations imposed by the short cruising range and reduced speed were of less significance. Thus the Marine Corps accepted 220 out of the total of 300 heavy tanks produced and proceeded to upgrade them to the M103A1 configuration. Later, after the introduction of the diesel powered M60, they supported a modernization program to bring their tanks up to the latest standard in propulsion and fire control systems. The modernized tank became the M103A2 and was the last of the series on active service. As in the Army, the heavy tank was eventually replaced in the Marine Corps by the M60 series of main battle tanks and the separate types of medium and heavy vehicles disappeared. The new M1 and M1A1 main battle tanks are, of course, heavy tanks, but they are driven by such powerful engines that their mobility exceeds that of some earlier light tanks.

The designers of the experimental heavy tanks attempted to produce a fighting vehicle which would meet the needs of future combat conditions. However, heavy armor has never been popular during

peacetime or even during wartime maneuvers. At those times, it is just so much dead weight that decreases vehicle mobility. The situation changes as soon as the troops come under enemy fire and the value of thick armor is greatly appreciated. From World War II to Vietnam, troops in action improvised additional protection for their tanks. These efforts ranged from extra track shoes attached to the hull and turret to layers of cement and sandbags. Another area neglected during peacetime years has been secondary armament. Most American tanks have been armed with a single rifle caliber coaxial machine gun and a .50 caliber machine gun for the tank commander. However, as soon as the tank goes into battle, all sorts of additional secondary armament are improvised. In Vietnam, these ranged from an additional coaxial machine gun replacing the gunner's telescope to an extra machine gun on the turret roof for the loader. Obviously, there is a need for greater secondary firepower when fighting enemy infantry. Perhaps the new main battle tanks with their heavy armor and additional machine gun will more adequately meet these true battlefield requirements.

Below, a U.S. Marine Corps 120mm gun tank M103A2 is operating at Camp Pendleton, California. This was the final version of the American heavy tank to see troop service before it was replaced by the all purpose or main battle tank.

PART III

REFERENCE DATA

A United States Marine Corps 120mm gun tank M103A2.

Above is a pilot 120mm gun tank M103A1E1. Note that this particular tank retains the full blast deflector on the cannon. Below is a Marine Corps M103A1 at Quantico, Virginia during 1959.

A 120mm gun tank T43E1 is shown above during tests at Aberdeen Proving Ground, Maryland on 10 September 1953. Below, another T43E1 is under evaluation by the Army Field Forces Board Number 2 at Fort Knox, Kentucky on 24 August 1955.

Above, superheavy tank T28, pilot number 1, is firing its 105mm gun at Aberdeen Proving Ground during the test program in March 1947. Below, a heavy recovery vehicle M51 from the 2nd Marine Division takes a light tank in tow during operations in the Dominican Republic on 13 May 1965.

There were many changes in the engineering test procedures used to evaluate the various vehicles during the period covered in this book. Also, the relative importance of certain vehicle characteristics shifted with changes in vehicle design and the mission that was to be accomplished. For example, trench crossing ability was a major consideration for the World War I designed Mark VIII and its ability to bridge a 16-foot gap was almost twice that of the last American heavy tank, the M103A2. Although the Mark VIII weighed over forty tons, its armor protection was equivalent only to the light tanks of the period. By the start of World War II, the concept of a heavy tank had changed to include heavy armor protection and firepower superior to that of the medium tank. Although the test methods varied during the period covered, an effort has been made to provide equivalent data to permit a better comparison of the different vehicles.

If available, original drawings were used to obtain dimensional data. If these could not be located, dimensions were taken from the characteristics sheets or the test reports from Aberdeen Proving Ground or Fort Knox. Some of the drawing dimensions were for reference only and would obviously vary on the actual tanks. For example, the ground clearance and the fire height, the latter defined as the distance from the ground to the center line of the main weapon bore at zero elevation, would change with load on the vehicle and increased spring compression. However, the design reference values are quoted to permit comparison between the vehicles.

A few other terms used in the data sheets might need clarification. The ground contact length at zero penetration is the distance between the centers of the front and rear road wheels. Unless otherwise specified, this is the value used to calculate the ground contact area and then the ground pressure using the combat weight of the vehicle. The tread is the distance between the centerlines of the tracks. When available, gross and net values are quoted for maximum engine horsepower and torque. The gross horsepower and torque refer to the output obtained with

only those accessories essential to engine operation. The effect of such items as generators and air cleaners is neglected. The net values are those obtained with the engine installed in the vehicle using all of its normal accessories.

Armor protection is specified by type, thickness and the angle with the vertical. This angle is measured between a vertical plane and the plate surface as indicated by the angle alpha in the sketch. Also, in this two dimensional drawing, the angle of obliquity is shown by the angle beta. This is defined as the angle between a line perpendicular to the armor plate and the path of a projectile impacting the armor. This angle is used to specify armor penetration performance.

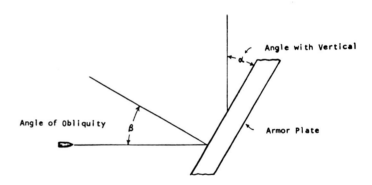

When available, weights are listed for the vehicles unstowed and combat loaded. The combat weight included the crew and a full load of fuel and ammunition. Actual weights often varied widely due to variations in casting thicknesses, vehicle stowage, etc. For single experimental vehicles, the exact weight is quoted if possible. However, for some of these tanks only approximate or estimated weights could be obtained. Average values for production vehicles are usually rounded off to the nearest 1000 pounds. Since the stowage frequently varied during the life of the vehicle, the data are quoted for the items that were standard during its period of greatest use.

HEAVY TANK Mark VIII

GENERAL DATA

Crew:	8 to 11	men
Length:	410.5	inches
Width: Over sponsons	144.0	inches
Width: Sponsons and guns retracted	108.0	inches
Height: Over commander's cupola	123.0	inches
Tread:	69.5	inches
Ground Clearance:	20.8	inches
Weight, Combat Loaded:	86,900	pounds
Weight, Unstowed:	81,000	pounds
Power to Weight Ration: Gross	7.8	hp/ton
Ground Pressure: Zero penetration	16.1	psi
1 inch penetration	15.0	psi
2 inch penetration	8.6	psi
5 inch penetration	5.9	psi

ARMOR

Type: Rolled face-hardened steel plate; Riveted assembly

Thickness:	Actual	Angle/Vertical
Hull, Upper Front	0.47 inches (12mm)	28 degrees
Hull Sides	0.47 inches (12mm)	0 degrees
* Hull Rear	0.63 inches (16mm)	0 degrees
Main Turret Sides	0.63 inches (16mm)	0 degrees
Cupola Sides	0.63 inches (16mm)	0 degrees
Sponson Sides	0.47 inches (12mm)	0 degrees
Top	0.24 inches (6mm)	80 to 90 degrees
* Top Rear	0.39 inches (10mm)	80 degrees
Floor	0.31-0.24 inches (8-6mm)	60 to 90 degrees

ARMANENT

(2) Hotchkiss 2.244 inch (57mm) 6 pounder Mark II Guns in side sponsons
** (5) .30 caliber Browning tank machine guns in ball mounts

AMMUNITION

208 rounds 6 pounder
15,100 rounds .30 caliber

SIGHTING AND VISION DEVICES

Driver: Flap in turret front, Vision slots (3), Hand held periscope (1)
Commnader: Hatch, Cupola vision slots (4), Hand held periscope (1)
Gunner, 6 pounder, left: Vision slots (4), Pistol ports (4), Telescopic sight (1)
Gunner, 6 pounder, right: Vision slots (3), Pistol ports (3), Telescopic sight (1)
Machine Gunner, turret front: Vision slots (3), Peepholes in MG ball mounts (2)
Machine Gunner, turret rear: Vision slots (3), Peephole in MG ball mount (1)
Machine Gunner, hull left: Peephole in MG ball mount (1), Pistol port (1)
Machine Gunner, hull right: Peephole in MG ball mount (1), Pistol port (1)
Total Vision Slots: (20), Pilot tank (22)
Total Pistol Ports: (9), Pilot tank (12)

* Thicker armor protects fuel tanks in rear of hull
** Pilot tank armed with (7) Hotchkiss .303 machine guns

ENGINE

Make and Model: Liberty 12
Type: 12 cylinder, 4 cycle, 45 degree vee
Cooling System: Liquid   Ignition: Delco

Displacement:	1649.34 cubic inches
Bore and Stroke:	5 x 7 inches
Compression Ratio:	4.9:1
Gross Horsepower:	338 hp at 1400 rpm
Weight:	850 pounds, dry
Fuel: Gasoline	240 gallons

POWER TRAIN

Clutch: Compound, friction cone and splined coupling
Bevel Gear Ratio: 14:46
Transmission: Epicyclic, 2 speeds forward, 2 reverse
    Gear Ratios: low 5:1 high 1.285:1 Both forward and reverse
Steering: Epicyclic
Brakes: Mechanical, external contracting
Final Drive: Chain and sprocket
    Ratio, rear chain sprocket to roller pinion: 12:23
    Ratio, roller pinion to road track driving wheel (sprocket): 9:35
Road Track Driving Wheel (Sprocket): At rear of vehicle with 35 teeth
    Diameter: 39.237 inches

RUNNING GEAR

Suspension: Rigid
    28 lower track rollers w/spacers and spring plates (14/track)
    30 lower track rollers w/o spacers and spring plates (15/track)
    2 top track return rollers (1/track)
    Adjustable idler at front of each track
    Idler Size: 40.187 inches in diameter
Tracks: Continuous linked
    Type: 0.31 inch (8mm) thick dished armor plate, 26.5 inch width,
        with integral grouser
    Pitch: 11.154 inches
    Shoes per Vehicle: 156 (78/track)
    Ground Contact Length: 102 inches, zero penetration
                           109 inches, 1 inch penetration
                           190 inches, 2 inch penetration
                           277 inches, 5 inch penetration

ELECTRICAL SYSTEM

Nominal Voltage: 6 and 12 volts DC (pilot tank 6 volts)
Generators: (1) 12 volt ignition generator, (2) 6 volt generators for lights,
        batteries, and spark
Battery: (2) 12 volts, (1) 6 volts (pilot tank (1) 6 volts)

COMMUNICATIONS

Semaphore signaling device on hull roof
Interphone connecting the tank commander with the driver, both 6
        pounder gunners, and the engine room mechanic

FIRE PROTECTION

(8) Pyrene fire extinguishers (3 on each side door, 2 in engine compartment)

PERFORMANCE

Maximum Speed: High gear	5.5 miles/hour
Low gear	1.4 miles/hour
Maximum Drawbar Pull:	48,000 pounds
Maximum Grade:	84 per cent
Maximum Trench:	16 feet
Maximum Vertical Wall:	54 inches
Maximum Fording Depth:	34 inches
Minimum Turning Circle: (diameter)	40.5 feet
Cruising Range: Roads	approx. 40 miles

HEAVY TANK T1E1

GENERAL DATA

Crew:	6	men
Length: Gun forward, w/stowage boxes	332.0	inches
Length: Gun to rear, w/stowage boxes	297.0	inches
Length: Without gun, w/stowage boxes	297.0	inches
Gun Overhang: Gun forward	35.0	inches
Width: Over track armor	123.0	inches
Height: To turret roof	118.0	inches
Tread:	93.9	inches
Ground clearance:	20.5	inches
Fire Height:	approx. 97	inches
Turret Ring Diameter: (inside)	69.0	inches
Weight, Combat Loaded:	127,000	pounds
Weight, Unstowed:	approx. 120,500	pounds
Power to Weight Ratio: Net	11.0	hp/ton
Gross	15.1	hp/ton
Ground Pressure: Zero penetration	13.1	psi

ARMOR

Type: Turret, cast homogenous steel; Hull, cast homogenous steel; Welded assembly

Hull Thickness:	Actual	Angle w/Vertical
Front, Upper	3.25 inches (83mm)	30 degrees
Lower	4.0-2.75 inches (102-70mm)	0 to 60 degrees
Sides, Upper	1.75 inches (44mm)	20 degrees
Lower	2.75 inches (70mm)	0 degrees (incl. track armor)
Rear	1.63 inches (41mm)	17 degrees
Top	1.0 inches (25mm)	90 degrees
Floor	1.0 inches (25mm)	90 degrees
Turret Thickness:		
Gun Shield	equals 4.0 inches (102mm)	0 degrees
Front	3.25 inches (83mm)	7 degrees
Sides	3.25 inches (83mm)	0 degrees
Rear	3.25 inches (83mm)	0 degrees
Top	1.0 inches (25mm)	90 degrees

ARMAMENT

Primary: 3 inch Gun M7 and 37mm Gun M6 in Combination Mount T49 in turret

Traverse: Electric and manual	360 degrees
Traverse Rate: (max)	20 seconds/360 degrees
Elevation: Manual	+30 to −10 degrees
Firing Rate: (max)	15 rounds/minute (3 inch)
	30 rounds/minute (37mm)
Loading System:	Manual
Stabilizer System:	Elevation only

Secondary:
- (2) .50 caliber MG HB M2 in Mount T52 in hull front
- (1) .30 caliber MG M1919A4 in bow mount (fixed)
- * (1) .30 caliber MG M1919A4 flexible AA mount on turret roof
- Provision for (2) .45 caliber SMG M1928A1

AMMUNITION

75 rounds 3 inch	24 hand grenades
202 rounds 37mm	
6900 rounds .50 caliber	
1200 rounds .45 caliber	
5500 rounds .30 caliber	

FIRE CONTROL AND VISION EQUIPMENT

Primary Weapon:	Direct	Indirect
	Periscope M8 with Telescope M39 Telescope M15	Gunner's Quadrant M1

Vision Devices:	Direct	Indirect
Driver	Hatch	Periscope M6 (2)
Bow Gunner	None	Periscope M6 (1) and Protectoscope (1)
Ammunition Passer	Hatch and hull pistol ports (2)	Protectoscopes (2) in hull pistol port covers
Commander	Hatch	Periscope M6 (1)
Gunner	None	Periscope M8 (1)
Loader	Pistol port (1)	Periscope M6 (1) and Protectoscope (1) in pistol port cover

Total Periscopes: M6 (5), M8 (1)
Total Protectoscopes: (4)
Total Pistol Ports: Hull (2), Turret (1)
* (1) .50 caliber MG HB M2 may be substituted for .30 caliber AA MG

ENGINE

Make and Model: Wright G-200 Model 795C9GC1	
Type: 9 cylinder, 4 cycle, radial	
Cooling System: Air Ignition: Magneto	
Displacement:	1823 cubic inches
Bore and Stroke:	6.125 x 6.875 inches
Compression Ratio:	4.92:1
Net Horsepower (max): Governed speed	700 hp at 1950 rpm
Gross Horsepower (max):	960 hp at 2300 rpm
Gross Torque (max): Governed speed	1810 ft-lb at 1950 rpm
Weight:	1350 pounds, dry
Fuel: 80 octane gasoline	464 gallons
Engine Oil:	72 quarts

POWER TRAIN

Transmission: Electric drive with speed infinitely variable both forward and reverse
Steering: Electric
Brakes: Electric

Final Drive: Spur gear	Gear Ratio: 10:1

Drive Sprocket: At rear of vehicle with 14 teeth
   Pitch Diameter: 26.806 inches

RUNNING GEAR

Suspension: Horizontal volute spring
   16 dual wheels in 8 bogies (4 bogies/track)
   Tire Size: 18 x 7 inches
   8 dual track return rollers (4/track)
   Dual adjustable idler at front of each track
   Idler Tire Size: 30 x 7 inches
   2 dual auxiliary idlers (1/track) between main idler and front bogie
Tracks: Outside guide T31*
   Type: (T31) Double pin, 25.75 inch width, rubber backed steel
   Pitch: 6 inches
   Shoes per Vehicle: 198 (99/track)
   Ground Contact Length: 187.9 inches

ELECTRICAL SYSTEM

Nominal Voltage: 24 volts DC
Battery Charging Generator: (1) 24 volts, 200 amperes, driven by power take-off from main engine
Auxiliary Generator: (1) 30 volts, 50 amperes, driven by the auxiliary engine
Battery: (2) 12 volts in series

COMMUNICATIONS

Radio: SCR 508, 528, or 538 in rear of turret, SCR 506 (command tanks only) in right sponson
Interphone: Part of radio, 6 stations

FIRE AND GAS PROTECTION

(6) 10 pound carbon dioxide, fixed
(2) 4 pound carbon dioxide, portable
(4) 1½ quart decontaminating apparatus M2

PERFORMANCE

Maximum Speed: Sustained, level road	20 miles/hour
Maximum Grade:	55 per cent
Maximum Trench:	11 feet
Maximum Vertical Wall:	36 inches
Maximum Fording Depth:	48 inches
Minimum Turning Circle: (diameter)	pivot
Cruising Range: Roads	approx. 100 miles

* Center guide added later to these tracks and the outside guides removed

HEAVY TANK T1E2, Pilot

GENERAL DATA

Crew:	6 or 7	men
Length: Gun forward	320	inches
Length: Gun to rear	285	inches
Length: Without gun	285	inches
Gun Overhang: Gun forward	35	inches
Width: Over track armor	123	inches
Height: Over cupola	122	inches
Tread:	93.9	inches
Ground Clearance:	21	inches
Fire Height:	approx. 97	inches
Turret Ring Diameter: (inside)	69.0	inches
Weight, Combat Loaded:	approx. 126,000	pounds
Weight, Unstowed:	approx. 120,000	pounds
Power to Weight Ratio: Net	13.1	hp/ton
Gross	15.2	hp/ton
Ground Pressure: Zero penetration	13.0	psi

ARMOR

Type: Turret, cast homogenous steel; Hull, cast homogenous steel; Welded assembly

Hull Thickness:	Actual	Angle w/Vertical
Front	equals 3.0 inches (76mm)	0 degrees
Sides, Front	equals 2.5 inches (64mm)	0 degrees
Rear	equals 2.0 inches (51mm)	0 degrees
Rear	equals 2.0 inches (51mm)	0 degrees
Top	1.0 inches (25mm)	90 degrees
Floor	1.0 inches (25mm)	90 degrees
Turret Thickness:		
Gun Shield	equals 3.0 inches (76mm)	0 degrees
Front	equals 3.0 inches (76mm)	0 degrees
Sides	equals 3.0 inches (76mm)	0 degrees
Rear	equals 3.0 inches (76mm)	0 degrees
Top	1.0 inches (25mm)	90 degrees

ARMAMENT

Primary: 3 inch Gun T12 and 37mm Gun M5E1 in combination mount in turret

Traverse: Electric and manual	360 degrees
Traverse Rate: (max)	20 seconds/360 degrees
Elevation: Manual	+30 to −10 degrees
Firing Rate: (max)	15 rounds/minute (3 inch)
	30 rounds/minute (37mm)
Loading System:	Manual
Stabilizer System:	Elevation only

Secondary:
- (1) .50 caliber MG HB M2 in AA rotor mount in rear of turret roof
- (2) .50 caliber MG HB M2 in flexible twin mount in hull front
- (2) .30 caliber MG M1919A4 in fixed bow mounts (elevation +10 to −5 deg.)
- (1) .30 caliber MG M1919A4 in commander's cupola
- Provision for (2) .45 caliber SMG M1928A1

AMMUNITION

75 rounds 3 inch	24 hand grenades
200 rounds 37mm	
8000 rounds .50 caliber	
1200 rounds .45 caliber	
10,000 rounds .30 caliber	

FIRE CONTROL AND VISION EQUIPMENT

Primary Weapon:	Direct	Indirect
	Periscope M1 with	Gunner's Quadrant M1
	Telescope T32	
	Telescope M15	

Vision Devices	Direct	Indirect
Driver	Hatch	Protectoscope (1)
Bow Gunner	None	Protectoscope (1)
Ammunition Passer	Hatch and hull pistol ports (2)	Protectoscopes (2) in pistol port covers
Commander	Hatch and vision slots (2)	Protectoscope (1)
Gunner	None	Periscope M1 (1)
Loader	Pistol port (1)	Protectoscope (1) in pistol port cover

Total Periscopes: M1 (1)
Total Protectoscopes: (6)
Total Pistol Ports: Hull (2), Turret (1)
Total Vision Slots: (2)

ENGINE

Make and Model: Wright G-200 Model 781C9GC1	
Type: 9 cylinder, 4 cycle, radial	
Cooling System: Air Ignition: Magneto	
Displacement:	1823 cubic inches
Bore and Stroke:	6.125 x 6.875 inches
Compression Ratio:	4.92:1
Net Horsepower (max):	825 hp at 2300 rpm
Gross Horsepower (max):	960 hp at 2300 rpm
Gross Torque (max):	1830 ft-lb at 2100 rpm
Weight:	1350 pounds, dry
Fuel: 80 octane gasoline	477 gallons
Engine Oil:	72 quarts

POWER TRAIN

Transmission: Timken mechanical w/Twin Disc torque converter model 16001, w/Hycon hydraulic control, 2 speeds forward, 1 reverse

Gear Ratios:	1st 1.61:1	reverse 1.61:1
	2nd 0.22:1	

Steering: Controlled differential
Gear Ratio: 0.62:1   Steering Ratio: 1.62:1
Brakes: Budd disc, mechanical and Hycon hydraulic control
Final Drive: Compensating differential   Gear Ratio: 5:1
Drive Sprocket: At rear of vehicle with 14 teeth
Pitch Diameter: 26.806 inches

RUNNING GEAR

Suspension: Horizontal volute spring
- 16 dual wheels in 8 bogies (4 bogies/track)
- Tire Size: 18 x 7 inches
- 8 dual track return rollers (4/track)
- Dual adjustable idler at front of each track
- Idler Tire Size: 30 x 7 inches
- 2 dual auxiliary idlers (1/track) between main idler and front bogie

Tracks: Outside guide w/removable rubber track pads
- Type: Double pin, 25.75 inch width, rubber backed steel
- Pitch: 6 inches
- Shoes per Vehicle: 198 (99/track)
- Ground Contact Length: 187.9 inches

ELECTRICAL SYSTEM

Nominal Voltage: 24 volts DC
Main Generator: (1) 24 volts, 50 amperes, driven by power take-off from main engine
Auxiliary Generator: (1) 30 volts, 50 amperes, driven by the auxiliary engine
Battery: (2) 12 volts in series

COMMUNICATIONS

Radio: SCR 508, 528, or 538 in rear of turret, SCR 506 (command tanks only) in right sponson.
Interphone: Part of radio, 6 stations

FIRE PROTECTION

- (6) 10 pound carbon dioxide, fixed
- (2) 4 pound carbon dioxide, portable

PERFORMANCE

Maximum Speed: Sustained, level road	22 miles/hour
Maximum Grade:	60 per cent
Maximum Trench:	11 feet
Maximum Vertical Wall:	36 inches
Maximum Fording Depth:	48 inches
Minimum Turning Circle: (diameter)	74 feet
Cruising Range: Roads	approx. 100 miles

GENERAL DATA

Crew:	6	men
Length: Gun forward, w/stowage boxes	332.0	inches
Length: Gun to rear, w/stowage boxes	297.0	inches
Length: Without gun, w/stowage boxes	297.0	inches
Gun Overhang: Gun forward	35.0	inches
Width: Over track armor	123.0	inches
Height: To turret roof	118.0	inches
Tread:	93.9	inches
Ground Clearance:	20.5	inches
Fire Height:	approx. 97	inches
Turret Ring Diameter: (inside)	69.0	inches
Weight, Combat Loaded:	approx. 126,500	pounds
Weight, Unstowed:	approx. 120,000	pounds
Power to Weight Ratio: Net	13.0	hp/ton
Gross	15.2	hp/ton
Ground Pressure: Zero penetration	13.1	psi

ARMOR

Type: Turret, cast homogenous steel; Hull, cast homogenous steel; Welded assembly

Hull Thickness:

	Actual	Angle w/Vertical
Front, Upper	3.25 inches (83mm)	30 degrees
Lower	4.0-2.75 inches (102-70mm)	0 to 60 degrees
Sides, Upper	1.75 inches (44mm)	20 degrees
Lower	2.75 inches (70mm)	0 degrees (incl. track armor)
Rear	1.63 inches (41mm)	17 degrees
Top	1.0 inches (25mm)	90 degrees
Floor	1.0 inches (25mm)	90 degrees

Turret Thickness:

Gun Shield	equals 4.0 inches (102mm)	0 degrees
Front	3.25 inches (83mm)	7 degrees
Sides	3.25 inches (83mm)	0 degrees
Rear	3.25 inches (83mm)	0 degrees
Top	1.0 inches (25mm)	90 degrees

ARMAMENT

Primary: 3 inch Gun M7 and 37mm Gun M6 in Combination Mount T49 in turret

Traverse: Electric and manual	360 degrees
Traverse Rate: (max)	20 seconds/360 degrees
Elevation: Manual	+30 to −10 degrees
Firing Rate: (max)	15 rounds/minute (3 inch)
	30 rounds/minute (37mm)
Loading System:	Manual
Stabilizer System:	Elevation only

Secondary:
  (2) .50 caliber MG HB M2 in Mount T52 in hull front
  (1) .30 caliber MG M1919A4 in bow mount (fixed)
  * (1) .30 caliber MG M1919A4 flexible AA mount on turret roof
  Provision for (2) .45 caliber SMG M1928A1

AMMUNITION

75 rounds 3 inch	24 hand grenades
202 rounds 37mm	
6900 rounds .50 caliber	
1200 rounds .45 caliber	
5500 rounds .30 caliber	

FIRE CONTROL AND VISION EQUIPMENT

	Direct	Indirect
Primary Weapon:	Periscope M8 with Telescope M39 Telescope M15	Gunner's Quadrant M1

Vision Devices:	Direct	Indirect
Driver	Hatch	Periscope M6 (2)
Bow Gunner	None	Periscope M6 (1) and Protectoscope (1)
Ammunition Passer	Hatch and hull pistol ports (2)	Protectoscopes (2) in hull pistol port covers
Commander	Hatch	Periscope M6 (1)
Gunner	None	Periscope M8 (1)
Loader	Pistol port (1)	Periscope M6 (1) and Protectoscope (1) in pistol port cover

Total Periscopes: M6 (5), M8 (1)
Total Protectoscopes: (4)
Total Pistol Ports: Hull (2), Turret (1)
  * (1) .50 caliber MG HB M2 may be substituted for .30 caliber AA MG

ENGINE

Make and Model: Wright G-200 Model 781C9GC1	
Type: 9 cylinder, 4 cycle, radial	
Cooling System: Air Ignition: Magneto	
Displacement:	1823 cubic inches
Bore and Stroke:	6.125 x 6.875 inches
Compression Ratio:	4.92:1
Net Horsepower (max):	825 hp at 2300 rpm
Gross Horsepower (max):	960 hp at 2300 rpm
Gross Torque (max):	1830 ft-lb at 2100 rpm
Weight:	1350 pounds, dry
Fuel: 80 octane gasoline	477 gallons
Engine Oil:	72 quarts

POWER TRAIN

Transmission: Timken mechanical w/Twin Disc torque converter model 16001, w/Hycon hydraulic control, 2 speeds forward, 1 reverse

Gear Ratios:	1st 1.61:1	reverse 1.61:1
	2nd 0.22:1	

Steering: Controlled differential
  Gear Ratio: 0.62:1   Steering Ratio: 1.62:1
Brakes: Budd disc, mechanical and Hycon hydraulic control
Final Drive: Compensating differential   Gear Ratio: 5:1
Drive Sprocket: At rear of vehicle with 14 teeth
  Pitch Diameter: 26.806 inches

RUNNING GEAR

Suspension: Horizontal volute spring
  16 dual wheels in 8 bogies (4 bogies/track)
  Tire Size: 18 x 7 inches
  8 dual track return rollers (4/track)
  Dual adjustable idler at front of each track
  Idler Tire Size: 30 x 7 inches
  2 dual auxiliary idlers (1/track) between main idler and front bogie
Tracks: Outside guide; T31*
  Type: (T31) Double pin, 25.75 inch width, rubber backed steel
  Pitch: 6 inches
  Shoes per Vehicle: 198 (99/track)
  Ground Contact Length: 187.9 inches

ELECTRICAL SYSTEM

Nominal Voltage: 24 volts DC
Main Generator: (1) 24 volts, 50 amperes, driven by power take-off from main engine
Auxiliary Generator: (1) 30 volts, 50 amperes, driven by the auxiliary engine
Battery: (2) 12 volts in series

COMMUNICATIONS

Radio: SCR 508, 528, or 538 in rear of turret, SCR 506 (command tanks only) in right sponson.
Interphone: Part of radio, 6 stations

FIRE AND GAS PROTECTION

  (6) 10 pound carbon dioxide, fixed
  (2) 4 pound carbon dioxide, portable
  (4) 1½ quart decontaminating apparatus M2

PERFORMANCE

Maximum Speed: Sustained, level road	22 miles/hour
Maximum Grade:	60 per cent
Maximum Trench:	11 feet
Maximum Vertical Wall:	36 inches
Maximum Fording Depth:	48 inches
Minimum Turning Circle: (diameter)	74 feet
Cruising Range: Roads	approx. 100 miles

  * Center guide added later to these tracks and outside guides removed

HEAVY TANK M6A1

GENERAL DATA

Crew:	6	men
Length: Gun forward, w/stowage boxes	332.0	inches
Length: Gun to rear, w/stowage boxes	297.0	inches
Length: Without gun, w/stowage boxes	297.0	inches
Gun Overhang: Gun forward	35.0	inches
Width: Over track armor	123.0	inches
Height: To turret roof	118.0	inches
Tread:	93.9	inches
Ground Clearance:	20.5	inches
Fire Height:	approx. 97	inches
Turret Ring Diameter: (inside)	69.0	inches
Weight, Combat Loaded:	approx. 126,300	pounds
Weight, Unstowed:	approx. 120,000	pounds
Power to Weight Ratio: Net	13.1	hp/ton
Gross	15.2	hp/ton
Ground Pressure: Zero penetration	13.1	psi

ARMOR

Type: Turret, cast homogenous steel; Hull, rolled and cast homogenous steel; Welded assembly

Hull Thickness:	Actual	Angle w/Vertical
Front, Upper	3.25 inches (83mm)	30 degrees
Lower	4.0-2.75 inches (102-70mm)	0 to 60 degrees
Sides, Upper	1.75 inches (44mm)	10 degrees
Lower	2.75 inches (70mm)	0 degrees
		(incl. track armor)
Rear	1.63 inches (41mm)	17 degrees
Top	1.0 inches (25mm)	90 degrees
Floor	1.0 inches (25mm)	90 degrees
Turret Thickness:		
Gun Shield	equals 4.0 inches (102mm)	0 degrees
Front	3.25 inches (83mm)	7 degrees
Sides	3.25 inches (83mm)	0 degrees
Rear	3.25 inches (83mm)	0 degrees
Top	1.0 inches (25mm)	90 degrees

ARMAMENT

Primary: 3 inch Gun M7 and 37mm Gun M6 in Combination Mount T49 in turret

Traverse: Electric and manual	360 degrees
Traverse Rate: (max)	20 seconds/360 degrees
Elevation: Manual	+30 to −10 degrees
Firing Rate: (max)	15 rounds/minute (3 inch)
	30 rounds/minute (37mm)
Loading System:	Manual
Stabilizer System:	Elevation only

Secondary:

(2) .50 caliber MG HB M2 in Mount T52 in hull front
(1) .30 caliber MG M1919A4 in bow mount (fixed)
* (1) .30 caliber MG M1919A4 flexible AA mount on turret roof
Provision for (2) .45 caliber SMG M1928A1

AMMUNITION

75 rounds 3 inch	24 hand grenades
202 rounds 37mm	
6900 rounds .50 caliber	
1200 rounds .45 caliber	
5500 rounds .30 caliber	

FIRE CONTROL AND VISION EQUIPMENT

Primary Weapon:	Direct	Indirect
	Periscope M8 with	Gunner's Quadrant M1
	Telescope M39	
	Telescope M15	

Vision Devices:	Direct	Indirect
Driver	Hatch	Periscope M6 (2)
Bow Gunner	None	Periscope M6 (1) and Protectoscope (1)
Ammunition Passer	Hatch and hull pistol ports (2)	Protectoscopes (2) in hull pistol port covers
Commander	Hatch	Periscope M6 (1)
Gunner	None	Periscope M8 (1)
Loader	Pistol port (1)	Periscope M6 (1) and Protectoscope (1) in pistol port cover

Total Periscopes: M6 (5), M8 (1)
Total Protectoscopes: (4)
Total Pistol Ports: Hull (2), Turret (1)
* (1) .50 caliber MG HB M2 may be substituted for .30 caliber AA MG

ENGINE

Make and Model: Wright G-200 Model 781C9GC1	
Type: 9 cylinder, 4 cycle, radial	
Cooling System: Air Ignition: Magneto	
Displacement:	1823 cubic inches
Bore and Stroke:	6.125 x 6.875 inches
Compression Ratio:	4.92:1
Net Horsepower (max):	825 hp at 2300 rpm
Gross Horsepower (max):	960 hp at 2300 rpm
Gross Torque (max):	1830 ft-lb at 2100 rpm
Weight:	1350 pounds, dry
Fuel: 80 octane gasoline	477 gallons
Engine Oil:	72 quarts

POWER TRAIN

Transmission: Timken mechanical w/Twin Disc torque converter model 16001, w/vacuum assist control, 2 speeds forward, 1 reverse

Gear Ratios:	1st 1.61:1	reverse 1.61:1
	2nd 0.22:1	

Steering: Controlled differential
Gear Ratio: 0.62:1   Steering Ratio: 1.62:1
Brakes: Budd disc, mechanical and vacuum assist control
Final Drive: Compensating differential   Gear Ratio: 5:1
Drive Sprocket: At rear of vehicle with 14 teeth
Pitch Diameter: 26.806 inches

RUNNING GEAR

Suspension: Horizontal volute spring
16 dual wheels in 8 bogies (4 bogies/track)
Tire Size: 18 x 7 inches
8 dual track return rollers (4/track)
Dual adjustable idler at front of each track
Idler Tire Size: 30 x 7 inches
2 dual auxiliary idlers (1/track) between main idler and front bogie
Tracks: Outside guide; T31*
Type: (T31) Double pin, 25.75 inch width, rubber backed steel
Pitch: 6 inches
Shoes per Vehicle: 198 (99/track)
Ground Contact Length: 187.9 inches

ELECTRICAL SYSTEM

Nominal Voltage: 24 volts DC
Main Generator: (1) 24 volts, 50 amperes, driven by power take-off from main engine
Auxiliary Generator: (1) 30 volts, 50 amperes, driven by the auxiliary engine
Battery: (2) 12 volts in series

COMMUNICATIONS

Radio: SCR 508, 528, or 538 in rear of turret, SCR 506 (command tanks only) in right sponson.
Interphone: Part of radio, 6 stations

FIRE AND GAS PROTECTION

(6) 10 pound carbon dioxide, fixed
(2) 4 pound carbon dioxide, portable
(4) 1½ quart decontaminating apprartus M2

PERFORMANCE

Maximum Speed: Sustained, level road	22 miles/hour
Maximum Grade:	60 per cent
Maximum Trench:	11 feet
Maximum Vertical Wall:	36 inches
Maximum Fording Depth:	48 inches
Minimum Turning Circle: (diameter)	74 feet
Cruising Range: Roads	approx. 100 miles

* Center guide added later to these tracks and outside guides removed

HEAVY TANK M6A2E1

GENERAL DATA

Crew:	5	men
Length: Gun forward, w/stowage boxes	440.0	inches
Length: Gun to rear, w/stowage boxes	390.0	inches
Length: Without gun, w/stowage boxes	297.0	inches
Gun Overhang: Gun forward	143.0	inches
Width: Over track armor	123.0	inches
Height: To turret roof	137.0	inches
Tread:	93.9	inches
Ground Clearance:	20.5	inches
Fire Height:	approx. 106	inches
Turret Ring Diameter: (inside)	80.0	inches
Weight, Combat Loaded:	approx. 154,000	pounds
Weight, Unstowed:	approx. 147,000	pounds
Power to Weight Ratio: Net	9.1	hp/ton
Gross	12.5	hp/ton
Ground Pressure: Zero penetration	15.9	psi

ARMOR

Type: Turret, cast homogenous steel; Hull, cast homogenous steel; Welded assembly

Hull Thickness:

	Actual	Angle w/Vertical
Front	equals 7.5 inches (191mm)	0 degrees
Sides, Upper	1.75 inches (44mm)	20 degrees
Lower	2.75 inches (70mm)	0 degrees (incl. track armor)
Rear	1.63 inches (41mm)	17 degrees
Top	1.0 inches (25mm)	90 degrees
Floor	1.0 inches (25mm)	90 degrees

Turret Thickness:

Gun Shield	7.5 inches (191mm)	0 degrees
Front	equals 7.5 inches (191mm)	0 degrees
Sides	3.5 inches (89mm)	0 degrees
Rear	8.2 inches (208mm)	0 degrees
Top	1.0 inches (25mm)	90 degrees

ARMAMENT

Primary: 105mm Gun T5E1 in combination mount in turret

Traverse: Electric and manual	360 degrees
Traverse Rate: (max)	20 seconds/360 degrees
Elevation: Manual	+20 to −10 degrees
Firing Rate: (max)	6 rounds/minute
Loading System:	Manual
Stabilizer System:	None

Secondary:

(1) .50 caliber MG HB M2 flexible AA mount on turret roof
(1) .30 caliber MG M1919A4 coaxial w/105mm gun in turret
Provision for (5) .45 caliber SMG M3

AMMUNITION

60 rounds 105mm	12 hand grenades
600 rounds .50 caliber	
900 rounds .45 caliber	
4000 rounds .30 caliber	

FIRE CONTROL AND VISION EQUIPMENT

Primary Weapon:	Direct	Indirect
	Periscopic Sight	Azimuth Indicator
	Telescope	Elevation Quadrant M9
		Gunner's Quadrant M1

Vision Devices:	Direct	Indirect
Driver	None	Periscope M6 (2)
Asst. Driver	None	Periscope M6 (1)
Commander	Vision blocks (6) in cupola, hatch	Periscope M6 (1)
Gunner	None	Periscopic Sight
Loader	Hatch and pistol port	Periscope M6 (1)

Total Periscopes: M6 (5), Periscopic Sight (1)
Total Pistol Ports: Hull (0), Turret (1)
Total Vision Blocks: (6) in cupola on turret top

ENGINE

Make and Model: Wright G-200 Model 795C9GC1	
Type: 9 cylinder, 4 cycle, radial	
Cooling System: Air Ignition: Magneto	
Displacement:	1823 cubic inches
Bore and Stroke:	6.125 x 6.875 inches
Compression Ratio:	4.92:1
Net Horsepower (max): Governed speed	700 hp at 1950 rpm
Gross Horsepower (max):	960 hp at 2300 rpm
Gross Torque (max): Governed speed	1810 ft-lb at 1950 rpm
Weight:	1350 pounds, dry
Fuel: 80 octane gasoline	464 gallons
Engine Oil:	72 quarts

POWER TRAIN

Transmission: Electric drive with speed infinitely variable both forward and reverse
Steering: Electric
Brakes: Electric
Final Drive: Spur gear   Gear Ratio: 10:1
Drive Sprocket: At rear of vehicle with 14 teeth
   Pitch Diameter: 26.806 inches

RUNNING GEAR

Suspension: Horizontal volute spring
   16 dual wheels in 8 bogies (4 bogies/track)
   Tire Size: 18 x 7 inches
   8 dual track return rollers (4/track)
   Dual adjustable idler at front of each track
   Idler Tire Size: 30 x 7 inches
   2 dual auxiliary idlers (1/track) between main idler and front bogie
Tracks: Outside guide T31*
   Type: (T31) Double pin, 25.75 inch width, rubber backed steel
   Pitch: 6 inches
   Shoes per Vehicle: 198 (99/track)
   Ground Contact Length: 187.9 inches

ELECTRICAL SYSTEM

Nominal Voltage: 24 volts DC
Battery Charging Generator: (1) 24 volts, 200 amperes, driven by power take-off from main engine
Auxiliary Generator: (1) 30 volts, 50 amperes, driven by the auxiliary engine
Battery: (2) 12 volts in series

COMMUNICATIONS

Radio: SCR 508, 528, or 538 in rear of turret, SCR 506 (command tanks only) in right sponson
Interphone: Part of radio, 6 stations

FIRE AND GAS PROTECTION

(6) 10 pound carbon dioxide, fixed
(2) 4 pound carbon dioxide, portable
(4) 1½ quart decontaminating apparatus M2

PERFORMANCE

Maximum Speed: Sustained, level road	18 miles/hour
Maximum Grade:	30 per cent
Maximum Trench:	11 feet
Maximum Vertical Wall:	36 inches
Maximum Fording Depth:	48 inches
Minimum Turning Circle: (diameter)	pivot
Cruising Range: Roads	approx. 100 miles

* Center guide added later to these tracks and the outside guides removed

SUPERHEAVY TANK T28 (105mm GUN MOTOR CARRIAGE T95)

GENERAL DATA

Crew:	4	men
Length: Gun forward	438.0	inches
Length: Without gun	295.1	inches
Gun Overhang: Gun forward	142.9	inches
Width: Over armor side skirts	179.3	inches
Without outboard tracks	124.0	inches
Height: Over AA MG	112.4	inches
Tread: With outboard tracks	126.5	inches
Without outboard tracks	104.5	inches
Ground Clearance:	19.5	inches
Fire Height:	approx. 60	inches
Weight, Combat Loaded:	approx. 190,000	pounds
Weight, Unstowed:	approx. 180,600	pounds
Weight, Without Outboard Tracks:	approx. 131,000	pounds
Power to Weight Ratio: Net	4.3	hp/ton
Gross	5.3	hp/ton
Ground Pressure: Zero penetration, w/outboard tracks	11.7	psi
Zero penetration, w/o outboard tracks	16.2	psi

ARMOR

Type: Turret, none; Hull, rolled and cast homogenous steel; Welded assembly

Hull Thickness:	Actual	Angle w/Vertical
Gun Shield	11.5 inches (292mm)	0 degrees
Front, Upper	12.0 inches (305mm)	0 degrees
Lower	5.25 inches (133mm)	60 degrees
Sides, Upper	2.5 inches (64mm)	57 degrees
* Lower	6.0 inches (152mm)	0 degrees
Rear	2.0 inches (51mm)	9 degrees
Top	1.5 inches (38mm)	90 degrees
Floor	1.0 inches (25mm)	90 degrees

ARMAMENT

Primary: 105mm Gun T5E1 in Mount T40 in front hull

Traverse: Manual	10 degrees right, 11 degrees left
Elevation: Manual	+19 degrees 30 minutes to −5 degrees
Firing Rate: (max)	4 rounds/minute (1 loader)
Loading System:	Manual
Stabilizer System:	None

Secondary:
(1) .50 caliber MG HB M2 flexible AA mount on hull roof
Provision for (1) .45 caliber SMG M3
Provision for (3) .30 caliber Carbine M2

AMMUNITION

62 rounds 105mm   12 hand grenades
660 rounds .50 caliber
180 rounds .45 caliber
225 rounds .30 caliber (carbine)

FIRE CONTROL AND VISION EQUIPMENT

Primary Weapon:	Direct	Indirect
	Telescope T139	Panoramic Telescope T141
	Periscope M10E3	Elevation Quadrant M9
Vision Devices:	Direct	Indirect
Driver	Vision blocks (6) in cupola, hatch	Periscope M13 (1)
Commander	Vision blocks (6) in cupola, hatch	Periscope M15 (1)
Gunner	None	Periscope M10E3 and Panoramic Telescope T141
Loader	None	None

Total Periscopes: M10E3 (1), M13 (1), M15 (1)
Total Cupolas: (2) each w/6 vision blocks on hull roof
* Includes 4 inch armor side skirt

ENGINE

Make and Model: Ford GAF	
Type: 8 cylinder, 4 cycle, 60 degree vee	
Cooling System: Liquid Ignition: Magneto	
Displacement:	1100 cubic inches
Bore and Stroke:	5.4 x 6 inches
Compression Ratio:	7.5:1
Net Horsepower (max):	410 hp at 2600 rpm
Gross Horsepower (max):	500 hp at 2600 rpm
Net Torque (max):	780 ft-lb at 2325 rpm
Gross Torque (max):	1050 ft-lb at 2200 rpm
Weight:	1414 pounds, dry
Fuel: 80 octane gasoline	400 gallons
Engine Oil:	32 quarts

POWER TRAIN

Transfer Case: Planetary reduction gears
    Gear Ratios: 1.377:1 engine to transmission
Transmission: Torqmatic, 3 speeds forward, 1 reverse
    Torque Converter Ratio: Varies from 1:1 to 4.8:1

Gear Ratios:	1st	1:1	3rd	0.244:1
	2nd	0.428:1	reverse	0.756:1

Steering: Controlled differential
    Steering Ratio: 2.08:1
Brakes: Mechanical, external contracting
Final Drive: Planetary Gear   Gear Ratio: 12.126:1
Drive Sprocket: At rear of vehicle with 14 teeth
    Pitch Diameter: 26.964 inches

RUNNING GEAR

Suspension: Double track horizontal volute spring, with separable outboard tracks
    32 dual wheels in 16 bogies (8 bogies/side or 4 bogies/track)
    Tire Size: 20.5 x 4.5 inches
    12 dual track return rollers (6/side or 3/track)
    8 single track return rollers (4/side or 2/track)
    Dual adjustable idler at front of each track
    Idler Tire Size: 22 x 4.5 inches
Tracks: Center guide
    Type: Double pin, 19.5 inch width, rubber and steel
    Pitch: 6 inches
    Shoes per Vehicle: 408 (204/side or 102/track)
    Ground Contact Length: 208 inches

ELECTRICAL SYSTEM

Nominal Voltage: 24 and 12 volts DC
Generator: (1) 28.5 volts, 150 amperes, belt driven by either the main engine or the auxiliary engine
Battery: (2) 12 volts in series

COMMUNICATIONS

Radio: SCR 508 and AN/VRC 3 on bulkhead in fighting compartment
Interphone: 4 stations

FIRE PROTECTION

(2) 10 pound carbon dioxide, fixed
(1) 4 pound carbon dioxide, portable

PERFORMANCE

Maximum Speed: Sustained, level road	8 miles/hour
Maximum Tractive Effort: TE at stall	143,000 pounds
Per Cent of Vehicle Weight: TE/W	75 per cent
Maximum Grade:	60 per cent
Maximum Trench:	9.5 feet
Maximum Vertical Wall:	24 inches
Maximum Fording Depth:	47 inches
Minimum Turning Circle: (diameter)	80 feet
Cruising Range: Roads	approx. 100 miles

GENERAL DATA

Crew:	6	men
Length: Gun forward	455.5	inches
Length: Gun in travel position	393.3	inches
Length: Without gun	299.6	inches
Gun Overhang: Gun forward	155.9	inches
Width: Over sandshields	149.7	inches
Height: Over cupola	126.9	inches
Tread: w/28 inch tracks	115.0	inches
w/23 inch tracks	110.0	inches
Ground Clearance:	18.8	inches
Fire Height:	approx. 85	inches
Turret Ring Diameter: (inside)	80.0	inches
Weight, Combat Loaded:	approx. 141,500	pounds
Weight, Unstowed:	approx. 132,500	pounds
Power to Weight Ratio: Net	9.2	hp/ton
Gross	10.9	hp/ton
Ground Pressure: Zero penetration, w/28 inch tracks	12.2	psi
Zero penetration, w/23 inch tracks	14.9	psi

ARMOR

Type: Turret, cast homogenous steel; Hull, rolled and cast homogenous steel; Welded assembly

Hull Thickness:	Actual	Angle w/Vertical
Front, Upper	4.0 inches (102mm)	54 degrees
Lower	2.75 inches (70mm)	58 degrees
Sides, Front	3.0 inches (76mm)	0 degrees
Rear	2.0 inches (51mm)	0 degrees
Rear, Upper	2.0 inches (51mm)	9 degrees
Lower	0.75 inches (19mm)	62 degrees
Top	1.5 inches (38mm)	90 degrees
Floor, Front	1.0 inches (25mm)	90 degrees
Rear	0.5 inches (13mm)	90 degrees

Turret Thickness:		
Gun Shield	8 to 11 inches (203 to 279mm)	0 degrees
Front	7.0 inches (178mm)	0 degrees
Sides	5.0 inches (127mm)	0 degrees
Rear	4.0 inches (102mm)	0 degrees
Top	1.5 inches (38mm)	90 degrees

ARMAMENT

Primary: 105mm Gun T5E2 in Mount T123E1 in turret

Traverse: Electric-hydraulic and manual	360 degrees
Traverse Rate: (max)	20 seconds/360 degrees
Elevation: Manual	+15 to −10 degrees
Firing Rate: (max)	6 rounds/minute (2 loaders)
Loading System:	Manual
Stabilizer System:	None

Secondary:
- (1) .50 caliber MG HB M2 flexible AA mount on turret
- (2) .50 caliber MG HB M2 coaxial w/105mm gun in turret
- (1) .30 caliber MG M1919A4 in bow mount
- Provision for (6) .45 caliber SMG M3

AMMUNITION

63 rounds 105mm	12 hand grenades
2420 rounds .50 caliber	
1080 rounds .45 caliber	
2500 rounds .30 caliber	

FIRE CONTROL AND VISION EQUIPMENT

Primary Weapon:	Direct	Indirect
	Telescope T143E1	Azimuth Indicator T19
	Periscope M10E5	Elevation Quadrant M9
		Gunner's Quadrant M1

Vision Devices:	Direct	Indirect
Driver	Hatch	Periscope M13 (1)
Asst. Driver	Hatch	Periscope M13 (1)
Commander	Vision blocks (6) in cupola, hatch	Periscope M15 (1)
Gunner	None	Periscope M10E5 (1)
Loader, left	Hatch	None
Loader, right	Hatch and pistol port	None

Total Periscopes: M10E5 (1), M13 (2), M15 (1)
Total Pistol Ports: Hull (0), Turret (1)
Total Vision Blocks: (6) in cupola on turret top

ENGINE

Make and Model: Ford GAC	
Type: 12 cylinder, 4 cycle, 60 degree vee	
Cooling System: Liquid Ignition: Magneto	
Displacement:	1649 cubic inches
Bore and Stroke:	5.4 x 6 inches
Compression Ratio:	7.5:1
Net Horsepower (max):	650 hp at 2800 rpm
Gross Horsepower (max):	770 hp at 2800 rpm
Net Torque (max):	1440 ft-lb at 1600 rpm
Gross Torque (max):	1560 ft-lb at 1600 rpm
Weight:	1850 pounds, dry
Fuel: 80 octane gasoline	300 gallons
Engine Oil:	55 quarts

POWER TRAIN

Transmission: Cross-drive CD-850-1, 2 ranges forward, 1 reverse
Three stage hydraulic torque converter
Stall Multiplication: 4.75:1

Overall Usable Ratios: low   12.7:1   reverse   20.6:1
high   6.2:1

Steering Control: Mechanical, wobble stick
Steering Rate: 5.7 rpm
Brakes: Multiple disc
Final Drive: Spur gear   Gear Ratio: 6.31:1
Drive Sprocket: At rear of vehicle with 15 teeth
Pitch Diameter: 28.89 inches

RUNNING GEAR

Suspension: Torsion bar
16 individually sprung dual road wheels (8/track)
Tire Size: 26 x 6 inches
14 dual track return rollers (7/track)
Dual compensating idler at front of each track
Idler Tire Size: 26 x 6 inches
Shock absorbers fitted on first 3 and last 2 road wheels on each side

Tracks: Center guide T80E3 and T84E3
* Type: (T80E3) Double pin, 28 inch width, rubber backed steel
(T84E3) Double pin 28 inch width, rubber chevron
Pitch: 6 inches
Shoes per Vehicle: 204 (102/track)
Ground Contact Length: 204.6 inches, left side
208.6 inches, right side

ELECTRICAL SYSTEM

Nominal Voltage: 24 volts DC
Main Generator: 28.5 volts, 175 amperes, gear driven by main engine
Auxiliary Generator: 28.5 volts, 175 amperes, driven by auxiliary engine
Battery: (2) 12 volts in series

COMMUNICATIONS

Radio: SCR 508 or 528 in turret bustle
AN/VRC-3 in turret bustle
Interphone: 6 stations plus external extension kit RC-298

FIRE PROTECTION

(2) 10 pound carbon dioxide, fixed
(2) 4 pound carbon dioxide, portable

PERFORMANCE

Maximum Speed: Sustained, level road	22 miles/hour
Maximum Tractive Effort: TE at stall	86,300 pounds
Per Cent of Vehicle Weight: TE/W	62 per cent
Maximum Grade:	60 per cent
Maximum Trench:	6.25 feet
Maximum Vertical Wall:	26 inches
Maximum Fording Depth:	42 inches
Minimum Turning Circle: (diameter)	pivot
Cruising Range: Roads	approx. 100 miles

* The T80E3 and T84E3 tracks are the 23 inch wide T80E1 and T84E1 tracks fitted with 5 inch extended end connectors.

HEAVY TANK T29E1

GENERAL DATA

Crew:	6	men
Length: Gun forward	455.5	inches
Length: Gun in travel position	393.3	inches
Length: Without gun	299.6	inches
Gun Overhang: Gun forward	155.9	inches
Width: Over sandshields	149.7	inches
Height: Over cupola	126.9	inches
Tread: w/28 inch tracks	115.0	inches
w/23 inch tracks	110.0	inches
Ground Clearance:	18.8	inches
Fire Height:	approx. 85	inches
Turret Ring Diameter: (inside)	80.0	inches
Weight, Combat Loaded:	approx. 141,000	pounds
Weight, Unstowed:	approx. 132,000	pounds
Power to Weight Ratio: Net	10.6	hp/ton
Gross	12.3	hp/ton
Ground Pressure: Zero penetration, w/28 inch tracks	12.2	psi
Zero penetration, w/23 inch tracks	14.8	psi

ARMOR

Type: Turret, cast homogenous steel; Hull, rolled and cast homogenous steel; Welded assembly

Hull Thickness:

	Actual	Angle w/Vertical
Front, Upper	4.0 inches (102mm)	54 degrees
Lower	2.75 inches (70mm)	58 degrees
Sides, Front	3.0 inches (76mm)	0 degrees
Rear	2.0 inches (51mm)	0 degrees
Rear, Upper	2.0 inches (51mm)	9 degrees
Lower	0.75 inches (19mm)	62 degrees
Top	1.5 inches (38mm)	90 degrees
Floor, Front	1.0 inches (25mm)	90 degrees
Rear	0.5 inches (13mm)	90 degrees

Turret Thickness:

Gun Shield	8 to 11 inches	0 degrees
	(203 to 279mm)	
Front	7.0 inches (178mm)	0 degrees
Sides	5.0 inches (127mm)	0 degrees
Rear	4.0 inches (102mm)	0 degrees
Top	1.5 inches (38mm)	90 degrees

ARMAMENT

Primary: 105mm Gun T5E1 in Mount T123 in turret

Traverse: Electric-hydraulic and manual	360 degrees
Traverse Rate: (max)	20 seconds/360 degrees
Elevation: Manual	+15 to −10 degrees
Firing Rate: (max)	6 rounds/minute (2 loaders)
Loading System:	Manual
Stabilizer System:	None

Secondary:
- (1) .50 caliber MG HB M2 flexible AA mount on turret
- (2) .50 caliber MG HB M2 coaxial w/105mm gun in turret
- (1) .30 caliber MG M1919A4 in bow mount
- Provision for (6) .45 caliber SMG M3

AMMUNITION

63 rounds 105mm	12 hand grenades
2420 rounds .50 caliber	
1080 rounds .45 caliber	
2500 rounds .30 caliber	

FIRE CONTROL AND VISION EQUIPMENT

Primary Weapon:	Direct	Indirect
	Telescope T143E1	Azimuth Indicator T19
	Periscope M10E5	Elevation Quadrant M9
		Gunner's Quadrant M1

Vision Devices:	Direct	Indirect
Driver	Hatch	Periscope M13 (1)
Asst. Driver	Hatch	Periscope M13 (1)
Commander	Vision blocks (6)	Periscope M15 (1)
	in cupola, hatch	
Gunner	None	Periscope M10E5 (1)
Loader, left	Hatch	None
Loader, right	Hatch and pistol port	None

Total Periscopes: M10E5 (1), M13 (2), M15 (1)
Total Pistol Ports: Hull (0), Turret (1)
Total Vision Blocks: (6) in cupola on turret top

ENGINE

Make and Model: General Motors Allison V-1710-E32	
Type: 12 cylinder, 4 cycle, 60 degree vee	
Cooling System: Liquid Ignition: Magneto	
Displacement:	1710.6 cubic inches
Bore and Stroke:	5.5 x 6.0 inches
Compression Ratio:	6.65:1
Net Horsepower (max):	750 hp at 2800 rpm
Gross Horsepower (max):	870 hp at 2800 rpm
Net Torque (max):	1700 ft-lb at 1700 rpm
Gross Torque (max):	1810 ft-lb at 1800 rpm
Weight:	1595 pounds, dry
Fuel: 80 octane gasoline	222 gallons
Engine Oil:	52 quarts

POWER TRAIN

Transmission: Cross-drive CD-850-1, 2 ranges forward, 1 reverse
 Three stage hydraulic torque converter
 Stall Multiplication: 4.75:1
 Overall Usable Ratios: low 12.7:1   reverse 20.6:1
                          high 6.2:1

Steering Control: Mechanical, wobble stick
 Steering Rate: 5.7 rpm
Brakes: Multiple disc
Final Drive: Spur gear   Gear Ratio: 6.31:1
Drive Sprocket: At rear of vehicle with 15 teeth
 Pitch Diameter: 28.89 inches

RUNNING GEAR

Suspension: Torsion bar
 16 individually sprung dual road wheels (8/track)
 Tire Size: 26 x 6 inches
 14 dual track return rollers (7/track)
 Dual compensating idler at front of each track
 Idler Tire Size: 26 x 6 inches
 Shock absorbers fitted on first 3 and last 2 road wheels on each side
Tracks: Center guide T80E3 and T84E3
 * Type: (T80E3) Double pin, 28 inch width, rubber backed steel
          (T84E3) Double pin 28 inch width, rubber chevron
 Pitch: 6 inches
 Shoes per Vehicle: 204 (102/track)
 Ground Contact Length: 204.6 inches, left side
                        208.6 inches, right side

ELECTRICAL SYSTEM

Nominal Voltage: 24 volts DC
Main Generator: 28.5 volts, 200 amperes, gear driven by main engine
Auxiliary Generator: 28.5 volts, 200 amperes, driven by auxiliary engine
Battery: (2) 12 volts in series

COMMUNICATIONS

Radio: SCR 508 or 528 in turret bustle
       AN/VRC-3 in turret bustle
Interphone: 6 stations plus external extension kit RC-298

FIRE PROTECTION

 (2) 10 pound carbon dioxide, fixed
 (2) 4 pound carbon dioxide, portable

PERFORMANCE

Maximum Speed: Sustained, level road	22 miles/hour
Maximum Grade:	60 per cent
Maximum Trench:	6.25 feet
Maximum Vertical Wall:	26 inches
Maximum Fording Depth:	42 inches
Minimum Turning Circle: (diameter)	pivot
Cruising Range: Roads	approx. 75 miles

 * The T80E3 and T84E3 tracks are the 23 inch wide T80E1 and T84E1 tracks fitted with 5 inch extended end connectors.

HEAVY TANK T29E3

GENERAL DATA

Crew:	6	men
Length: Gun forward	455.5	inches
Length: Gun in travel position	393.3	inches
Length: Without gun	299.6	inches
Gun Overhang: Gun forward	155.9	inches
Width: Over sandshields	149.7	inches
Height: Over cupola	126.9	inches
Tread: w/28 inch tracks	115.0	inches
w/23 inch tracks	110.0	inches
Ground Clearance:	18.8	inches
Fire Height:	approx. 85	inches
Turret Ring Diameter: (inside)	80.0	inches
Weight, Combat Loaded:	approx. 144,000	pounds
Weight, Unstowed:	approx. 135,000	pounds
Power to Weight Ratio: Net	9.0	hp/ton
Gross	10.7	hp/ton
Ground Pressure: Zero penetration, w/28 inch tracks	12.4	psi
Zero penetration, w/23 inch tracks	15.2	psi

ARMOR

Type: Turret, cast homogenous steel; Hull, rolled and cast homogenous steel;
Welded assembly

Hull Thickness:

	Actual	Angle w/Vertical
Front, Upper	4.0 inches (102mm)	54 degrees
Lower	2.75 inches (70mm)	58 degrees
Sides, Front	3.0 inches (76mm)	0 degrees
Rear	2.0 inches (51mm)	0 degrees
Rear, Upper	2.0 inches (51mm)	9 degrees
Lower	0.75 inches (19mm)	62 degrees
Top	1.5 inches (38mm)	90 degrees
Floor, Front	1.0 inches (25mm)	90 degrees
Rear	0.5 inches (13mm)	90 degrees

Turret Thickness:

Gun Shield	8 to 11 inches (203 to 279mm)	0 degrees
Front	7.0 inches (178mm)	0 degrees
Sides	5.0 inches (127mm)	0 degrees
Rear	4.0 inches (102mm)	0 degrees
Top	1.5 inches (38mm)	90 degrees

ARMAMENT

Primary: 105mm Gun T5E1 in Mount T123 in turret

Traverse: Electric-hydraulic and manual	360 degrees
Traverse Rate: (max)	20 seconds/360 degrees
Elevation: Manual	+15 to −10 degrees
Firing Rate: (max)	6 rounds/minute (2 loaders)
Loading System:	Manual
Stabilizer System:	None

Secondary:
(1) .50 caliber MG HB M2 flexible AA mount on turret
(2) .50 caliber MG HB M2 coaxial w/105mm gun in turret
(1) .30 caliber MG M1919A4 in bow mount
Provision for (6) .45 caliber SMG M3

AMMUNITION

63 rounds 105mm   12 hand grenades
2420 rounds .50 caliber
1080 rounds .45 caliber
2500 rounds .30 caliber

FIRE CONTROL AND VISION EQUIPMENT

Primary Weapon:	Direct	Indirect
	Range Finder T31E1	Panoramic Telescope T141
	Telescope T93E2	Panoramic Telescope T144
	Periscope M10E5 (1)	Panoramic Telescope T145
		Azimuth Indicator T19
		Elevation Quadrant M9
		Gunner's Quadrant M1

Vision Devices:	Direct	Indirect
Driver	Hatch	Periscope M13 (1)
Asst. Driver	Hatch	Periscope M13 (1)
Commander	Vision blocks (6) in cupola, hatch	Periscope M15 (1)
		Range Finder T31E1
Gunner	None	Periscope M10E5 (1)
		Panoramic Telescopes T141, T144, or T145
Loader, left	Hatch	None
Loader, right	Hatch and pistol port	None

Total Periscopes: M10E5 (1), M13 (2), M15 (1)
Total Pistol Ports: Hull (0), Turret (1)
Total Vision Blocks: (6) in cupola on turret top

ENGINE

Make and Model: Ford GAC	
Type: 12 cylinder, 4 cycle, 60 degree vee	
Cooling System: Liquid Ignition: Magneto	
Displacement:	1649 cubic inches
Bore and Stroke:	5.4 x 6 inches
Compression Ratio:	7.5:1
Net Horsepower (max):	650 hp at 2800 rpm
Gross Horsepower (max):	770 hp at 2800 rpm
Net Torque (max):	1440 ft-lb at 1600 rpm
Gross Torque (max):	1560 ft-lb at 1600 rpm
Weight:	1850 pounds, dry
Fuel: 80 octane gasoline	300 gallons
Engine Oil:	55 quarts

POWER TRAIN

Transmission: Cross-drive CD-850-1, 2 ranges forward, 1 reverse
Three stage hydraulic torque converter
Stall Multiplication: 4.75:1

Overall Usable Ratios:	low 12.7:1	reverse 20.6:1
	high 6.2:1	

Steering Control: Mechanical, wobble stick
Steering Rate: 5.7 rpm
Brakes: Multiple disc
Final Drive: Spur gear   Gear Ratio: 6.31:1
Drive Sprocket: At rear of vehicle with 15 teeth
Pitch Diameter: 28.89 inches

RUNNING GEAR

Suspension: Torsion bar
16 individually sprung dual road wheels (8/track)
Tire Size: 26 x 6 inches
14 dual track return rollers (7/track)
Dual compensating idler at front of each track
Idler Tire Size: 26 x 6 inches
Shock absorbers fitted on first 3 and last 2 road wheels on each side

Tracks: Center guide T80E3 and T84E3
 * Type: (T80E3) Double pin, 28 inch width, rubber backed steel
      (T84E3) Double pin 28 inch width, rubber chevron
Pitch: 6 inches
Shoes per Vehicle: 204 (102/track)
Ground Contact Length: 204.6 inches, left side
                       208.6 inches, right side

ELECTRICAL SYSTEM

Nominal Voltage: 24 volts DC
Main Generator: 28.5 volts, 175 amperes, gear driven by main engine
Auxiliary Generator: 28.5 volts, 175 amperes, driven by auxiliary engine
Battery: (2) 12 volts in series

COMMUNICATIONS

Radio: SCR 508 or 528 in turret bustle
       AN/VRC-3 in turret bustle
Interphone: 6 stations plus external extension kit RC-298

FIRE PROTECTION

(2) 10 pound carbon dioxide, fixed
(2) 4 pound carbon dioxide, portable

PERFORMANCE

Maximum Speed: Sustained, level road	22 miles/hour
Maximum Tractive Effort: TE at stall	86,300 pounds
Per Cent of Vehicle Weight:	62 per cent
Maximum Grade:	60 per cent
Maximum Trench:	6.25 feet
Maximum Vertical Wall:	26 inches
Maximum Fording Depth:	42 inches
Minimum Turning Circle: (diameter)	pivot
Cruising Range: Roads	approx. 75 miles

 * The T80E3 and T84E3 tracks are the 23 inch wide T80E1 and T84E1 tracks
fitted with 5 inch extended end connectors.

HEAVY TANK T30

GENERAL DATA
Crew:	6	men
Length: Gun forward	429.0	inches
Length: Gun in travel position	365.0	inches
Length: Without gun	299.6	inches
Gun Overhang: Gun forward	129.4	inches
Width: Over sandshields	149.7	inches
Height: Over cupola	126.9	inches
Tread: w/28 inch tracks	115.0	inches
w/23 inch tracks	110.0	inches
Ground Clearance:	18.8	inches
Fire Height:	approx. 85	inches
Turret Ring Diameter: (inside)	80.0	inches
Weight, Combat Loaded:	approx. 142,600	pounds
Weight, Unstowed:	approx. 133,600	pounds
Power to Weight Ratio: Net	9.9	hp/ton
Gross	11.4	hp/ton
Ground Pressure: Zero penetration, w/28 inch tracks	12.3	psi
Zero penetration, w/23 inch tracks	15.0	psi

ARMOR
Type: Turret, cast homogenous steel; Hull, rolled and cast homogenous steel;
 Welded assembly

Hull Thickness:

	Actual	Angle w/Vertical
Front, Upper	4.0 inches (102mm)	54 degrees
Lower	2.75 inches (70mm)	58 degrees
Sides, Front	3.0 inches (76mm)	0 degrees
Rear	2.0 inches (51mm)	0 degrees
Rear, Upper	2.0 inches (51mm)	9 degrees
Lower	0.75 inches (19mm)	62 degrees
Top	1.5 inches (38mm)	90 degrees
Floor, Front	1.0 inches (25mm)	90 degrees
Rear	0.5 inches (13mm)	90 degrees

Turret Thickness:

Gun Shield	8 to 11 inches	0 degrees
	(203 to 279mm)	
Front	7.0 inches (178mm)	0 degrees
Sides	5.0 inches (127mm)	0 degrees
Rear	4.0 inches (102mm)	0 degrees
Top	1.5 inches (38mm)	90 degrees

ARMAMENT
Primary: 155mm Gun T7 in Mount T124 in turret

Traverse: Electric-hydraulic and manual	360 degrees
Traverse Rate: (max)	20 seconds/360 degrees
Elevation: Manual	+15 to −10 degrees
Firing Rate: (max)	2 rounds/minute (2 loaders)
Loading System:	Manual w/hoist and spring rammer
Stabilizer System:	None

Secondary:
 (1) .50 caliber MG HB M2 flexible AA mount on turret
 (1) .50 caliber MG HB M2 coaxial w/155mm gun in turret
 (1) .30 caliber MG M1919A4 in bow mount
 Provision for (6) .45 caliber SMG M3

AMMUNITION
34 rounds 155mm	12 hand grenades
2200 rounds .50 caliber	
1080 rounds .45 caliber	
2500 rounds .30 caliber	

FIRE CONTROL AND VISION EQUIPMENT
Primary Weapon:	Direct	Indirect
	Telescope T143E1	Azimuth Indicator T19
	Periscope M10E9	Elevation Quadrant M9
		Gunner's Quadrant M1

Vision Devices:	Direct	Indirect
Driver	Hatch	Periscope M13 (1)
Asst. Driver	Hatch	Periscope M13 (1)
Commander	Vision blocks (6) in cupola, hatch	Periscope M15 (1)
Gunner	None	Periscope M10E9 (1)
Loader, left	Hatch	None
Loader, right	Hatch and pistol port	None

Total Periscopes: M10E9 (1), M13 (2), M15 (1)
Total Pistol Ports: Hull (0), Turret (1)
Total Vision Blocks: (6) in cupola on turret top

ENGINE
Make and Model: Continental AV-1790-3	
Type: 12 cylinder, 4 cycle, 90 degree vee	
Cooling System: Air Ignition: Magneto	
Displacement:	1791.7 cubic inches
Bore and Stroke:	5.75 x 5.75 inches
Compression Ratio:	6.5:1
Net Horsepower (max):	704 hp at 2800 rpm
Gross Horsepower (max):	810 hp at 2800 rpm
Net Torque (max):	1440 ft-lb at 2000 rpm
Gross Torque (max):	1610 ft-lb at 2200 rpm
Weight:	2332 pounds, dry
Fuel: 80 octane gasoline	320 gallons
Engine Oil:	72 quarts

POWER TRAIN
Transmission: Cross-drive CD-850-1, 2 ranges forward, 1 reverse
 Three stage hydraulic torque converter
 Stall Multiplication: 4.75:1
 Overall Usable Ratios: low   12.7:1   reverse 20.6:1
                                          high   6.2:1

Steering Control: Mechanical, wobble stick
 Steering Rate: 5.7 rpm
Brakes: Multiple disc
Final Drive: Spur gear   Gear Ratio: 6.31:1
Drive Sprocket: At rear of vehicle with 15 teeth
 Pitch Diameter: 28.89 inches

RUNNING GEAR
Suspension: Torsion bar
 16 individually sprung dual road wheels (8/track)
 Tire Size: 26 x 6 inches
 14 dual track return rollers (7/track)
 Dual compensating idler at front of each track
 Idler Tire Size: 26 x 6 inches
 Single track tension idler in front of each sprocket
 Shock absorbers fitted on first 3 and last 2 road wheels on each side
Tracks: Center guide T80E3 and T84E3
 * Type: (T80E3) Double pin, 28 inch width, rubber backed steel
          (T84E3) Double pin, 28 inch width, rubber chevron
 Pitch: 6 inches
 Shoes per Vehicle: 204 (102/track)
 Ground Contact Length: 204.6 inches, left side
                                    208.6 inches, right side

ELECTRICAL SYSTEM
Nominal Voltage: 24 volts DC
Main Generator: 28.5 volts, 200 amperes, gear driven by main engine
Auxiliary Generator: 28.5 volts, 200 amperes, driven by auxiliary engine
Battery: (2) 12 volts in series

COMMUNICATIONS
Radio: SCR 508 or 528 in turret bustle
 AN/VRC-3 in turret bustle
Interphone: 6 stations plus external extension kit RC-298

FIRE PROTECTION
 (3) 10 pound carbon dioxide, fixed
 (2) 5 pound carbon dioxide, portable

PERFORMANCE
Maximum Speed: Sustained, level road	22 miles/hour
Maximum Tractive Effort: TE at stall	91,700 pounds
Per Cent of Vehicle Weight: TE/W	64 per cent
Maximum Grade:	60 per cent
Maximum Trench:	6.25 feet
Maximum Vertical Wall:	26 inches
Maximum Fording Depth:	42 inches
Minimum Turning Circle: (diameter)	pivot
Cruising Range: Roads	approx. 100 miles

 * The T80E3 and T84E3 tracks are the 23 inch wide T80E1 and T84E1 tracks
   fitted with 5 inch extended end connectors.

HEAVY TANK T32

GENERAL DATA

Crew:	5	men
Length: Gun forward	426.6	inches
Length: Gun in travel position	375.0	inches
Length: Without gun	278.4	inches
Gun Overhang: Gun forward	148.2	inches
Width: Over sandshields	148.3	inches
Height: To top of cupola	110.7	inches
Tread: w/28 inch tracks	115.0	inches
w/23 inch tracks	110.0	inches
Ground Clearance:	18.3	inches
Fire Height:	approx. 78	inches
Turret Ring Diameter: (inside)	69.0	inches
Weight, Combat Loaded:	approx. 120,000	pounds
Weight, Unstowed:	approx. 112,000	pounds
Power to Weight Ratio: Net	10.8	hp/ton
Gross	12.8	hp/ton
Ground Pressure: Zero penetration, w/28 inch tracks	11.6	psi
Zero penetration, w/23 inch tracks	14.2	psi

ARMOR

Type: Turret, cast homogenous steel; Hull, rolled and cast homogenous steel; Welded assembly

Hull Thickness:	Actual	Angle w/Vertical
Front, Upper	5.0 inches (127mm)	54 degrees
Lower	3.75 inches (95mm)	59 degrees
Sides	3.0 inches (76mm)	0 degrees
Rear	2.0 inches (51mm)	9 degrees
Top	1.5 inches (38mm)	90 degrees
Floor, Front	1.0 inches (25mm)	90 degrees
Rear	0.5 inches (13mm)	90 degrees
Turret Thickness:		
Gun Shield	11.75 inches (298mm)	0 degrees
Front	11.75 inches (298mm)	15 degrees
Sides	7.75 to 6 inches (197 to 152mm)	9 degrees
Rear	6.0 inches (152mm)	0 degrees
Top	1.0 inches (25mm)	90 degrees

ARMAMENT

Primary: 90mm Gun T15E2 in Mount T119 in turret

Traverse: Electric-hydraulic and manual	360 degrees
Traverse Rate: (max)	15 seconds/360 degrees
Elevation: Manual	+20 to −10 degrees
Firing Rate: (max)	4 rounds/minute
Loading System:	Manual
Stabilizer System:	None

Secondary:
- (1) .50 caliber MG HB M2 flexible AA mount on turret
- (1) .30 caliber MG M1919A4 coaxial w/90mm gun in turret
- (1) .30 caliber MG M1919A4 in bow mount
- Provision for (5) .45 caliber SMG M3

AMMUNITION

54 rounds 90mm	12 hand grenades
550 rounds .50 caliber	
900 rounds .45 caliber	
4000 rounds .30 caliber	

FIRE CONTROL AND VISION EQUIPMENT

Primary Weapon:	Direct	Indirect
	Telescope M77E1 or	Azimuth Indicator M20
	Telescope M71E4	Elevation Quadrant M9
	Periscope M10E4	Gunner's Quadrant M1
Vision Devices:	Direct	Indirect
Driver	Hatch	Periscope M13 (1)
Asst. Driver	Hatch	Periscope M13 (1)
Commander	Vision blocks (6) in cupola, hatch	Periscope M15 (1)
Gunner	None	Periscope M10E4 (1)
Loader	Hatch and pistol port	Periscope M13 (1)

Total Periscopes: M10E4 (1), M13 (3), M15 (1)
Total Pistol Ports: Hull (0), Turret (1)
Total Vision Blocks: (6) in cupola on turret top

ENGINE

Make and Model: Ford GAC	
Type: 12 cylinder, 4 cycle, 60 degree vee	
Cooling System: Liquid Ignition: Magneto	
Displacement:	1649 cubic inches
Bore and Stroke:	5.4 x 6 inches
Compression Ratio:	7.5:1
Net Horsepower (max):	650 hp at 2800 rpm
Gross Horsepower (max):	770 hp at 2800 rpm
Net Torque (max):	1440 ft-lb at 1600 rpm
Gross Torque (max):	1560 ft-lb at 1600 rpm
Weight:	1850 pounds, dry
Fuel: 80 octane gasoline	255 gallons
Engine Oil:	55 quarts

POWER TRAIN

Transmission: Cross-drive EX-120, 2 ranges forward, 1 reverse
    Three stage hydraulic torque converter
    Stall Multiplication: 4.75:1

Overall Usable Ratios:	low 12:1	reverse 22:1
	high 6:1	

Steering Control: Mechanical, wobble stick
    Steering Rate: 5.7 rpm
Brakes: Multiple disc
Final Drive: Planetary gear   Gear Ratio: 5.47:1
Drive Sprocket: At rear of vehicle with 13 teeth
    Pitch Diameter: 25.038 inches

RUNNING GEAR

Suspension: Torsion bar
    14 individually sprung dual road wheels (7/track)
    Tire Size: 26 x 6 inches
    12 dual track return rollers (6/track)
    Dual compensating idler at front of each track
    Idler Tire Size: 26 x 6 inches
    Shock absorbers fitted on first 2 and last 2 road wheels on each side
Tracks: Center guide, T80E3 and T84E3
  * Type: (T80E3) Double pin, 28 inch width, rubber backed steel
    (T84E3) Double pin, 28 inch width, rubber chevron
    Pitch: 6 inches
    Shoes per Vehicle: 188 (94/track)
    Ground Contact Length: 182.1 inches, left side
        185.9 inches, right side

ELECTRICAL SYSTEM

Nominal Voltage: 24 volts DC
Main Generator: (1) 28.5 volts, 150 amperes, gear driven by main engine
Auxiliary Generator: (1) 28.5 volts, 150 amperes, driven by auxiliary engine
Battery: (2) 12 volts in series

COMMUNICATIONS

Radio: SCR 508 and AN/VRC-3 in turret bustle
Interphone: 5 stations

FIRE PROTECTION

(2) 10 pound carbon dioxide, fixed
(2) 4 pound carbon dioxide, portable

PERFORMANCE

Maximum Speed: Sustained, level road	22 miles/hour
Maximum Tractive Effort: TE at stall	90,000 pounds
Per Cent of Vehicle Weight: TE/W	75 per cent
Maximum Grade:	60 per cent
Maximum Trench:	8.5 feet
Maximum Vertical Wall:	46 inches
Maximum Fording Depth:	48 inches
Minimum Turning Circle: (diameter)	pivot
Cruising Range: Roads	approx. 100 miles

  * The T80E3 and T84E3 tracks are the 23 inch wide T80E1 and T84E1 tracks fitted with 5 inch extended end connectors.

HEAVY TANK T32E1

GENERAL DATA

Crew:	5	men
Length: Gun forward	426.6	inches
Length: Gun in travel position	375.0	inches
Length: Without gun	278.4	inches
Gun Overhang: Gun forward	148.2	inches
Width: Over sandshields	148.3	inches
Height: To top of cupola	110.7	inches
Tread: w/28 inch tracks	115.0	inches
w/23 inch tracks	110.0	inches
Ground Clearance:	18.3	inches
Fire Height:	approx. 78	inches
Turret Ring Diameter: (inside)	69.0	inches
Weight, Combat Loaded:	approx. 120,000	pounds
Weight, Unstowed:	approx. 112,000	pounds
Power to Weight Ratio: Net	10.8	hp/ton
Gross	12.8	hp/ton
Ground Pressure: Zero penetration, w/28 inch tracks	11.6	psi
Zero penetration, w/23 inch tracks	14.2	psi

ARMOR

Type: Turret, cast homogenous steel; Hull, rolled and cast homogenous steel; Welded assembly

Hull Thickness:

	Actual	Angle w/Vertical
Front, Upper	5.0 inches (127mm)	54 degrees
Lower	3.75 inches (95mm)	59 degrees
Sides	3.0 inches (76mm)	0 degrees
Rear	2.0 inches (51mm)	9 degrees
Top	1.5 inches (38mm)	90 degrees
Floor, Front	1.0 inches (25mm)	90 degrees
Rear	0.5 inches (13mm)	90 degrees

Turret Thickness:

Gun Shield	11.75 inches (298mm)	0 degrees
Front	11.75 inches (298mm)	15 degrees
Sides	7.75 to 6 inches (197 to 152mm)	9 degrees
Rear	6.0 inches (152mm)	0 degrees
Top	1.0 inches (25mm)	90 degrees

ARMAMENT

Primary: 90mm Gun T15E2 in Mount T119 in turret

Traverse: Electric-hydraulic and manual	360 degrees
Traverse Rate: (max)	15 seconds/360 degrees
Elevation: Manual	+20 to −10 degrees
Firing Rate: (max)	4 rounds/minute
Loading System:	Manual
Stabilizer System:	None

Secondary:

(1) .50 caliber MG HB M2 flexible AA mount on turret
(1) .30 caliber MG M1919A4 coaxial w/90mm gun in turret
Provision for (5) .45 caliber SMG M3

AMMUNITION

54 rounds 90mm	12 hand grenades
550 rounds .50 caliber	
900 rounds .45 caliber	
2000 rounds .30 caliber	

FIRE CONTROL AND VISION EQUIPMENT

Primary Weapon:	Direct	Indirect
	Telescope M77E1 or	Azimuth Indicator M20
	Telescope M71E4	Elevation Quadrant M9
	Periscope M10E4	Gunner's Quadrant M1

Vision Devices:	Direct	Indirect
Driver	Hatch	Periscope M25 (1)
Asst. Driver	Hatch	Periscope M25 (1)
Commander	Vision blocks (6) in cupola, hatch	Periscope M15 (1)
Gunner	None	Periscope M10E4 (1)
Loader	Hatch and pistol port	Periscope M13 (1)

Total Periscopes: M10E4 (1), M13 (1), M15 (1), M25 (2)
Total Pistol Ports: Hull (0), Turret (1)
Total Vision Blocks: (6) in cupola on turret top

ENGINE

Make and Model: Ford GAC	
Type: 12 cylinder, 4 cycle, 60 degree vee	
Cooling System: Liquid Ignition: Magneto	
Displacement:	1649 cubic inches
Bore and Stroke:	5.4 x 6 inches
Compression Ratio:	7.5:1
Net Horsepower (max):	650 hp at 2800 rpm
Gross Horsepower (max):	770 hp at 2800 rpm
Net Torque (max):	1440 ft-lb at 1600 rpm
Gross Torque (max):	1560 ft-lb at 1600 rpm
Weight:	1850 pounds, dry
Fuel: 80 octane gasoline	255 gallons
Engine Oil:	55 quarts

POWER TRAIN

Transmission: Cross-drive EX-120, 2 ranges forward, 1 reverse
   Three stage hydraulic torque converter
   Stall Multiplication: 4.75:1

Overall Usable Ratios:	low 12:1	reverse 22:1
	high 6:1	

Steering Control: Mechanical, wobble stick
   Steering Rate: 5.7 rpm
Brakes: Multiple disc
Final Drive: Planetary gear   Gear Ratio: 5.47:1
Drive Sprocket: At rear of vehicle with 13 teeth
   Pitch Diameter: 25.038 inches

RUNNING GEAR

Suspension: Torsion bar
   14 individually sprung dual road wheels (7/track)
   Tire Size: 26 x 6 inches
   12 dual track return rollers (6/track)
   Dual compensating idler at front of each track
   Idler Tire Size: 26 x 6 inches
   Shock absorbers fitted on first 2 and last 2 road wheels on each side
Tracks: Center guide, T80E3 and T84E3
 * Type: (T80E3) Double pin, 28 inch width, rubber backed steel
     (T84E3) Double pin, 28 inch width, rubber chevron
   Pitch: 6 inches
   Shoes per Vehicle: 188 (94/track)
   Ground Contact Length: 182.1 inches, left side
                185.9 inches, right side

ELECTRICAL SYSTEM

Nominal Voltage: 24 volts DC
Main Generator: (1) 28.5 volts, 150 amperes, gear driven by main engine
Auxiliary Generator: (1) 28.5 volts, 150 amperes, driven by auxiliary engine
Battery: (2) 12 volts in series

COMMUNICATIONS

Radio: SCR 508 and AN/VRC-3 in turret bustle
Interphone: 5 stations

FIRE PROTECTION

(2) 10 pound carbon dioxide, fixed
(2) 4 pound carbon dioxide, portable

PERFORMANCE

Maximum Speed: Sustained, level road	22 miles/hour
Maximum Tractive Effort: TE at stall	90,000 pounds
Per Cent of Vehicle Weight: TE/W	75 per cent
Maximum Grade:	60 per cent
Maximum Trench:	8.5 feet
Maximum Vertical Wall:	46 inches
Maximum Fording Depth:	48 inches
Minimum Turning Circle: (diameter)	pivot
Cruising Range: Roads	approx. 100 miles

 * The T80E3 and T84E3 tracks are the 23 inch wide T80E1 and T84E1 tracks fitted with 5 inch extended end connectors.

GENERAL DATA

Crew:	6	men
Length: Gun forward	463.5	inches
Length: Gun in travel position	398.2	inches
Length: Without gun	299.6	inches
Gun Overhang: Gun forward	163.9	inches
Width: Over sandshields	149.7	inches
Height: Over cupola	126.9	inches
Tread: w/28 inch tracks	115.0	inches
w/23 inch tracks	110.0	inches
Ground Clearance:	18.8	inches
Fire Height:	approx. 85	inches
Turret Ring Diameter: (inside)	80.0	inches
Weight, Combat Loaded:	approx. 143,600	pounds
Weight, Unstowed:	approx. 134,600	pounds
Power to Weight Ratio: Net	9.8	hp/ton
Gross	11.3	hp/ton
Ground Pressure: Zero penetration, w/28 inch tracks	12.4	psi
Zero penetration, w/23 inch tracks	15.1	psi

ARMOR

Type: Turret, cast homogenous steel; Hull, rolled and cast homogenous steel;
  Welded assembly

Hull Thickness:	Actual	Angle w/Vertical
Front, Upper	4.0 inches (102mm)	54 degrees
Lower	2.75 inches (70mm)	58 degrees
Sides, Front	3.0 inches (76mm)	0 degrees
Rear	2.0 inches (51mm)	0 degrees
Rear, Upper	2.0 inches (51mm)	9 degrees
Lower	0.75 inches (19mm)	62 degrees
Top	1.5 inches (38mm)	90 degrees
Floor, Front	1.0 inches (25mm)	90 degrees
Rear	0.5 inches (13mm)	90 degrees
Turret Thickness:		
Gun Shield	8 to 11 inches (203 to 279mm)	0 degrees
Front	7.0 inches (178mm)	0 degrees
Sides	5 inches (127mm)	0 degrees
Rear	8.0 inches (203mm)	0 degrees
Top	1.5 inches (38mm)	90 degrees

ARMAMENT

Primary: 120mm Gun T53 in Mount T125 in turret

Traverse: Electric-hydraulic and manual	360 degrees
Traverse Rate: (max)	20 seconds/360 degrees
Elevation: Manual	+15 to −10 degrees
Firing Rate: (max)	5 rounds/minute (2 loaders)
Loading System:	Manual
Stabilizer System:	None

Secondary:
  (1) .50 caliber MG HB M2 flexible AA mount on turret
  (2) .50 caliber MG HB M2 coaxial w/120mm gun in turret
  (1) .30 caliber MG M1919A4 in bow mount
  Provision for (6) .45 caliber SMG M3

AMMUNITION

34 rounds 120mm	12 hand grenades
2090 rounds .50 caliber	
1080 rounds .45 caliber	
2500 rounds .30 caliber	

FIRE CONTROL AND VISION EQUIPMENT

Primary Weapon:	Direct	Indirect
	Telescope T143E2	Azimuth Indicator T19
	Periscope M10E10	Elevation Quadrant M9
		Gunner's Quadrant M1

Vision Devices:	Direct	Indirect
Driver	Hatch	Periscope M13 (1)
Asst. Driver	Hatch	Periscope M13 (1)
Commander	Vision blocks (6) in cupola, hatch	Periscope M15 (1)
Gunner	None	Periscope M10E10 (1)
Loader, left	Hatch	None
Loader, right	Hatch and pistol port	None

Total Periscopes: M10E10 (1), M13 (2), M15 (1)
Total Pistol Ports: Hull (0), Turret (1)
Total Vision Blocks: (6) in cupola on turret top

ENGINE

Make and Model: Continental AV-1790-3	
Type: 12 cylinder, 4 cycle, 90 degree vee	
Cooling System: Air Ignition: Magneto	
Displacement:	1791.7 cubic inches
Bore and Stroke:	5.75 x 5.75 inches
Compression Ratio:	6.5:1
Net Horsepower (max):	704 hp at 2800 rpm
Gross Horsepower (max):	810 hp at 2800 rpm
Net Torque (max):	1440 ft-lb at 2000 rpm
Gross Torque (max):	1610 ft-lb at 2200 rpm
Weight:	2332 pounds, dry
Fuel: 80 octane gasoline	320 gallons
Engine Oil:	72 quarts

POWER TRAIN

Transmission: Cross-drive CD-850-1, 2 ranges forward, 1 reverse
  Three stage hydraulic torque converter
  Stall Multiplication: 4.75:1
  Overall Usable Ratios: low   12.7:1   reverse   20.6:1
                 high   6.2:1

Steering Control: Mechanical, wobble stick	
Steering Rate: 5.7 rpm	
Brakes: Multiple disc	
Final Drive: Spur gear Gear Ratio: 6.31:1	
Drive Sprocket: At rear of vehicle with 15 teeth	
Pitch Diameter: 28.89 inches	

RUNNING GEAR

Suspension: Torsion bar
  16 individually sprung dual road wheels (8/track)
  Tire Size: 26 x 6 inches
  14 dual track return rollers (7/track)
  Dual compensating idler at front of each track
  Idler Tire Size: 26 x 6 inches
  Single track tension idler in front of each sprocket
  Shock absorbers fitted on first 3 and last 2 road wheels on each side
Tracks: Center guide, T80E3 and T84E3
  * Type: (T80E3) Double pin, 28 inch width, rubber backed steel
      (T84E3) Double pin, 28 inch width, rubber chevron
  Pitch: 6 inches
  Shoes per Vehicle: 204 (102/track)
  Ground Contact Length: 204.6 inches, left side
                208.6 inches, right side

ELECTRICAL SYSTEM

Nominal Voltage: 24 volts DC
Main Generator: 28.5 volts, 200 amperes, gear driven by main engine
Auxiliary Generator: 28.5 volts, 200 amperes, driven by auxiliary engine
Battery: (2) 12 volts in series

COMMUNICATIONS

Radio: SCR 508 or 528 in turret bustle
Interphone: 6 stations plus external extension kit RC-298

FIRE PROTECTION

  (3) 10 pound carbon dioxide, fixed
  (2) 5 pound carbon dioxide, portable

PERFORMANCE

Maximum Speed: Sustained, level road	22 miles/hour
Maximum Tractive Effort: TE at stall	91,700 pounds
Per Cent of Vehicle Weight: TE/W	64 per cent
Maximum Grade:	60 per cent
Maximum Trench:	6.25 feet
Maximum Vertical Wall:	26 inches
Maximum Fording Depth:	42 inches
Minimum Turning Circle: (diameter)	pivot
Cruising Range: Roads	approx. 100 miles

* The T80E3 and T84E3 tracks are the 23 inch wide T80E1 and T84E1 tracks
  fitted with 5 inch extended end connectors.

GENERAL DATA

Crew:	5	men
Length: Gun forward	448.6	inches
Length: Gun in travel position	397.5	inches
Length: Without gun	275.3	inches
Gun Overhang: Gun forward	173.3	inches
Width: Over sandshields	147.6	inches
Height: Over cupola	126.7	inches
Tread:	115.0	inches
Ground Clearance:	16.1	inches
Fire Height:	approx. 82	inches
Turret Ring Diameter: (inside)	85.0	inches
Weight, Combat Loaded:	approx. 120,000	pounds
Weight, Unstowed:	approx. 110,000	pounds
Power to Weight Ratio: Net	10.8	hp/ton
Gross	13.5	hp/ton
Ground Pressure: Zero penetration	12.4	psi

ARMOR

Type: Turret, cast homogenous steel; Hull, rolled and cast homogenous steel; Welded assembly

Hull Thickness:

	Actual	Angle w/Vertical
Front, Upper	5.0 inches (127mm)	60 degrees
Lower	4.0 inches (102mm)	45 degrees
Sides, Upper	equals 3.0 inches (76mm)	0 degrees
Lower	equals 3.0 inches (76mm)	0 degrees
Rear, Upper	1.5 inches (38mm)	30 degrees
Lower	1.0 inches (25mm)	62 degrees
Top	1.0 inches (25mm)	90 degrees
Floor, Front	1.5 inches (38mm)	90 degrees
Center	1.0 inches (25mm)	90 degrees
Rear	0.5 inches (13mm)	90 degrees

Turret Thickness:

Gun Shield	10.5 to 4 inches (267 to 102mm)	0 to 45 degrees
Front	5.0 inches (127mm)	60 degrees
Sides	3.25-2.75 inches (83-70mm)	40 degrees
Rear	2.0 inches (51mm)	40 degrees
Top	1.5 inches (38mm)	85 to 90 degrees

ARMAMENT

Primary: 120mm Gun T122 in Mount T140 in turret

Traverse: Electric-hydraulic and manual	360 degrees
Traverse Rate: (max)	20 seconds/360 degrees
Elevation: Electric-hydraulic and manual	+15 to −8 degrees
Elevation Rate: (max)	4 degrees/second
Firing Rate: (max)	5 rounds/minute (2 loaders)
Loading System:	Manual
Stabilizer System:	None

Secondary:
(1) .50 caliber MG HB M2 flexible AA mount on turret
* (2) .50 caliber MG HB M2E1 coaxial w/120mm gun in turret
Provision for (1) .45 caliber SMG M3
Provision for (1) .30 caliber Carbine M2 w/grenade launcher

AMMUNITION

34 rounds 120mm
4000 rounds .50 caliber (w/2 .50 caliber coax MG)
2800 rounds .50 caliber (w/1 .50 caliber coax MG)
5225 rounds .30 caliber (w/1 .30 caliber coax MG)
180 rounds .45 caliber
90 rounds .30 caliber (carbine)

12 hand grenades

FIRE CONTROL AND VISION EQUIPMENT

Primary Weapon:	Direct	Indirect
	Range Finder T42	Azimuth Indicator T25
	Periscope T35	Elevation Quadrant T21
		Gunner's Quadrant M1

Vision Devices:	Direct	Indirect
Driver	Hatch	Periscope T36 (3)
Commander	Vision blocks (5) in cupola, hatch	Periscope T35 (1)
Gunner	None	Periscope T35 (1)
Loader, left	Pistol port	None
Loader, right	Hatch	None

Total Periscopes: T35 (2), T36 (3)
Total Pistol Ports: Hull (0), Turret (1)
Total Vision Blocks: (5) in cupola on turret top

* A .30 caliber MG M1919A4E1 or T153 may be substituted for one of the coaxial .50 caliber machine guns.

ENGINE

Make and Model: Continental AV-1790-5C
Type: 12 cylinder, 4 cycle, 90 degree vee
Cooling System: Air   Ignition: Magneto

Displacement:	1791.7 cubic inches
Bore and Stroke:	5.75 x 5.75 inches
Compression Ratio:	6.5:1
Net Horsepower (max):	650 hp at 2400 rpm
Gross Horsepower (max):	810 hp at 2800 rpm
Net Torque (max):	1250 ft-lb at 2100 rpm
Gross Torque (max):	1575 ft-lb at 2200 rpm
Weight:	2554 pounds, dry
Fuel: 80 octane gasoline	280 gallons
Engine Oil:	72 quarts

POWER TRAIN

Transmission: Cross-drive CD-850-4, 2 ranges forward, 1 reverse
Single stage multiphase hydraulic torque converter
Stall Multiplication: 4.3:1

Overall Usable Ratios: low 13.0:1   reverse 17.8:1
high 4.5:1

Steering Control: Mechanical, wobble stick
Steering Rate: 5.6 rpm
Brakes: Multiple disc
Final Drive: Spur gear   Gear Ratio: 7.077:1
Drive Sprocket: At rear of vehicle with 13 teeth
Pitch Diameter: 28.802 inches

RUNNING GEAR

Suspension: Torsion bar
14 individually sprung dual road wheels (7/track)
Tire Size: 26 x 6 inches
12 dual track return rollers (6/track)
Dual compensating idler at front of each track
Idler Tire Size: 26 x 6 inches
Single track tension idler in front of each sprocket
Shock absorbers fitted on first 3 and last 2 road wheels on each side
Tracks: Center guide T96 and T97
Type: (T96) Double pin, 28 inch width, rubber backed steel
(T97) Double pin, 28 inch width, rubber chevron
Pitch: 6.94 inches
Shoes per Vehicle: 164 (82/track)
Ground Contact Length: 173.4 inches

ELECTRICAL SYSTEM

Nominal Voltage: 24 volts DC
Main Generator: 24 volts, 200 amperes, gear driven by main engine
Auxiliary Generator: 28.5 volts, 300 amperes, driven by auxiliary engine
Battery: (4) 12 volts, 2 sets of 2 in series connected in parallel

COMMUNICATIONS

Radio: AN/GRC-3 thru 8 series or SCR 508 or SCR 528 in turret bustle
Interphone: 4 stations plus external extension kit AN/VIA-1

FIRE PROTECTION

(3) 10 pound carbon dioxide, fixed
(1) 5 pound carbon dioxide, portable

PERFORMANCE

Maximum Speed: Sustained, level road	25 miles/hour
Maximum Tractive Effort: TE at stall	92,000 pounds
Per Cent of Vehicle Weight: TE/W	77 per cent
Maximum Grade:	60 per cent
Maximum Trench:	7.5 feet
Maximum Vertical Wall:	27 inches
Maximum Fording Depth:	48 inches
Minimum Turning Circle: (diameter)	pivot
Cruising Range: Roads	approx. 80 miles

120mm GUN TANK M103

GENERAL DATA

Crew:	5	men
Length: Gun forward	448.6	inches
Length: Gun in travel position	400.3	inches
Length: Without gun	275.3	inches
Gun Overhang: Gun forward	173.3	inches
Width: Over tracks	143.0	inches
Height: Over cupola MG	140.1	inches
Tread:	115.0	inches
Ground Clearance:	15.4	inches
Fire Height:	approx. 82	inches
Turret Ring Diameter: (inside)	85.0	inches
Weight, Combat Loaded:	approx. 125,000	pounds
Weight, Unstowed:	approx. 117,000	pounds
Power to Weight Ratio: Net	11.0	hp/ton
Gross	13.0	hp/ton
Ground Pressure: Zero penetration	12.9	psi

ARMOR

Type: Turret, cast homogenous steel; Hull, rolled and cast homogenous steel; Welded assembly

Hull Thickness:

	Actual	Angle w/Vertical
Front, Upper	5.0 inches (127mm)	60 degrees
Lower	4.5 inches (114mm)	50 degrees
Sides, Upper	equals 2.0 inches (51mm)	40 degrees
Lower	equals 1.75 inches (44mm)	30 degrees
Rear, Upper	1.5 inches (38mm)	30 degrees
Lower	1.0 inches (25mm)	60 degrees
Top	1.0 inches (25mm)	90 degrees
Floor, Front	1.5 inches (38mm)	90 degrees
Rear	1.25 inches (32mm)	90 degrees

Turret Thickness:

Gun Shield	10 to 4 inches (254 to 102mm)	0 to 45 degrees
Front	5.0 inches (127mm)	50 degrees
Sides	5.38-2.75 inches (137-70mm)	20 to 40 degrees
Rear	2.0 inches (51mm)	40 degrees
Top	1.5 inches (38mm)	85 to 90 degrees

ARMAMENT

Primary: 120mm Gun M58 (T123E1) in Mount M89 (T154) in turret

Traverse: Electric-hydraulic and manual	360 degrees
Traverse Rate: (max)	20 seconds/360 degrees
Elevation: Electric-hydraulic and manual	+15 to −8 degrees
Elevation Rate: (max)	4 degrees/second
Firing Rate: (max)	5 rounds/minute (2 loaders)
Loading System:	Manual
Stabilizer System:	None

Secondary:
(1) .50 caliber MG HB M2 in remote control mount on commander's cupola M4
(2) .30 caliber MG M1919A4E1 or M37 coaxial w/120mm gun in turret
Provision for (1) .45 caliber SMG M3A1
Provision for (1) .30 caliber Carbine M2 w/grenade launcher

AMMUNITION

33 rounds 120mm   8 hand grenades
900 rounds .50 caliber
180 rounds .45 caliber
8150 rounds .30 caliber
180 rounds .30 caliber (carbine)

FIRE CONTROL AND VISION EQUIPMENT

Primary Weapon:	Direct	Indirect
	Range Finder M14	Azimuth Indicator M30
	Periscope M20A1	Elevation Quadrant M13
	Ballistic Drive M6	Gunner's Quadrant M1A1
Vision Devices:	Direct	Indirect
Driver	Hatch	Early: Periscope M26 (3)
		Late: Periscope M27 (3) and Periscope M24, infrared (1)
Commander	Hatch	Periscope M17 (4)
Gunner	None	Periscope M20A1 (1) Range Finder M14
Loader, left	None	None
Loader, right	Hatch	None

Total Periscopes: M17 (4), M20A1 (1), M24 (infrared) (1), M26 or 27 (3)

ENGINE

Make and Model: Continental AV-1790-5B, AV-1790-7, AV-1790-7B or AV-1790-7C (data for AV-1790-7C)

Type: 12 cylinder, 4 cycle, 90 degree vee	
Cooling System: Air Ignition: Magneto	
Displacement:	1791.7 cubic inches
Bore and Stroke:	5.75 x 5.75 inches
Compression Ratio:	6.5:1
Net Horsepower (max):	690 hp at 2800 rpm
Gross Horsepower (max):	810 hp at 2800 rpm
Net Torque (max):	1410 ft-lb at 2200 rpm
Gross Torque (max):	1600 ft-lb at 2200 rpm
Weight:	2647 pounds, dry
Fuel: 80 octane gasoline	280 gallons
Engine Oil:	64 quarts

POWER TRAIN

Transmission: Cross-drive CD-850-4A or CD-850-4B (data for CD-850-4B)
2 ranges forward, 1 reverse
Single stage multiphase hydraulic torque converter
Stall Multiplication: 4.0:1
Overall Usable Ratios: low 13.0:1   reverse 18.1:1
                   high 4.5:1
Steering Control: Mechanical, steering wheel
Steering Rate: 5.7 rpm
Brakes: Multiple disc
Final Drive: Spur gear   Gear Ratio: 7.077:1
Drive Sprocket: At rear of vehicle with 11 teeth
Pitch Diameter: 24.504 inches

RUNNING GEAR

Suspension: Torsion bar
14 individually sprung dual road wheels (7/track)
Tire Size: 26 x 6 inches
12 dual track return rollers (6/track)
Dual compensating idler at front of each track
Idler Tire Size: 26 x 6 inches
Shock absorbers fitted on first 3 and last 2 road wheels on each side
Tracks: Center guide T96, T97, T97E1, or T97E2
Type: (T96) Double pin, 28 inch width, rubber backed steel
(T97) Double pin, 28 inch width, rubber chevron
(T97E1) Double pin, 28 inch width, rubber chevron
(T97E2) Double pin, 28 inch width, rubber chevron
Pitch: 6.94 inches
Shoes per Vehicle: 164 (early), 162 (late), 82 or 81/track
Ground Contact Length: 173.4 inches

ELECTRICAL SYSTEM

Nominal Voltage: 24 volts DC
Main Generator: 24 volts, 300 amperes, gear driven by main engine
Auxiliary Generator: 24 volts, 300 amperes, driven by auxiliary engine
Battery: (4) 12 volts, 2 sets of 2 in series connected in parallel

COMMUNICATIONS

Radio: AN/GRC-3 thru 8 series in turret bustle
AN/ARC-3 or AN/ARC-27 (air to ground) also may be fitted
Interphone: 4 stations plus external extension kit AN/VIA-1

FIRE PROTECTION

(3) 10 pound carbon dioxide, fixed
(1) 5 pound carbon dioxide, portable

PERFORMANCE

Maximum Speed: Sustained, level road	21 miles/hour
Maximum Tractive Effort: TE at stall	110,000 pounds
Per Cent of Vehicle Weight: TE/W	88 per cent
Maximum Grade:	60 per cent
Maximum Trench:	7.5 feet
Maximum Vertical Wall:	36 inches
Maximum Fording Depth:	48 inches
Minimum Turning Circle: (diameter)	pivot
Cruising Range: Roads	approx. 80 miles

120mm GUN TANK M103A1

GENERAL DATA

Crew:	5	men
Length: Gun forward	448.6	inches
Length: Gun in travel position	400.3	inches
Length: Without gun	275.3	inches
Gun Overhang: Gun forward	173.3	inches
Width: Over tracks	143.0	inches
Height: Over cupola MG	140.1	inches
Tread:	115.0	inches
Ground Clearance:	15.4	inches
Fire Height:	approx. 82	inches
Turret Ring Diameter: (inside)	85.0	inches
Weight, Combat Loaded:	approx. 125,000	pounds
Weight, Unstowed:	approx. 117,000	pounds
Power to Weight Ratio: Net	11.0	hp/ton
Gross	13.0	hp/ton
Ground Pressure: Zero penetration	12.9	psi

ARMOR

Type: Turret, cast homogenous steel; Hull, rolled and cast homogenous steel;
Welded assembly

Hull Thickness:	Actual	Angle w/Vertical
Front, Upper	5.0 inches (127mm)	60 degrees
Lower	4.5 inches (114mm)	50 degrees
Sides, Upper	equals 2.0 inches (51mm)	40 degrees
Lower	equals 1.75 inches (44mm)	30 degrees
Rear, Upper	1.5 inches (38mm)	30 degrees
Lower	1.0 inches (25mm)	60 degrees
Top	1.0 inches (25mm)	90 degrees
Floor, Front	1.5 inches (38mm)	90 degrees
Rear	1.25 inches (32mm)	90 degrees

Turret Thickness:		
Gun Shield	10 to 4 inches (254 to 102mm)	0 to 45 degrees
Front	5.0 inches (127mm)	50 degrees
Sides	5.38-2.75 inches (137-70mm)	20 to 40 degrees
Rear	2.0 inches (51mm)	40 degrees
Top	1.5 inches (38mm)	85 to 90 degrees

ARMAMENT

Primary: 120mm Gun M58 in Mount M89A1 in turret

Traverse: Amplidyne and manual	360 degrees
Traverse Rate: (max)	17 seconds/360 degrees
Elevation: Amplidyne and manual	+15 to −8 degrees
Elevation Rate: (max)	4 degrees/second
Firing Rate: (max)	5 rounds/minute (2 loaders)
Loading System:	Manual
Stabilizer System:	None

Secondary:

(1) .50 caliber MG HB M2 in flexible mount on commander's cupola M11
(1) .30 caliber MG M37 coaxial w/120mm gun in turret
Provision for (2) .45 caliber SMG M3A1 (USMC)

AMMUNITION

38 rounds 120mm   8 hand grenades
1000 rounds .50 caliber
360 rounds .45 caliber
5250 rounds .30 caliber

FIRE CONTROL AND VISION EQUIPMENT

Primary Weapon:	Direct	Indirect
	Range Finder M15	Azimuth Indicator M28
	Periscope M29	Elevation Quadrant M13
	Ballistic Computer M14	Gunner's Quadrant M1A1
	Telescope M102	

Vision Devices:	Direct	Indirect
Driver	Hatch	Periscope M27 (3) and Periscope M24, infrared (1)
Commander	Hatch	Periscope M17 (4) and Range Finder M15
Gunner	None	Periscope M29 (1)
Loader, left	None	None
Loader, right	Hatch	None

Total Periscopes: M17 (4), M24 (infrared) (1), M27 (3), M29 (1)

ENGINE

Make and Model: Continental AV-1790-5B, AV-1790-7, AV-1790-7B or AV-1790-7C
(data for AV-1790-7C)
Type: 12 cylinder, 4 cycle, 90 degree vee
Cooling System: Air   Ignition: Magneto

Displacement:	1791.7 cubic inches
Bore and Stroke:	5.75 x 5.75 inches
Compression Ratio:	6.5:1
Net Horsepower (max):	690 hp at 2800 rpm
Gross Horsepower (max):	810 hp at 2800 rpm
Net Torque (max):	1410 ft-lb at 2200 rpm
Gross Torque (max):	1600 ft-lb at 2200 rpm
Weight:	2647 pounds, dry
Fuel: 80 octane gasoline	280 gallons
Engine Oil:	64 quarts

POWER TRAIN

Transmission: Cross-drive CD-850-4A or CD-850-4B (data for CD-850-4B)
2 ranges forward, 1 reverse
Single stage multiphase hydraulic torque converter
Stall Multiplication: 4.0:1

Overall Usable Ratios:	low 13.0:1	reverse 18.1:1
	high 4.5:1	

Steering Control: Mechanical, steering wheel
Steering Rate: 5.7 rpm
Brakes: Multiple disc
Final Drive: Spur gear   Gear Ratio: 7.077:1
Drive Sprocket: At rear of vehicle with 11 teeth
Pitch Diameter: 24.504 inches

RUNNING GEAR

Suspension: Torsion bar
14 individually sprung dual road wheels (7/track)
Tire Size: 26 x 6 inches
12 dual track return rollers (6/track)
Dual compensating idler at front of each track
Idler Tire Size: 26 x 6 inches
Shock absorbers fitted on first 3 and last 2 road wheels on each side
Tracks: Center guide T96, T97, T97E1, or T97E2
Type: (T96) Double pin, 28 inch width, rubber backed steel
(T97) Double pin, 28 inch width, rubber chevron
(T97E1) Double pin, 28 inch width, rubber chevron
(T97E2) Double pin, 28 inch width, rubber chevron
Pitch: 6.94 inches
Shoes per Vehicle: 164 (early), 162 (late), 82 or 81/track
Ground Contact Length: 173.4 inches

ELECTRICAL SYSTEM

Nominal Voltage: 24 volts DC
Main Generator: 24 volts, 300 amperes, gear driven by main engine
Auxiliary Generator: 24 volts, 300 amperes, driven by auxiliary engine
Battery: (4) 12 volts, 2 sets of 2 in series connected in parallel

COMMUNICATIONS

Radio: AN/GRC-3 thru 8 series or AN/VRC-7 in turret bustle
AN/ARC-3 or AN/ARC-27 (air to ground) also may be fitted
Interphone: 4 stations plus external extension kit AN/VIA-1

FIRE PROTECTION

(3) 10 pound carbon dioxide, fixed (1 shot, 30 pounds)
(1) 5 pound carbon dioxide, portable

PERFORMANCE

Maximum Speed: Sustained, level road	21 miles/hour
Maximum Tractive Effort: TE at stall	110,000 pounds
Per Cent of Vehicle Weight: TE/W	88 per cent
Maximum Grade:	60 per cent
Maximum Trench:	7.5 feet
Maximum Vertical Wall:	36 inches
Maximum Fording Depth: w/o deep water kit	48 inches
w/deep water kit	96 inches
Minimum Turning Circle: (diameter)	pivot
Cruising Range: Roads, w/o jettison tank kit	approx. 80 miles
Roads, w/jettison tank kit	approx. 145 miles

120mm GUN TANK M103A2

GENERAL DATA

Crew:	5	men
Length: Gun forward	442.2	inches
Length: Gun in travel position	393.9	inches
Length: Without gun	275.3	inches
Gun Overhang: Gun forward	166.9	inches
Width: Over tracks	143.0	inches
Height: Over cupola MG	140.1	inches
Tread:	115.0	inches
Ground Clearance:	15.4	inches
Fire Height:	approx. 82	inches
Turret Ring Diameter: (inside)	85.0	inches
Weight, Combat Loaded:	approx. 128,000	pounds
Weight, Unstowed:	approx. 123,000	pounds
Power to Weight Ratio: Net	10.0	hp/ton
Gross	11.7	hp/ton
Ground Pressure: Zero penetration	13.2	psi

ARMOR

Type: Turret, cast homogenous steel; Hull, rolled and cast homogenous steel; Welded assembly

Hull Thickness:	Actual	Angle w/Vertical
Front, Upper	5.0 inches (127mm)	60 degrees
Lower	4.5 inches (114mm)	50 degrees
Sides, Upper	equals 2.0 inches (51mm)	40 degrees
Lower	equals 1.75 inches (44mm)	30 degrees
Rear, Upper	1.5 inches (38mm)	30 degrees
Lower	1.0 inches (25mm)	60 degrees
Top	1.0 inches (25mm)	90 degrees
Floor, Front	1.5 inches (38mm)	90 degrees
Rear	1.25 inches (32mm)	90 degrees

Turret Thickness:		
Gun Shield	10 to 4 inches (254 to 102mm)	0 to 45 degrees
Front	5.0 inches (127mm)	50 degrees
Sides	5.38-2.75 inches (137-70mm)	20 to 40 degrees
Rear	2.0 inches (51mm)	40 degrees
Top	1.5 inches (38mm)	85 to 90 degrees

ARMAMENT

Primary: 120mm Gun M58 in Mount M89A1 in turret

Traverse: Amplidyne and manual	360 degrees
Traverse Rate: (max)	17 seconds/360 degrees
Elevation: Amplidyne and manual	+15 to −8 degrees
Elevation Rate: (max)	4 degrees/second
Firing Rate: (max)	5 rounds/minute (2 loaders)
Loading System:	Manual
Stabilizer System:	None

Secondary:
(1) .50 caliber MG HB M2 flexible mount on commander's cupola M11
(1) .30 caliber MG M37 coaxial w/120mm gun in turret
Provision for (2) .45 caliber SMG M3A1 (USMC)

AMMUNITION

38 rounds 120mm
1000 rounds .50 caliber
360 rounds .45 caliber
5250 rounds .30 caliber

8 hand grenades

FIRE CONTROL AND VISION EQUIPMENT

Primary Weapon:	Direct	Indirect
	Range Finder M24	Azimuth Indicator M28A1
	Periscope M29	Elevation Quadrant M13B1
	Ballistic Computer M14A1	Gunner's Quadrant M1A1
	Telescope M102C	

Vision Devices:	Direct	Indirect
Driver	Hatch	Periscope M27 (3) and Periscope M24, infrared (1)
Commander	Hatch	Periscope M17 (4) and Range Finder M24
Gunner	None	Periscope M29 (1)
Loader, left	None	None
Loader, right	Hatch	None

Total Periscopes: M17 (4), M24 (infrared) (1), M27 (3), M29 (1)

ENGINE

Make and Model: Continental AVDS-1790-2A	
Type: 12 cylinder, 4 cycle, 90 degree vee	
Cooling System: Air Ignition: Compression	
Displacement:	1791.7 cubic inches
Bore and Stroke:	5.75 x 5.75 inches
Compression Ratio:	16:1
Net Horsepower (max):	643 hp at 2400 rpm
Gross Horsepower (max):	750 hp at 2400 rpm
Net Torque (max):	1575 ft-lb at 1750 rpm
Gross Torque (max):	1710 ft-lb at 1800 rpm
Weight:	4700 pounds, dry
Fuel: 40 cetane diesel	440 gallons
Engine Oil:	72 quarts

POWER TRAIN

Transmission: Cross-drive CD-850-6 or CD-850-6A (data for CD-850-6A)
2 ranges forward, 1 reverse
Single stage multiphase hydraulic torque converter
Stall Multiplication: 4.0:1
Overall Usable Ratios: low 12.0:1   reverse 16.9:1
high 4.3:1

Steering Control: Mechanical, steering wheel
Steering Rate: 5.7 rpm
Brakes: Multiple disc
Final Drive: Spur gear   Gear Ratio: 7.077:1
Drive Sprocket: At rear of vehicle with 11 teeth
Pitch Diameter: 25.000 inches

RUNNING GEAR

Suspension: Torsion bar
14 individually sprung dual road wheels (7/track)
Tire Size: 26 x 6 inches
12 dual track return rollers (6/track)
Dual compensating idler at front of each track
Idler Tire Size: 26 x 6 inches
Shock absorbers fitted on first 3 and last 2 road wheels on each side
Tracks: Center guide T107
Type: (T107) Double pin, 28 inch width, rubber chevron
Pitch: 7.09 inches
Shoes per Vehicle: 162 (81/track)
Ground Contact Length: 173.4 inches

ELECTRICAL SYSTEM

Nominal Voltage: 24 volts DC
Main Generator: 24 volts, 300 amperes, gear driven by main engine
Auxiliary Generator: None
Battery: (6) 3 sets of 2 in series connected in parallel

COMMUNICATIONS

Radio: AN/GRC-3 thru 8 series in turret bustle
AN/ARC-3 or AN/ARC-27 (air to ground) also may be fitted
Interphone: 4 stations plus external extension kit AN/VIA-1

FIRE PROTECTION

(3) 10 pound carbon dioxide, fixed (2 shot; 1st 10 lb., 2nd 20 lb.)
(1) 5 pound carbon dioxide, portable

PERFORMANCE

Maximum Speed: Sustained, level road	23 miles/hour
Maximum Tractive Effort: TE at stall	93,000 pounds
Per Cent of Vehicle Weight: TE/W	73 per cent
Maximum Grade:	60 per cent
Maximum Trench:	8.5 feet
Maximum Vertical Wall:	36 inches
Maximum Fording Depth: w/o deep water kit	48 inches
w/deep water kit	96 inches
Minimum Turning Circle: (diameter)	pivot
Cruising Range: Roads	approx. 300 miles

120mm GUN TANK T57

GENERAL DATA

Crew:	4	men
Length: Gun forward	449.3	inches
Length: Gun in travel position	401.0	inches
Length: Without gun	275.3	inches
Gun Overhang: Gun forward	174.0	inches
Width: Over tracks	143.0	inches
Height: Over turret roof	104.5	inches
Tread:	115.0	inches
Ground Clearance:	18.0	inches
Fire Height:	88.3	inches
Turret Ring Diameter: (inside)	85.0	inches
Weight, Combat Loaded:	120,000	pounds
Weight, Unstowed:	116,000	pounds
Power to Weight Ratio: Net	10.8	hp/ton
Gross	13.5	hp/ton
Ground Pressure: Zero penetration	12.4	psi

ARMOR

Type: Turret, cast homogenous steel; Hull, rolled and cast homogenous steel; Welded assembly

Hull Thickness:

	Actual	Angle w/Vertical
Front, Upper	5.0 inches (127mm)	60 degrees
Lower	4.5 inches (114mm)	50 degrees
Sides, Upper	equals 2.0 inches (51mm)	40 degrees
Lower	equals 1.75 inches (44mm)	30 degrees
Rear, Upper	1.5 inches (38mm)	30 degrees
Lower	1.0 inches (25mm)	60 degrees
Top	1.0 inches (25mm)	90 degrees
Floor, Front	1.5 inches (38mm)	90 degrees
Rear	1.25 inches (32mm)	90 degrees

Turret Thickness:

Front	5.0 inches (127mm)	60 degrees
Sides	5.38 inches (137mm)	20 to 40 degrees
Rear	equals 2.0 inches (51mm)	40 degrees
Top	1.5 inches (38mm)	86 to 90 degrees (0 elevation)

ARMAMENT

Primary: 120mm Gun T179 in Mount T169 (rigid) in turret

Traverse: Amplidyne and manual	360 degrees
Traverse Rate: (max)	15 seconds/360 degrees
Elevation: Amplidyne and manual	+15 to −8 degrees
Elevation Rate: (max)	4 degrees/second
Firing Rate: (max w/auto load)	30 rounds/minute (design rate)
Loading System:	Automatic w/8 round magazine
Stabilizer System:	None

Secondary:
(1) .50 caliber MG HB M2 flexible AA mount on turret hatch
(1) .30 caliber MG HB M1919A4E1 or T153 coaxial w/120mm gun in turret
Provision for (1) .45 caliber SMG M3A1
Provision for (1) .30 caliber Carbine M2 w/grenade launcher

AMMUNITION

18 rounds 120mm	8 hand grenades
3425 rounds .50 caliber	
180 rounds .45 caliber	
3000 rounds .30 caliber	
180 rounds .30 caliber (carbine)	

FIRE CONTROL AND VISION EQUIPMENT

Primary Weapon:	* Direct	Indirect
	Range Finder T50	Azimuth Indicator T28
	Range Drive T33E2	Elevation Quadrant M13
	Periscope M20A1	Gunner's Quadrant M1 or M1A1
	Range Drive T32E2	
	Telescope T170	

Vision Devices:	Direct	Indirect
Driver	Hatch	Periscope T36 (3)
Commander	Hatch	Periscope T36 (6)
		Range Finder T50
Gunner	None	Periscope M20A1 (1)
Loader	Hatch	Periscope M13 (1)

Total Periscopes: M13 (1), M20A1 (1), T36 (9)
* Space provided for Ballistic Computer T34

ENGINE

Make and Model: Continental AV-1790-5C	
Type: 12 cylinder, 4 cycle, 90 degree vee	
Cooling System: Air Ignition: Magneto	
Displacement:	1791.7 cubic inches
Bore and Stroke:	5.75 x 5.75 inches
Compression Ratio:	6.5:1
Net Horsepower (max):	650 hp at 2400 rpm
Gross Horsepower (max):	810 hp at 2800 rpm
Net Torque (max):	1250 ft-lb at 2100 rpm
Gross Torque (max):	1575 ft-lb at 2200 rpm
Weight:	2554 pounds, dry
Fuel: 80 octane gasoline	280 gallons
Engine Oil:	72 quarts

POWER TRAIN

Transmission: Cross-drive CD-850-4, 2 ranges forward, 1 reverse
Single stage multiphase hydraulic torque converter
Stall Multiplication: 4.3:1

Overall Usable Ratios:	low 13.0:1	reverse 17.8:1
	high 4.5:1	

Steering Control: Mechanical, steering wheel
Steering Rate: 5.6 rpm
Brakes: Multiple disc
Final Drive: Spur gear   Gear Ratio: 7.077:1
Drive Sprocket: At rear of vehicle with 11 teeth
Pitch Diameter: 24.504 inches

RUNNING GEAR

Suspension: Torsion bar
14 individually sprung dual road wheels (7/track)
Tire Size: 26 x 6 inches
12 dual track return rollers (6/track)
Dual compensating idler at front of each track
Idler Tire Size: 26 x 6 inches
Shock absorbers fitted on first 3 and last 2 road wheels on each side
Tracks: Center guide T96 and T97
Type: (T96) Double pin, 28 inch width, rubber backed steel
(T97) Double pin, 28 inch width, rubber chevron
Pitch: 6.94 inches
Shoes per Vehicle: 164 (82/track)
Ground Contact Length: 173.4 inches

ELECTRICAL SYSTEM

Nominal Voltage: 24 volts DC
Main Generator: 24 volts, 200 amperes, gear driven by main engine
Auxiliary Generator: 24 volts, 300 amperes, driven by auxiliary engine
Battery: (4) 12 volts, 2 sets of 2 in series connected in parallel

COMMUNICATIONS

Radio: AN/GRC-3 thru 8 series in turret bustle
Interphone: 4 stations plus external extension kit AN/VIA-1

FIRE PROTECTION

(3) 10 pound carbon dioxide, fixed
(2) 5 pound carbon dioxide, portable

PERFORMANCE

Maximum Speed: Sustained, level road	22 miles/hour
Maximum Tractive Effort: TE at stall	105,400 pounds
Per Cent of Vehicle Weight: TE/W	88 per cent
Maximum Grade:	60 per cent
Maximum Trench:	7.5 feet
Maximum Vertical Wall:	27 inches
Maximum Fording Depth:	48 inches
Minimum Turning Circle: (diameter)	pivot
Cruising Range: Roads	approx. 80 miles

155mm GUN TANK T58

GENERAL DATA

Crew:	4	men
Length: Gun forward	425.8	inches
Length: Gun in travel position	379.0	inches
Length: Without gun	275.3	inches
Gun Overhang: Gun forward	150.5	inches
Width: Over tracks	143.0	inches
Height: Over turret hatch	125.0	inches
Tread:	115.0	inches
Ground Clearance:	15.0	inches
Fire Height:	approx. 92	inches
Turret Ring Diameter: (inside)	85.0	inches
Weight, Combat Loaded:	approx. 132,000	pounds
Weight, Unstowed:	126,270	pounds
Power to Weight Ratio: Net	9.8	hp/ton
Gross	12.3	hp/ton
Ground Pressure: Zero penetration	13.6	psi

ARMOR

Type: Turret, cast homogenous steel; Hull, rolled and cast homogenous steel; Welded assembly

Hull Thickness:

	Actual	Angle w/Vertical
Front, Upper	5.0 inches (127mm)	60 degrees
Lower	4.5 inches (114mm)	50 degrees
Sides, Upper	equals 2.0 inches (51mm)	40 degrees
Lower	equals 1.75 inches (44mm)	30 degrees
Rear, Upper	1.5 inches (38mm)	30 degrees
Lower	1.0 inches (25mm)	60 degrees
Top	1.0 inches (25mm)	90 degrees
Floor, Front	1.5 inches (38mm)	90 degrees
Rear	1.25 inches (32mm)	90 degrees

Turret Thickness:

Front	5.0 inches (127mm)	60 degrees
Sides	3.25-2.75 inches (83-70mm)	40 degrees
Rear	2.0 inches (51mm)	40 degrees
Top	1.5 inches (38mm)	80 to 90 degrees (0 elevation)

ARMAMENT

Primary: 155mm Gun T180 in Mount T170 in turret

Traverse: Amplidyne and manual	360 degrees
Traverse Rate: (max)	20 seconds/360 degrees
Elevation: Amplidyne and manual	+12 to −8 degrees
Elevation Rate: (max)	4 degrees/second
Firing Rate: (max w/auto load)	23 rounds/minute (design rate)
Loading System:	Automatic w/6 round magazine
Stabilizer System:	None

Secondary:
(1) .50 caliber MG HB M2 flexible AA mount on turret hatch
(1) .30 caliber MG HB M1919A4E1 coaxial w/155mm gun in turret
Provision for (1) .45 caliber SMG M3A1
Provision for (1) .30 caliber Carbine M2 w/grenade launcher

AMMUNITION

32 rounds 155mm	8 hand grenades
1200 rounds .50 caliber	
180 rounds .45 caliber	
6500 rounds .30 caliber	
180 rounds .30 caliber (carbine)	

FIRE CONTROL AND VISION EQUIPMENT

Primary Weapon:

	* Direct	Indirect
	Range Finder T50E1	Azimuth Indicator T28
	Range Drive T33E3	Elevation Quadrant M13
	Periscope M20 (T35)	Gunner's Quadrant M1 or M1A1
	Range Drive T32E3	
	Telescope T170	

Vision Devices:

	Direct	Indirect
Driver	Hatch	Periscope T36 (3)
Commander	Hatch	Periscope T36 (7)
		Range Finder T50E1
Gunner	None	Periscope M20 (T35) (1)
Loader	Hatch	Periscope M13 (1)

Total Periscopes: M13 (1), M20 (1), T36 (10)
* Space provided for Ballistic Computer T34E2

ENGINE

Make and Model: Continental AV-1790-5C	
Type: 12 cylinder, 4 cycle, 90 degree vee	
Cooling System: Air Ignition: Magneto	
Displacement:	1791.7 cubic inches
Bore and Stroke:	5.75 x 5.75 inches
Compression Ratio:	6.5:1
Net Horsepower (max):	650 hp at 2400 rpm
Gross Horsepower (max):	810 hp at 2800 rpm
Net Torque (max):	1250 ft-lb at 2100 rpm
Gross Torque (max):	1575 ft-lb at 2200 rpm
Weight:	2554 pounds, dry
Fuel: 80 octane gasoline	280 gallons
Engine Oil:	72 quarts

POWER TRAIN

Transmission: Cross-drive CD-850-4, 2 ranges forward, 1 reverse
Single stage multiphase hydraulic torque converter
Stall Multiplication: 4.3:1

Overall Usable Ratios:	low 13.0:1	reverse 17.8:1
	high 4.5:1	

Steering Control: Mechanical, steering wheel
Steering Rate: 5.6 rpm
Brakes: Multiple disc
Final Drive: Spur gear   Gear Ratio: 7.077:1
Drive Sprocket: At rear of vehicle with 11 teeth
Pitch Diameter: 24.504 inches

RUNNING GEAR

Suspension: Torsion bar
14 individually sprung dual road wheels (7/track)
Tire Size: 26 x 6 inches
12 dual track return rollers (6/track)
Dual compensating idler at front of each track
Idler Tire Size: 26 x 6 inches
Shock absorbers fitted on first 3 and last 2 road wheels on each side
Tracks: Center guide, T96 and T97
Type: (T96) Double pin, 28 inch width, rubber backed steel
(T97) Double pin, 28 inch width, rubber chevron
Pitch: 6.94 inches
Shoes per Vehicle: 164 (82/track)
Ground Contact Length: 173.4 inches

ELECTRICAL SYSTEM

Nominal Voltage: 24 volts DC
Main Generator: 24 volts, 200 amperes, gear driven by main engine
Auxiliary Generator: 24 volts, 300 amperes, driven by auxiliary engine
Battery: (4) 12 volts, 2 sets of 2 in series connected in parallel

COMMUNICATIONS

Radio: AN/GRC-3 thru 8 series in turret bustle
Interphone: 4 stations plus external extension kit AN/VIA-1

FIRE PROTECTION

(3) 10 pound carbon dioxide, fixed
(2) 5 pound carbon dioxide, portable

PERFORMANCE

Maximum Speed: Sustained, level road	22 miles/hour
Maximum Tractive Effort: TE at stall	105,400 pounds
Per Cent of Vehicle Weight: TE/W	80 per cent
Maximum Grade:	60 per cent
Maximum Trench:	7.5 feet
Maximum Vertical Wall:	27 inches
Maximum Fording Depth:	48 inches
Minimum Turning Circle: (diameter)	pivot
Cruising Range: Roads	approx. 80 miles

HEAVY RECOVERY VEHICLE M51

GENERAL DATA

Crew:	4	men
Length: Boom and spade in travel position	399	inches
Width: Over tracks	143	inches
Height: Over AA MG	approx. 129	inches
Tread:	115	inches
Ground Clearance:	18	inches
Weight, Combat Loaded:	approx. 120,000	pounds
Weight, Unstowed:	approx. 112,500	pounds
Power to Weight Ratio: Net	12.8	hp/ton
Gross	16.3	hp/ton
Ground Pressure: Zero penetration	11.5	psi

ARMOR

Type: Hull and Cab, rolled homogenous steel; Welded assembly

Hull and Cab

Thickness:	Actual	Angle w/Vertical
Front, Upper	0.75 inches (19mm)	36 degrees
Lower	1.5 inches (38mm)	0 degrees
Sides, Upper	0.75 inches (19mm)	0 degrees
Lower	1.0 inches (25mm)	0 degrees
Rear, Upper	0.75 inches (19mm)	0 degrees
Lower	1.5 inches (38mm)	0 degrees
Top	0.75 inches (19mm)	90 degrees
Floor, Front	1.5 inches (38mm)	90 degrees
Rear	1.0 inches (25mm)	90 degrees

ARMAMENT

(1) .50 caliber MG HB M2 flexible AA mount on commander's cupola
Provision for (1) 3.5 inch Rocket Launcher M20
Provision for (1) .45 caliber SMG M3A1
Provision for (1) .30 caliber Carbine M2

AMMUNITION

1500 rounds .50 caliber	32 hand grenades
6 rockets 3.5 inch	
180 rounds .45 caliber	
540 rounds .30 caliber (carbine)	

RECOVERY EQUIPMENT

Spade: One on front and one on rear of vehicle operated by the auxiliary winch
Auxiliary Winch: 10,000 pound capacity, hydraulic power
Main Winch: 90,000 pound capacity, hydraulic power
Crane: 60,000 pound capacity, 4 feet from rear of vehicle, boom retracted
    30,000 pound capacity, 8 feet from rear of vehicle, boom extended

VISION EQUIPMENT

	Direct	Indirect
Driver	Hatch	Periscope M17 (4) and Periscope M19 (1) infrared
Commander	Hatch	Periscope M17 (4)
Crane Operator	Hatch and rear vision door	None
Rigger	None	None

Total Periscopes: M17 (8), M19 infrared (1)

ENGINE

Make and Model: Continental AVSI-1790-6	
Type: 12 cylinder, 4 cycle, 90 degree vee, supercharged, fuel injection	
Cooling System: Air Ignition: Magneto	
Displacement:	1791.7 cubic inches
Bore and Stroke:	5.75 x 5.75 inches
Compression Ratio:	5.5:1
Net Horsepower (max):	765 hp at 2800 rpm
Gross Horsepower (max):	980 hp at 2800 rpm
Net Torque (max):	1670 ft-lb at 2100 rpm
Gross Torque (max):	1870 ft-lb at 2400 rpm
Weight:	3050 pounds, dry
Fuel: 80 octane gasoline	400 gallons
Engine Oil:	64 quarts

POWER TRAIN

Transmission: Cross-drive XT-1400-2A, 3 ranges forward, 1 reverse
    Single stage multiphase hydraulic torque converter w/lock-up clutch
    Stall Multiplication: 3.6:1
    Overall Usable Ratios: low 112:1   reverse 121.3:1
                intermediate 52.3:1
                high 24.4:1
Steering Control: Mechanical, T-bar
    Steering Rate: 5.6 rpm
Brakes: Multiple disc
Final Drive: Planetary gear   Gear Ratio: 4.63:1
Drive Sprocket: At rear of vehicle with 11 teeth
    Pitch Diameter: 25.000 inches

RUNNING GEAR

Suspension: Torsion bar
    14 individually sprung dual road wheels (7/track)
    Tire Size: 26 x 6 inches
    8 dual track return rollers (4/track)
    Dual compensating idler at front of each track
    Idler Tire Size: 26 x 6 inches
    Shock absorbers (snubbers) fitted on first 2 and last 2 road wheels on each side
Tracks: Center guide, T107
    Type: (T107) Double pin, 28 inch width, rubber chevron
    Pitch: 7.09 inches
    Shoes per Vehicle: 162 (81/track)
    Ground Contact Length: 186.25 inches

ELECTRICAL SYSTEM

Nominal Voltage: 24 volts DC
Main Generator: (1) 24 volts, 300 amperes, gear driven by main engine
Auxiliary Generator: (1) 28 volts, 300 amperes, driven by auxiliary engine
Battery: (4) 12 volts, 2 sets of 2 in series connected in parallel

COMMUNICATIONS

Radio: AN/GRC-3, 6, or 8 or AN/VRC 13, 14, or 15 in the center rear of cab
Interphone: AN/UIC-1, 4 stations

FIRE PROTECTION

(8) 10 pound carbon dioxide, fixed (2 shot)
(2) 5 pound carbon dioxide, portable
(2) 15 pound carbon dioxide, portable

PERFORMANCE

Maximum Speed: Sustained, level road	30 miles/hour
Maximum Tractive Effort: TE at stall	179,500 pounds
Per Cent of Vehicle Weight: TE/W	150 per cent
Maximum Grade:	60 per cent
Maximum Trench:	9.1 feet
Maximum Vertical Wall:	36 inches (w/o pintle)
Maximum Fording Depth:	60 inches
Minimum Turning Circle: (diameter)	pivot
Cruising Range: Roads	approx. 150 miles

Data describing the general characteristics and performance of the armor piercing weapons mounted on American heavy tanks are tabulated on the following pages. The various dimensions included are defined in the sketch below.

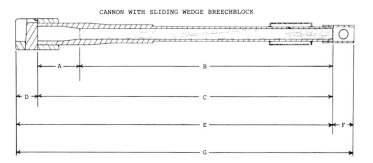

CANNON WITH SLIDING WEDGE BREECHBLOCK

A. Length of Chamber (to rifling)
B. Length of Rifling
C. Length of Bore
D. Depth of Breech Recess
E. Length, Muzzle to Rear Face of Breech
F. Additional Length, Blast Deflector, Etc.
G. Overall Length

Ammunition is listed by the official nomenclature in use during its period of greatest service. However, since this terminology frequently changed during the service life, a standard nomenclature is added in parentheses to prevent confusion. These standard terms which are used separately and in combination are defined below.

AP	Armor piercing, uncapped
APBC	Armor piercing with ballistic cap
APCBC	Armor piercing with armor piercing cap and ballistic cap
APCR	Armor piercing, composite rigid
HE	High explosive
HEAT	High explosive antitank, shaped charge
TP	Target practice
TPBC	Target practice with ballistic cap
TPCR	Target practice, composite rigid
-T	Tracer

Armor penetration performance for the various types of ammunition is quoted for various angles of obliquity. As mentioned in the introduction to the vehicle data sheets, this angle is defined as the angle between a line perpendicular to the armor plate and the projectile path. However, in three dimensions, the calculation of the true angle of obliquity is a little more complicated as indicated in these drawings. Here the true angle of obliquity is shown to be the angle whose cosine equals the product of the cosines for the vertical and lateral attack angles.

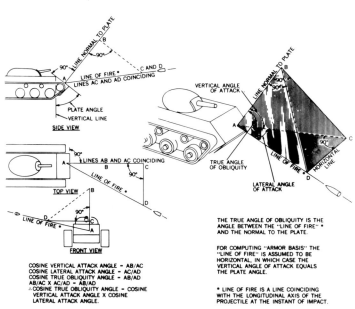

During the World War II period, penetration performance was usually provided for 30 degree angles of obliquity. However, with the appearance of highly sloped armor on the later tanks, these data were of limited value. Postwar penetration performance data were quoted for angles of 60 degrees allowing a more realistic evaluation of the effectiveness against an actual vehicle. Where possible these data sheets include penetration performance for the armor piercing ammunition at both 30 and 60 degree angles of obliquity. If values for 60 degrees are unknown, data for the largest available angle are included. Note that the relative performance of the various types of ammunition at 30 degrees obliquity is not necessarily maintained at 60 degrees.

37mm GUN M6

Carriage and Mount	Heavy Tanks M6, M6A1, and T1E1		
Length of Chamber (to rifling)	9.55 inches		
Length of Rifling	68.45 inches		
Length of Chamber (to projectile base)	8.1 inches (square base projectiles)		
Travel of Projectile in Bore	69.9 inches (square base projectiles)		
Length of Bore	78.0 inches, 53.5 calibers		
Depth of Breech Recess	4.5 inches		
Length, Muzzle to Rear Face of Breech	82.5 inches		
Additional Length, Muzzle Brake, etc.	None		
Overall Length	82.5 inches		
Diameter of Bore	1.457 inches		
Chamber Capacity	19.35 cubic inches (APC M51), 19.19 cubic inches (HE M63)		
Weight, Tube	138 pounds		
Total Weight	185 pounds		
Type of Breechblock	Semiautomatic, vertical sliding wedge		
Rifling	12 grooves, uniform right-hand twist, one turn in 25 calibers		
Ammunition	Fixed		
Primer	Percussion		
Weight, Complete Round	APC M51 Shot (APCBC-T)		3.48 pounds (1.6 kg)
	AP M74 Shot (AP-T)		3.34 pounds (1.5 kg)
	HE M63 Shell (HE)		3.13 pounds (1.4 kg)
	Canister M2		3.49 pounds (1.6 kg)
Weight, Projectile	APC M51 Shot (APCBC-T)		1.92 pounds (0.9 kg)
	AP M74 Shot (AP-T)		1.92 pounds (0.9 kg)
	HE M63 Shell (HE)		1.61 pounds (0.7 kg)
	Canister M2 (122 steel balls)		1.94 pounds (0.9 kg)
Maximum Powder Pressure	50,000 psi		
Maximum Rate of Fire	30 rounds/minute		
Muzzle Velocity	APC M51 Shot (APCBC-T)		2900 ft/sec (844 m/sec)
	AP M74 Shot (AP-T)		2900 ft/sec (884 m/sec)
	HE M63 Shell (HE)		2600 ft/sec (792 m/sec)
	Canister M2		2500 ft/sec (762 m/sec)
Muzzle Energy of Projectile, KE=½MV² Rotational energy is neglected and values are based on long tons (2240 pounds)	APC M51 Shot (APCBC-T)		112 ft-tons
	AP M74 Shot (AP-T)		112 ft-tons
	HE M63 Shell (HE)		75 ft-tons
	Canister M2		84 ft-tons
Maximum Range (independent of mount)	APC M51 Shot (APCBC-T)		12,850 yards (11,750 m)
	AP M74 Shot (AP-T)		8725 yards (7978 m)
	HE M63 Shell (HE)		9500 yards (8687 m)
	Canister M2 approx.		200 yards (183 m)

Penetration Performance Range	1000 yards (914 m)	2000 yards (1829 m)
	Homogenous Armor at 30 degrees obliquity	
APC M51 Shot (APCBC-T)	1.8 inches (46mm)	1.4 inches (35mm)
	Homogenous Armor at 60 degrees obliquity	
APC M51 Shot (APCBC-T)	0.8 inches (20mm)	0.7 inches (17mm)

3 inch GUN M7

Carriage and Mount	Heavy Tanks M6, M6A1, and T1E1
Length of Chamber (to rifling)	23.15 inches
Length of Rifling	126.85 inches
Length of Chamber (to projectile base)	21.5 inches (square base projectiles)
Travel of Projectile in Bore	128.5 inches (square base projectiles)
Length of Bore	150.0 inches, 50.0 calibers
Depth of Breech Recess	8.10 inches
Length, Muzzle to Rear Face of Breech	158.10 inches
Additional Length, Muzzle Brake, etc.	None
Overall Length	158.10 inches
Diameter of Bore	3.000 inches
Chamber Capacity	205.585 cubic inches (APC M62), 203.50 cubic inches (HE M42A1)
Total Weight	1990 pounds
Type of Breechblock	Semiautomatic, vertical sliding wedge
Rifling	28 grooves, uniform right-hand twist, one turn in 40 calibers
Ammunition	Fixed
Primer	Percussion

Weight, Complete Round	APC M62 Projectile (APCBC/HE-T)	27.24 pounds (12.4 kg)
	HVAP M93 Shot (APCR-T)	20.77 pounds (9.4 kg)
	AP M79 Shot (AP-T)	26.56 pounds (12.0 kg)
	HE M42A1 Shell (HE)	24.91 pounds (11.3 kg)
	HC BI M88 Shell (Smoke)	15.40 pounds (7.0 kg)
Weight, Projectile	APC M62 Projectile (APCBC/HE-T)	15.44 pounds (7.0 kg)
	HVAP M93 Shot (APCR-T)	9.40 pounds (4.3 kg)
	AP M79 Shot (AP-T)	15.00 pounds (6.8 kg)
	HE M42A1 Shell (HE)	12.87 pounds (5.8 kg)
	HC BI M88 Shell (Smoke)	7.38 pounds (3.3 kg)
Maximum Powder Pressure	38,000 psi	
Maximum Rate of Fire	15 rounds/minute	
Muzzle Velocity	APC M62 Projectile (APCBC/HE-T)	2600 ft/sec (792 m/sec)
	HVAP M93 Shot (APCR-T)	3400 ft/sec (1036 m/sec)
	AP M79 Shot (AP-T)	2600 ft/sec (792 m/sec)
	HE M42A1 Shell (HE)	2800 ft/sec (853 m/sec)
	HC BI M88 Shell (Smoke)	900 ft/sec (274 m/sec)
Muzzle Energy of Projectile, $KE=\frac{1}{2}MV^2$	APC M62 Projectile (APCBC/HE-T)	724 ft-tons
Rotational energy is neglected and values are based on long tons (2240 pounds)	HVAP M93 Shot (APCR-T)	753 ft-tons
	AP M79 Shot (AP-T)	703 ft-tons
	HE M42A1 Shell (HE)	699 ft-tons
Maximum Range (independent of mount)	APC M62 Projectile (APCBC/HE-T)	16,100 yards (14,722 m)
	HVAP M93 Shot (APCR-T)	13,100 yards (11,979 m)
	AP M79 Shot (AP-T)	12,770 yards (11,677 m)
	HE M42A1 Shell (HE)	14,780 yards (13,515 m)
	HC BI M88 Shell (Smoke) at 12 degrees elevation	2000 yards (1829 m)

Penetration Performance Range

	1000 yards (914 m)	2000 yards (1829 m)
	Homogenous Armor at 30 degrees obliquity	
APC M62 Projectile (APCBC/HE-T)	3.5 inches (88mm)	3.0 inches (75mm)
HVAP M93 Shot (APCR-T)	5.3 inches (135mm)	3.9 inches (98mm)
AP M79 Shot (AP-T)	3.6 inches (92mm)	2.5 inches (64mm)
	Homogenous Armor at 55 degrees obliquity	
APC M62 Projectile (APCBC/HE-T)	2.0 inches (51mm)	1.7 inches (43mm)
HVAP M93 Shot (APCR-T)	2.1 inches (53mm)	1.5 inches (38mm)

213

90mm GUN M3 (T7)

Carriage and Mount	Mounted experimentally in Heavy Tank T1E1
Length of Chamber (to rifling)	24.8 inches
Length of Rifling	152.4 inches
Length of Chamber (to projectile base)	20.8 inches (boat-tailed projectiles)
Travel of Projectile in Bore	156.4 inches (boat-tailed projectiles)
Length of Bore	177.15 inches, 50.0 calibers
Depth of Breech Recess	9.00 inches
Length, Muzzle to Rear Face of Breech	186.15 inches
Additional Length, Muzzle Brake M3	16.0 inches (late production guns only)
Overall Length	202.2 inches
Diameter of Bore	3.543 inches
Chamber Capacity	300 cubic inches
Weight, Complete (w/o muzzle brake)	2300 pounds
Weight, Muzzle Brake M3	149.5 pounds
Total Weight approx.	2450 pounds
Type of Breechblock	Semiautomatic, vertical sliding wedge
Rifling	32 grooves, uniform right-hand twist, one turn in 32 calibers
Ammunition	Fixed
Primer	Percussion

Weight, Complete Round		
	APC M82 Projectile (APCBC/HE-T) early	42.75 pounds (19.4 kg)
	APC M82 Projectile (APCBC/HE-T) late	43.87 pounds (19.9 kg)
	HVAP M304 (T30E16) Shot (APCR-T)	37.13 pounds (16.9 kg)
	AP T33 Shot (APBC-T)	43.82 pounds (19.9 kg)
	HE M71 Shell (HE)	41.93 pounds (19.1 kg)
Weight, Projectile	APC M82 Projectile (APCBC/HE-T)	24.11 pounds (11.0 kg)
	HVAP M304 (T30E16) Shot (APCR-T)	16.80 pounds (7.6 kg)
	AP T33 Shot (APBC-T)	24.06 pounds (10.9 kg)
	HE M71 Shell (HE)	23.29 pounds (10.6 kg)

Maximum Powder Pressure	38,000 psi	
Maximum Rate of Fire	8 rounds/minute	
Muzzle Velocity	APC M82 Projectile (APCBC/HE-T) early	2650 ft/sec (808 m/sec)
	APC M82 Projectile (APCBC/HE-T) late	2800 ft/sec (853 m/sec)
	HVAP M304 (T30E16) Shot (APCR-T)	3350 ft/sec (1021 m/sec)
	AP T33 Shot (APBC-T)	2800 ft/sec (853 m/sec)
	HE M71 Shell (HE)	2700 ft/sec (823 m/sec)

Muzzle Energy of Projectile, $KE = \frac{1}{2}MV^2$
Rotational energy is neglected and values are based on long tons (2240 pounds)

APC M82 Projectile (APCBC/HE-T) early	1174 ft-tons
APC M82 Projectile (APCBC/HE-T) late	1310 ft-tons
HVAP M304 (T30E16) Shot (APCR-T)	1307 ft-tons
AP T33 Shot (APBC-T)	1310 ft-tons
HE M71 Shell (HE)	1177 ft-tons

Maximum Range (independent of mount)	
APC M82 Projectile (APCBC/HE-T) early	20,400 yards (18,654 m)
APC M82 Projectile (APCBC/HE-T) late	21,400 yards (19,568 m)
HVAP M304 (T30E16) Shot (APCR-T)	15,700 yards (14,356 m)
AP T33 Shot (APBC-T)	21,000 yards (19,202 m)
HE M71 Shell (HE)	19,560 yards (17,886 m)

Penetration Performance Range	1000 yards (914 m)	2000 yards (1829 m)
	Homogenous Armor at 30 degrees obliquity	
APC M82 Projectile (APCBC/HE-T) early	4.4 inches (112mm)	3.8 inches (96mm)
APC M82 Projectile (APCBC/HE-T) late	4.8 inches (122mm)	4.2 inches (106mm)
HVAP M304 (T30E16) Shot (APCR-T)	7.9 inches (199mm)	6.1 inches (156mm)
AP T33 Shot (APBC-T)	4.6 inches (117mm)	4.3 inches (109mm)
	Homogenous Armor at 55 degrees obliquity	
APC M82 Projectile (APCBC/HE-T) early	2.3 inches (58mm)	2.0 inches (51mm)
APC M82 Projectile (APCBC/HE-T) late	2.5 inches (64mm)	2.2 inches (56mm)
HVAP M304 (T30E16) Shot (APCR-T)	2.9 inches (74mm)	1.8 inches (46mm)
AP T33 Shot (APBC-T)	2.5 inches (64mm)	2.3 inches (58mm)

90mm GUN T15E2

Carriage and Mount	Heavy Tanks T32 and T32E1 in Mount T119
Length of Chamber (to rifling)	40.7 inches
Length of Rifling	207.2 inches
Length of Chamber (to projectile base)	36.7 inches (boat-tailed projectiles)
Travel of Projectile in Bore	211.2 inches (boat-tailed projectiles)
Length of Bore	247.9 inches, 70.0 calibers
Depth of Breech Recess	9.0 inches
Length, Muzzle to Rear Face of Breech	256.9 inches
Additional Length, Muzzle Brake M3	16.0 inches
Overall Length	272.9 inches
Diameter of Bore	3.543 inches
Chamber Capacity	488 cubic inches (estimated)
Weight, Complete (w/o muzzle brake)	3270 pounds
Weight, Muzzle Brake M3	150 pounds
Total Weight	3420 pounds
Type of Breechblock	Semiautomatic, vertical sliding wedge
Rifling	32 grooves, uniform right-hand twist, one turn in 32 calibers
Ammunition	Separated
Primer	Percussion
Weight, Complete Round	AP T43 Shot (APBC-T)	51.2 pounds (23.2 kg)
	HVAP T44 Shot (APCR-T)	44 pounds (20.0 kg)
	HE T42 Shell (HE)	50.4 pounds (22.9 kg)
Weight, Projectile	AP T43 Shot (APBC-T)	24.06 pounds (10.9 kg)
	HVAP T44 Shot (APCR-T)	16.70 pounds (7.6 kg)
	HE T42 Shell (HE)	23.3 pounds (10.6 kg)
Maximum Powder Pressure	41,500 psi
Maximum Rate of Fire	4 rounds/minute
Muzzle Velocity	AP T43 Shot (APBC-T)	3200 ft/sec (975 m/sec)
	HVAP T44 Shot (APCR-T)	3750 ft/sec (1143 m/sec)
	HE T42 Shell (HE)	3200 ft/sec (975 m/sec)
Muzzle Energy of Projectile, KE=½MV²	AP T43 Shot (APBC-T)	1711 ft-tons
Rotational energy is neglected and values	HVAP T44 Shot (APCR-T)	1628 ft-tons
are based on long tons (2240 pounds)	HE T42 Shell (HE)	1654 ft-tons
Maximum Range (independent of mount)	HE T42 Shell (HE)	27,000 yards (24,689 m)

Muzzle Energy of Projectile, $KE = \frac{1}{2}MV^2$

Penetration Performance Range

	1000 yards (914 m)	2000 yards (1829 m)
Homogenous Armor at 30 degrees obliquity		
AP T43 Shot (APBC-T)	5.0 inches (127mm)	4.8 inches (122mm)
HVAP T44 Shot (APCR-T)	8.7 inches (221mm)	6.8 inches (173mm)
Homogenous Armor at 55 degrees obliquity		
AP T43 Shot (APBC-T)	2.9 inches (74mm)	2.8 inches (71mm)
HVAP T44 Shot (APCR-T)	3.7 inches (94mm)	2.5 inches (64mm)

105mm GUNS T5E1 and T5E2

Carriage and Mount	Heavy Tank M6A2E1 (T5E1 Gun), Heavy Tank T28 (105mm GMC T95) in Mount T40 (T5E1 Gun), Heavy Tank T29 in Mount T123E1 (T5E2 Gun), Heavy Tank T29E1 in Mount T123 (T5E1 Gun), Heavy Tank T29E2 in Mount T123E2 (T5E2 Gun), Heavy Tank T29E3 in Mount T123 (T5E1 Gun)
Length of Chamber (to rifling)	32.72 inches
Length of Rifling	236.09 inches
Length of Chamber (to projectile base)	28.81 inches
Travel of Projectile in Bore	240.00 inches
Length of Bore	268.81 inches, 65.0 calibers
Depth of Breech Recess	9.25 inches
Length, Muzzle to Rear Face of Breech	278.06 inches
Additional Length, Muzzle Brake T10	18.5 inches
Overall Length	296.5 inches
Diameter of Bore	4.134 inches
Chamber Capacity	615 cubic inches
Weight, Tube (w/o muzzle brake)	5170 pounds
Weight, Complete (w/o muzzle brake)	6300 pounds
Weight, Muzzle Brake T10	184 pounds
Total Weight approx.	6484 pounds
Type of Breechblock	Semiautomatic, vertical sliding wedge
Rifling	36 grooves, uniform right-hand twist, one turn in 30 calibers
Ammunition	Separated
Primer	Percussion
Weight, Complete Round	AP-T T32 Shot (APBC-T)	74 pounds (34 kg)
	HVAP-T T29E3 Shot (APCR-T)	60 pounds (27 kg)
	HE T30E1 Shell (HE)	69 pounds (31 kg)
Weight, Projectile	AP-T T32 Shot (APBC-T)	39.0 pounds (17.7 kg)
	HVAP-T T29E3 Shot (APCR-T)	24.6 pounds (11.2 kg)
	HE T30E1 Shell (HE)	33.5 pounds (15.2 kg)
Maximum Powder Pressure	42,000 psi
Maximum Rate of Fire	6 rounds/minute, two loaders
Muzzle Velocity	AP-T T32 Shot (APBC-T)	3000 ft/sec (914 m/sec)
	HVAP-T T29E3 Shot (APCR-T)	3700 ft/sec (1128 m/sec)
	HE T30E1 Shell (HE)	3100 ft/sec (945 m/sec)
	HE T30E1 Shell (HE) red. vel.	2500 ft/sec (762 m/sec)

Muzzle Energy of Projectile, $KE = \frac{1}{2}MV^2$
Rotational energy is neglected and values
are based on long tons (2240 pounds)

AP-T T32 Shot (APBC-T)	2433 ft-tons
HVAP-T T29E3 Shot (APCR-T)	2335 ft-tons
HE T30E1 Shell (HE)	2232 ft-tons
HE T30E1 Shell (HE) red. vel.	1451 ft-tons

Maximum Range (independent of mount)	Undetermined*	
Penetration Performance Range Estimated*	1000 yards (914 m)	2000 yards (1829 m)
AP-T T32 Shot (APBC-T)	Homogenous Armor at 30 degrees obliquity	
	5.3 inches (135mm)	4.7 inches (119mm)
AP-T T32 Shot (APBC-T)	Homogenous Armor at 60 degrees obliquity	
	3.3 inches (84mm)	2.7 inches (69mm)

*Ammunition development terminated prior to the completion of the testing program.

120mm GUN T53

Carriage and Mount	Heavy Tank T34 in Mount T125	
Length of Chamber (to rifling)	38.05 inches	
Length of Rifling	243.95 inches	
Length of Chamber (to projectile base)	33.7 inches	
Travel of Projectile in Bore	248.3 inches	
Length of Bore	282.00 inches, 60 calibers	
Depth of Breech Recess	9.00 inches	
Length, Muzzle to Rear Face of Breech	291.00 inches	
Additional Length, Muzzle Brake T18	11.3 inches	
Overall Length	302.3 inches	
Diameter of Bore	4.7 inches	
Chamber Capacity	1046 cubic inches	
Weight, Tube (w/o muzzle brake)	6180 pounds	
Weight, Complete (w/o muzzle brake)	7300 pounds	
Weight, Muzzle Brake T18	105 pounds	
Total Weight approx.	7405 pounds	
Type of Breechblock	Semiautomatic, vertical sliding wedge	
Rifling	42 grooves, uniform right-hand twist, one turn in 25 calibers	
Ammunition	Separated	
Primer	Percussion	
Weight, Complete Round	Test Shot T20E3	100 pounds (45 kg)
Weight, Projectile	Test Shot T20E3	50 pounds (23 kg)
Maximum Powder Pressure	38,000 psi	
Maximum Rate of Fire	5 rounds/minute, two loaders	
Muzzle Velocity	Test Shot T20E3	3100 ft/sec (945 m/sec)
Muzzle Energy of Projectile, $KE = \frac{1}{2}MV^2$ Rotational energy is neglected and values are based on long tons (2240 pounds)	Test Shot T20E3	3331 ft-tons
Maximum Range (independent of mount)	Undetermined*	

Penetration Performance Range Estimated*	1000 yards (914 m)	2000 yards (1829 m)
	Homogenous Armor at 30 degrees obliquity	
AP Shot (APBC)	7.8 inches (198mm)	6.8 inches (173mm)
HVAP Shot (APCR)	15.0 inches (381mm)	12.5 inches (318mm)
	Homogenous Armor at 60 degrees obliquity	
AP Shot (APBC)	4.0 inches (102mm)	3.6 inches (91mm)
HVAP Shot (APCR)	4.4 inches (112mm)	3.0 inches (76mm)

*Program for the T53 gun terminated prior to completion of the ammunition development.

120mm GUN T122

Carriage and Mount	Heavy Tank T43 (1st pilot) in Mount T140 (concentric)
Length of Chamber (to rifling)	38.05 inches
Length of Rifling	243.95 inches
Length of Chamber (to projectile base)	33.7 inches
Travel of Projectile in Bore	248.3 inches
Length of Bore	282.00 inches, 60 calibers
Depth of Breech Recess	9.00 inches
Length, Muzzle to Rear Face of Breech	291.00 inches
Additional Length, Muzzle Brake	11.3 inches
Overall Length	302.3 inches
Diameter of Bore	4.7 inches
Chamber Capacity	1015 cubic inches
Weight, Tube (w/o muzzle brake)	4601 pounds
Weight, Complete (w/o muzzle brake)	6215 pounds, estimated
Weight, Muzzle Brake	105 pounds
Total Weight approx.	6320 pounds
Type of Breechblock	Semiautomatic, vertical sliding wedge
Rifling	42 grooves, uniform right-hand twist, one turn in 25 calibers

Ammunition	Separated	
Primer	Percussion	
Weight, Complete Round	AP Shot (APBC)	100 pounds (45 kg)
Weight, Projectile	AP Shot (APBC)	50 pounds (23 kg)
Maximum Powder Pressure	38,000 psi	
Maximum Rate of Fire	5 rounds/minute, two loaders	
Muzzle Velocity	AP Shot (APBC)	3100 ft/sec (945 m/sec)
Muzzle Energy of Projectile, $KE = \frac{1}{2}MV^2$ Rotational energy is neglected and values are based on long tons (2240 pounds)	AP Shot (APBC)	3331 ft-tons
Maximum Range (independent of mount)	Undetermined*	

	1000 yards (914 m)	2000 yards (1829 m)
Penetration Performance Range Estimated*	Homogenous Armor at 30 degrees obliquity	
AP Shot (APBC)	7.8 inches (198mm)	6.8 inches (173mm)
HVAP Shot (APCR)	15.0 inches (381mm)	12.5 inches (318mm)
	Homogenous Armor at 60 degrees obliquity	
AP Shot (APBC)	4.0 inches (102mm)	3.6 inches (91mm)
HVAP Shot (APCR)	4.4 inches (112mm)	3.0 inches (76mm)

*Program for the T122 gun terminated prior to completion of the ammunition development.

120mm GUNS M58 (T123E1) and T179

Carriage and Mount	120mm Gun Tank M103 in Mount M89 and 120mm Gun Tanks M103A1 and M103A2 in Mount M89A1 (M58 Gun)
	120mm Gun Tank T57 in Mount T169 (T179 Gun)
Length of Chamber (to rifling)	38.05 inches
Length of Rifling	243.95 inches
Length of Chamber (to projectile base)	33.7 inches
Travel of Projectile in Bore	248.3 inches
Length of Bore	282.00 inches, 60.0 calibers
Depth of Breech Recess	9.50 inches
Length, Muzzle to Rear Face of Breech	291.50 inches
Additional Length, Blast Deflector	7.25 inches
Overall Length	298.75 inches
Diameter of Bore	4.7 inches
Chamber Capacity	1021 cubic inches
Weight, Tube	4600 pounds
Total Weight	6280 pounds
Type of Breechblock	Semiautomatic, vertical sliding wedge
Rifling	42 grooves, uniform right-hand twist, one turn in 25 calibers
Ammunition	Separated
Primer	Percussion or percussion-electric

Weight, Complete Round	*AP-T M358 Shot (APBC-T)	107.31 pounds (48.8 kg)
	★HEAT-T M469 (T153E15) Shell (HEAT-T)	52.55 pounds (23.9 kg)
	**HE-T M356 (T15E3) Shell (HE-T)	89.15 pounds (40.5 kg)
	**WP-T M357 (T16E4) Shell (Smoke)	89.15 pounds (40.5 kg)
	*TP-T M359E2 (T147E7) Shot (TPBC-T)	107.31 pounds (48.8 kg)
Weight, Projectile	AP-T M358 Shot (APBC-T)	50.85 pounds (23.1 kg)
	HEAT-T M469 (T153E15) Shell (HEAT-T)	31.11 pounds (14.1 kg)
	HE-T M356 (T15E3) Shell (HE-T)	50.41 pounds (22.9 kg)
	WP-T M357 (T16E4) Shell (Smoke)	50.41 pounds (22.9 kg)
	TP-T M359E2 (T147E7) Shot (TPBC-T)	50.85 pounds (23.1 kg)
Maximum Powder Pressure	48,000 psi	
Maximum Rate of Fire	5 rounds/minute, manual loading, two loaders (M58 gun)	
Muzzle Velocity	AP-T M358 Shot (APBC-T)	3500 ft/sec (1067 m/sec)
	HEAT-T M469 (T153E15) Shell (HEAT-T)	3750 ft/sec (1143 m/sec)
	HE-T M356 (T15E3) Shell (HE-T)	2500 ft/sec (762 m/sec)
	WP-T M357 (T16E4) Shell (Smoke)	2500 ft/sec (762 m/sec)
	TP-T M359E2 (T147E7) Shot (TPBC-T)	3500 ft/sec (1067 m/sec)
Muzzle Energy of Projectile, KE=½MV²	AP-T M358 Shot (APBC-T)	4318 ft-tons
Rotational energy is neglected and values are based on long tons (2240 pounds)	HEAT-T M469 (T153E15) Shell (HEAT-T)	3033 ft-tons
	HE-T M356 (T15E3) Shell (HE-T)	2184 ft-tons
	WP-T M357 (T16E4) Shell (Smoke)	2184 ft-tons
	TP-T M359E2 (T147E7) Shot (TPBC-T)	4318 ft-tons
Maximum Range (independent of mount)	AP-T M358 Shot (APBC-T)	25,290 yards (23,125 m)
	HEAT-T M469 (T153E15) Shell (HEAT-T)	25,290 yards (23,125 m)
	HE-T M356 (T15E3) Shell (HE-T)	19,910 yards (18,206 m)
	WP-T M357 (T16E4) Shell (Smoke)	19,910 yards (18,206 m)
	TP-T M359E2 (T147E7) Shot (TPBC-T)	25,290 yards (23,125 m)

Penetration Performance Range	1000 yards (914 m)	2000 yards (1829 m)
	Homogenous Armor at 30 degrees obliquity	
AP-T M358 Shot (APBC-T)	8.7 inches (221mm)	7.7 inches (196mm)
HEAT-T M469 (T153E15) Shell (HEAT-T)	13.0 inches (330mm)	13.0 inches (330mm)
	Homogenous Armor at 60 degrees obliquity	
AP-T M358 Shot (APBC-T)	4.9 inches (124mm)	4.5 inches (114mm)
HEAT-T M469 (T153E15) Shell (HEAT-T)	7.5 inches (191mm)	7.5 inches (191mm)

*With propelling charge assembly M46 (T38E1) in cartridge case M109 (T25)
**With propelling charge assembly M45 (T21E1) in cartridge case M109 (T25)
★With propelling charge assembly M99 (T42E1) in cartridge case M111

The T179 gun was similar to the M58 gun, but it was inverted in the T169 mount for use with an automatic loader. The T169 was a rigid mount without a recoil system.

155mm GUNS T7 and T7E1

Carriage and Mount	Heavy Tank T30 in Mount T124 (T7 Gun) and Heavy Tank T30E1 in Mount T124E1 (T7E1 Gun)
Length of Chamber (to rifling)	27.22 inches
Length of Rifling	216.78 inches
Length of Chamber (to projectile base)	26 inches
Travel of Projectile in Bore	218 inches
Length of Bore	244 inches, 40 calibers
Depth of Breech Recess	8.5 inches
Length, Muzzle to Rear Face of Breech	252.5 inches
Additional Length, Muzzle Brake T19	13.0 inches
Overall Length	265.5 inches
Diameter of Bore	6.102 inches
Chamber Capacity	800 cubic inches
Weight, Tube (w/o muzzle brake)	3955 pounds
Weight, Complete (w/o muzzle brake)	5100 pounds
Weight, Muzzle Brake T19	155 pounds
Total Weight approx.	5255 pounds
Type of Breechblock	Semiautomatic, horizontal sliding wedge
Rifling	48 grooves, uniform right-hand twist, one turn in 25 calibers

Ammunition	Separated	
Primer	Percussion	
Weight, Complete Round	HE	135 pounds (61 kg)
Weight, Projectile	HE	95 pounds (43 kg)
Maximum Powder Pressure	32,000 psi	
Maximum Rate of Fire	2 rounds/minute, manual loading, two loaders (T7 gun)	
Muzzle Velocity	HE	2300 ft/sec (717 m/sec)
Muzzle Energy of Projectile, $KE = \frac{1}{2}MV^2$ Rotational energy is neglected and values are based on long tons (2240 pounds)	HE	3484 ft-tons
Maximum Range (independent of mount)	Undetermined*	

*Development was terminated prior to the completion of the test program.

The T7E1 gun differed from the T7 in that it was modified for use with a power rammer and ejection equipment.

155mm GUN T180

Carriage and Mount	155mm Gun Tank T58 in Mount T170	
Length of Chamber (to rifling)	28 inches	
Length of Rifling	216 inches	
Length of Chamber (to projectile base)	27 inches	
Travel of Projectile in Bore	217 inches	
Length of Bore	244 inches, 40 calibers	
Depth of Breech Recess	8.5 inches	
Length, Muzzle to Rear Face of Breech	252.5 inches	
Additional Length, Blast Deflector	11.6 inches	
Overall Length	264.1 inches	
Diameter of Bore	6.102 inches	
Chamber Capacity	800 cubic inches	
Total Weight	5588 pounds	
Type of Breechblock	Semiautomatic, vertical sliding wedge	
Rifling	48 grooves, uniform right-hand twist, one turn in 25 calibers	
Ammunition	Separated	
Primer	Percussion	
Weight, Complete Round	HE	135 pounds (61 kg)
	HEAT T267	105 pounds (48 kg)
Weight, Projectile	HE	95 pounds (43 kg)
	HEAT T267	64 pounds (29 kg)
Maximum Powder Pressure	32,000 psi	
Maximum Rate of Fire	23 rounds/minute (design rate w/automatic loader)	
Muzzle Velocity	HE	2300 ft/sec (717 m/sec)
	HEAT T267	2650 ft/sec (826 m/sec)
Muzzle Energy of Projectile, KE=½MV²	HE	3484 ft-tons
Rotational energy is neglected and values are based on long tons (2240 pounds)	HEAT T267	3116 ft-tons
Maximum Range (independent of mount)	Undetermined*	
Penetration Performace	Homogenous Armor at all ranges	
HEAT T267, Estimated*	13.9 inches (353mm) at 30 degrees obliquity	
	8.0 inches (203mm) at 60 degrees obliquity	

*Development was terminated prior to the completion of the test program.

REFERENCES AND SELECTED BIBLIOGRAPHY

Books and Published Articles

Ament, First Lieutenant Robert L., ''The 120mm Gun Tank Company'', Armor, May-June 1960

Jones, Major Ralph E., Rarey, Captain George H., Icks, First Lieutenant Robert J.,''The Fighting Tanks Since 1916'', The National Service Publishing Company, Washington, D.C., June 1933

Stern, Lieutenant Colonel Sir Albert G., ''Tanks 1914-1918, The Log-Book of a Pioneer'', Hodder and Stoughton, London, 1919

Reports and Official Documents

''Army Equipment Development Guide'', U.S. Army, Fort Monroe, Virginia, 29 December 1950

''Army Equipment Development Guide'', Department of the Army, Washington, D.C., 3 May 1954

''Mark VIII Tank, Preliminary Handbook'', Washington, D.C., 15 November 1918

''Notes on Materiel, Gun, 90mm, T7'', Watervliet Arsenal, Watervliet, New York, December 1942

''Notes on Materiel, Gun, 90mm, T15'', Watervliet Arsenal, Watervliet, New York, January 1946

''Notes on Materiel, Gun, 105mm, T5'', Watervliet Arsenal, Watervliet, New York, February 1944

''Notes on Materiel, Gun, 105mm, T5E2'', Watervliet Arsenal, Watervliet, New York, October 1946

''Notes on Materiel, Gun, 120mm, T53'', Watervliet Arsenal, Watervliet, New York, February 1948

''Notes on Materiel, Gun, 120mm, T122'', Watervliet Arsenal, Watervliet, New York, May 1951

''Notes on Materiel, Gun, 120mm, T123'', Watervliet Arsenal, Watervliet, New York, October 1951

''Notes on Materiel, Gun, 120mm, T123E1'', Watervliet Arsenal, Watervliet, New York, January 1952

''Notes on Materiel, Gun, 155mm, T7'', Watervliet Arsenal, Watervliet, New York, August 1946

''Notes on Materiel, Gun, Motor Carriage T95'', Pacific Car and Foundry Company for Office Chief of Ordnance, Detroit, Michigan, 1 February 1946

''Notes on Materiel, Heavy Tank T29'', Pressed Steel Car Company for Office Chief of Ordnance, Detroit, Michigan, 1 April 1946

''Notes on Materiel, Heavy Tank T30'', Detroit Arsenal, Center Line, Michigan, June 1948

''Notes on Materiel, Heavy Tank T32 and Heavy Tank T32E1'', Chrysler Corporation for Detroit Ordnance District, Michigan, 1 February 1946

''Notes on Materiel, Heavy Tank T34'', Detroit Arsenal, Center Line, Michigan, June 1948

''Notes on Development Type Materiel, 120mm Gun Tank T43'', Detroit Arsenal, Center Line, Michigan, 1 October 1951

''Notes on Development Type Materiel, 120mm Gun Tanks T57 and T77, Trunnion Mounted Turrets with Automatic Loading Equipment'', Detroit Arsenal, Center Line, Michigan, 31 August 1956

''Operation Questionmark'', Detroit Arsenal, Center Line, Michigan, March 1952

''Questionmark III'', Detroit Arsenal, Center Line, Michigan, June 1954

''Questionmark IV'', Detroit Arsenal, Center Line, Michigan, August 1955

''Report of the Army Ground Forces Equipment Review Board'', Washington, D.C., 20 June 1945

''Report of the War Department Equipment Board'' (Stilwell Board), Washington, D.C., 19 January 1946

''Technical Manual TM9-323 3-inch Gun M7 Mounted in Combat Vehicles'', War Department, Washington, D.C., 25 March 1944

''Technical Manual TM9-500 Ordnance Equipment Data Sheets'', Department of the Army, Washington, D.C., September 1962

''Technical Manual TM9-721 Heavy Tank M6 and M6A1'', War Department, Washington, D.C., 5 February 1943

''Technical Manual TM9-1300-203 Artillery Ammunition for Guns, Howitzers, Mortars and Recoilless Rifles'', Department of the Army, Washington, D.C., April 1967

''Technical Manual TM9-2320-204-12 Heavy Tank Recovery Vehicle M51'', Department of the Army, Washington, D.C., 28 April 1958

''Technical Manual TM9-2350-206-12 Tank, Combat, Full Tracked, 120mm Gun M103 (T43E1)'', Department of the Army, Washington, D.C., 24 October 1958

''Technical Manual TM9-2350-214-10 Tank, Combat, Full Tracked, 120mm Gun M103A1 (T43E2)'', Department of the Army, Washington, D.C., 16 December 1960

''Technical Manual TM-00590B-10/1 Tank, Combat, Full Tracked, 120mm Gun M103A2'', Headquarters, U.S. Marine Corps, Washington, D.C., 10 March 1964

''Trunnion Mounted Turret with Automatic Loading Equipment for the 155mm Gun Tank'', Final Report by United Shoe Machinery Corporation for Detroit Arsenal, Center Line, Michigan, February 1957

''The Hunter Heavy Tank Design'', Final Report on concept study by Rheem Manufacturing Company for Detroit Arsenal, Center Line, Michigan, 15 June 1955

''Proposal Tank, 120mm Gun T110 with 360 Degree Traverse'', Chrysler Corporation, Detroit, Michigan, undated

INDEX